THE
Westminster Pulpit

VOLUME V

THE
Westminster
Pulpit

VOLUME V

The Preaching of
G. CAMPBELL MORGAN

WIPF & STOCK · Eugene, Oregon

Wipf and Stock Publishers
199 W 8th Ave, Suite 3
Eugene, OR 97401

The Westminster Pulpit vol. V
The Preaching of G. Campbell Morgan
By Morgan, G. Campbell
Copyright©1954 by The Morgan Trust
ISBN 13: 978-1-60899-314-7
Publication date 1/15/2012
Previously published by Fleming H. Revell, Co., 1954

CONTENTS

CHAPTER		PAGE
I	PEACE	9
II	THINGS NEW AND OLD	23
III	EXALTATION AND HUMBLING	36
IV	THE ATONEMENT	48
V	FELLOWSHIP WITH GOD	60
VI	THE PASSION-BAPTISM	74
VII	THE TRIUMPHAL ENTRY	87
VIII	DEATH ABOLISHED	100
IX	THE TEACHING OF THE RESURRECTION	113
X	WAS THOMAS MISTAKEN?	126
XI	CHRISTIAN CITIZENSHIP: NO ABIDING CITY	140
XII	CHRISTIAN CITIZENSHIP: THE SEARCH FOR THE CITY	153
XIII	CHRISTIAN CITIZENSHIP: THE BUILDING OF THE CITY	167
XIV	CHRISTIAN CITIZENSHIP: CO-OPERATION IN THE BUILDING	179
XV	CHURCH IDEALS: THE CHURCH INSTITUTED	191
XVI	CHURCH IDEALS: THE CHURCH GOVERNED	205
XVII	CHURCH IDEALS: THE CHURCH DISCIPLINED	219
XVIII	CHURCH IDEALS: THE CHURCH AT WORK	233
XIX	THE KINGDOM: THE KING	247
XX	THE KINGDOM: "THY KINGDOM"	260
XXI	THE KINGDOM: "OF SUCH IS THE KINGDOM"	274
XXII	THE KINGDOM: THE OATH OF ALLEGIANCE	287
XXIII	THE KINGDOM: TRAITORS	299
XXIV	"IN THE BEGINNING GOD"	312
XXV	WHAT IS MAN	325
XXVI	THE BEGINNING OF SIN	338

THE
Westminster
Pulpit

VOLUME V

CHAPTER I

PEACE

His name shall be called . . . Prince of Peace.
ISAIAH 9:6

I came not to send peace, . . . but a sword.
MATTHEW 10:34

The wisdom that is from above is first pure, then peaceable.
JAMES 3:17

THAT IS A STARTLING COMBINATION OF TEXT. THE FIRST IS part of one of the sublimest of Messianic prophecies. It occurs in that great passage of Isaiah in which out of circumstances of tumult and turmoil, of war and strife and perplexity, the prophet foretells the day when all the things of war shall be destroyed; and he bases his hope upon the great fact that a child is born, a son is given. Whatever local meaning there may have been in the words of the prophet; whatever first application there may have been in his own domestic relationships, it is quite certain that he looked through, and saw emerging, amid the mists somewhere—how far I think he could not have told—the figure of One, a great and wonderful Deliverer, Whom he described by the four titles, Wonderful Counsellor, God-hero, Father of eternity, and finally Prince of peace; which titles constitute a key to the interpretation of Scripture, and of all human history so far as that history has been written, either in what we call sacred or profane literature. The complete title gives us an account of the unveiling of God, of the growing understanding of God on the part of man.

He was known first in Creation as the "Wonderful Counsellor," and then of necessity, in human history as the "Mighty God," the God-hero, the God of battles, the warrior God. Then in revealed religion, He was progressively revealed as the "Everlasting Father," or as the margin has it, the Father of eternity. If we take the Hebrew word here, and translate it quite literally we are grievously disappointed. It would then read, the Father of the terminus. Can anything be more disappointing than that? Yet that is that! As another Hebrew word—"everlasting"—means vanishing point; this Hebrew word, not from the same root, and not having exactly the same meaning signifies the terminus; that is, that which is beyond the vanishing point. God is the Father of that. So if the first uttering disappoint, we find that the suggestiveness is vast. The Father of the banishing point, and of that which is beyond, the terminus. Therefore He is the abiding One both as to time and space. And finally, the "Prince of peace."

If we accept the suggestion, which this morning it is not my purpose to argue, that here a progressive unveiling of God is indicated; then you will notice that there is first the thought of the "Wonderful Counsellor," the One of perfect thought and perfect will, from Whom must come a perfect law. And immediately following it, the "Mighty God," the God-hero, the God of battles, the God of war. And out of that, and following it, the further revelation of the "Father of eternity." And at last, that of the "Prince of peace."

So that if we take the whole of this description, there is here also a recognition of conflict. "I came not to cast peace"

PEACE

—and I adopt that marginal reading very definitely, not "I came not to send it," but I came not to cast it promiscuously, carelessly. There must be the God of battles before there can be the Prince of peace. There must be the coming of the sword ere there can be peace. And yet why? And the answer is postponed for a moment.

The second of these texts is the word of the Prince Himself. The centuries have run their course. Others have also climbed the heights of vision, and have gazed in hope and longing; and men have again, and yet again, been encouraged as the dreamers have told of lights upon the eastern sky, and have sung to them some refrain caught in high moments of meditation; and all the songs have been those of a coming One. At last we stand by the side of the One long looked for; and what this prophet said of Him long before is true; "when we see Him there is no beauty that we should desire Him." The Prince of peace is now speaking to His messengers as He prepares them for their work; and as He is sending them forth to proclaim the Kingdom He is warning them of the fact that they will have to do their work in the presence of, and in spite of persecution. "Think not that I came to cast peace on the earth: I came not to cast peace, but a sword!" That text is meaningless and valueless, and may be misinterpreted immediately unless we keep it in relation to its context. Where does the subject really begin? In the previous chapter, with Matthew's declaration that when Jesus went through all the cities and villages He saw the multitudes, and He was moved with compassion, because He saw them as sheep scattered, harried by wolves, without a shepherd. Out of that compassion comes the rule of the sword; and if you will take time to look at the context you will see that from that declaration of the moving of His heart with compassion in the presence of what He saw, the story moves right on to my text. It is continuous! The text belongs to that. He saw the multitudes, He was moved with compassion. He said to His disciples, Go ye, and then He began to instruct them as they went. He said, You will go as sheep in the midst of wolves. It is not going to be easy work, this work I bring to you. What is the work? To bring peace. The multitudes are harried by wolves, scattered, spoiled, harmed; therefore, I must fight! What for? To bring peace to the multitudes. The passion for peace creates the necessity for the sword.

The third text is the word of the most practical of the New Testament writers, and if you will take all the context here in this letter of James you will see that he is protesting against conflict amongst the brethren of the Prince. Brother of the Prince Himself, according to the flesh, he writes to those scattered by the dispersion, and speaks to them again and again as "My brethren," "My brethren," "My brethren." I am constrained to wait a moment here, because there is light upon that thought which is of value to us. There was a day when Jesus was in the midst of His work, and His mother and His brethren—this man amongst them in all probability—took a long journey as far as from Nazareth to Capernaum, to find Him, and to persuade Him to give up His work, because He was over-wearying Himself. Jesus was in the house, with a handful of disciples, and He then inquired "Who is My mother? and who are My brethren . . . For whosoever shall do the will of My Father which is in heaven, he is My brother, and sister, and mother." A great deal has happened since then. His brother has become His brother in a new sense, because he is doing the will of His Father. And it is very significant to me, that when he writes, this brother of the Lord after the flesh, he says to those to whom he writes, "My brethren." He is protesting against conflict amongst them, faction and strife among the brethren of the

Lord. How will it be cured? In these circumstances, which are very local, and for the correction of conditions which do not universally obtain among the saints of God, there flames out a principle of interpretation, which helps me in an understanding of all the things of difficulty which have oppressed me as I have read the prophecies of the coming of the Prince of peace, and then heard this self-same Prince of peace say, "I came not to cast peace, but a sword."

Think of the history of the centuries, the nineteen centuries of the Christian era or dispensation. Look back for a moment to the Person with Whom we are so familiar now, the Person of this Lord Jesus Christ of ours. Remember that He is the One to Whom all the prophets give witness; the Prince of peace for Whom men had been waiting, and for Whose coming they had been longing. Remember this also, even though it but increase the perplexity of the situation, that before He went away He said to a little group of His disciples, "Peace I leave with you; My peace I give unto you: not as the world giveth, give I unto you." Remembering all these things, then look at Him, and if there is one matter that impresses the mind more than another as you watch this man Jesus, from the moment when His public ministry began, to the close of that ministry, it is that of the restlessness of the life of this Lord of peace. I know you are in revolt against that statement because you are in sympathy with the underlying riches of His quietness. All that is true. I am speaking now of the external things. No home! Oh my masters, did you ever think of it? Oh, the tragedy of it! We recite it carelessly, or with merely sentimental sympathy, but listen to it, and at this Christmastide try to understand it: "Foxes have holes, and the birds of the heaven have nests; but the Son of man hath not where to lay His head." Homeless! Friendless! Do you challenge me? Well, then I shall ask your definition of a friend, and I will give you one from inspiration, and this is it. "A friend loveth at all times, And a brother is born for adversity."

Test the friends of Jesus by that, and He had not one. When the darkness gathered, and the tempest swept, He was left alone. There are some passages in this New Testament that to my own heart are passages which flame with fire. "They all"—they, that little group of disciples, whom He in grace called friends only by virtue of what He would make them presently, "they all forsook Him and fled." No, I am not angry with them. I admire them for staying so long. I am such a coward myself that I should have gone long before they did. But the fact, consider it, wherever He went, unrest; no place to lay His head; no friend. He tried to tell them of His Cross, but they never understood it until after His resurrection. All about Him were the men of light and leading, planning and plotting to catch Him in His talk, to entrap Him, He was a storm-center from the beginning of his ministry to its close. No peace.

Then look at the story of His first disciples, and the appalling thing is that when you begin now to look at the inner circle, strife is discovered amongst them. Oh, that dreadful picture of the New Testament of those last days, in which there was strife amongst them, as to which of them should be the greatest, repeated as you read the story, until you are weary of it. Conflict!

And then we come outside, and look generally through the centuries; and we look abroad today; where is peace? In the Church? Would God it were, but it is not. Brethren are divided, fighting; wasting the energies of their spiritual life which ought to be devoted to the warfare against the devil; hindering one another. Do you admire the divisions of Christendom? Then so do not I. Do you care to argue that all these things are willed by Him Who prayed that we all might be one? The divided condition of the Christian Church is a shame and a disgrace. Where is peace?

And my brethren, if I lift my eyes and look outside, if I look at the world, where is peace? If I look at that section of the world over which, sooner or later during these centuries, the messengers of the Cross have passed, that section of the world which is spoken of as Christian, or Christianized, where is peace? Well, I need say very little. I do not know, and I do not ask, and I care absolutely nothing for your particular convictions as to national politics, but I ask you to look from the height of your Christian experience at the world. We talk about peace. We thank God in speeches from the throne and elsewhere that there is peace, but is there peace?

To take that first text, "His name shall be called . . . Prince of peace" is to be faced by apparent contradiction. Nineteen centuries, well nigh two millenniums have run their course, and where is peace?

But to take the second text, "I came not to cast peace, but a sword" is to find a description of all that we have seen, but it seems to contradict the idea that He is the Prince of peace.

To take the third is to find the explanation, and to deny both the apparent contradictions.

Mark then I pray you, how these three texts are a revelation, and in order that we may profit by the revelation let us understand its method.

The first text is the announcement of ultimate purpose. He is the Prince of peace. This one Book of Isaiah, is the Book of the Servant of God, Whose mission is one. What is that mission? To establish peace. How does He do it? By the way of judgment; and the first division of the prophecy describes the peace resulting from judgment. In that second division;

first, the purpose is declared; secondly, the Prince is presented; and finally, the program is announced. If I were to write one word across the prophecy of Isaiah, a word that catches the underlying motive, what would it be? Peace, God's great purpose of peace. He is the Prince of peace.

When the Prince came, He described the process toward the peace as being the way of the sword. Jesus did not come to sing a lullaby to humanity, and to tell it that its sin does not matter, and its wickedness is nothing, that presently it will all be forgotten. He came in the name of God and eternity to declare war upon all the things that prevent peace. The sword is necessary in the interests of peace.

The third of these texts reveals for us the underlying principle. "First pure, then peaceable."

In the few moments that remain to us, let us make some applications of the teaching; first, in individual life; secondly, in social life; thirdly, in national life; finally, in international matters.

He is the Prince of peace. Think of individual life today. Was it ever more restless than it is now? What are the causes of unrest in individual life? Now I pray you, shut out of view, if it be possible to you for the moment, all other people than yourself. Think of the individual, think of the restlessness of individual life. What are the causes of unrest? Sin. And if the word is not understood outside, I think it is understood here, even if it is a word you are not inclined to make use of. Sir Oliver Lodge says the intelligent man does not speak of sin today. I deny it absolutely. The intelligent man speaks of every fact, it is ignorance that declines to look facts in the face. We may differ as to the interpretation of what is the underlying cause of the unrest; but the Bible teaches that it is lack of God. I take any individual life you please, and where there is no recognition of God, no practical, everyday, actual, positive traffic with God or commerce with eternity, then you have a life hot, restless, feverish. And by way of contrast, find me the life of the man, or the woman, or the little child, who knows God; and I will find you a life of quietness and peace, in spite of all the circumstances of stress and strain and conflict. Oh, do we not know them! How they help us, the quiet saints of the most high God, many of them devoid of all the things that minister to man's supposed well-being, but whose hearts are firm and steady and quiet, until it may be said of them, "He that believeth shall not make haste." All the restlessness of individual life today is due to man's lack of God.

What is the way of peace? First pure. And what is purity of heart? It is the heart undivided in its allegiance to God. So this Prince of peace comes. He will come this morning. He is coming this morning. He comes into the pulpit, for this Prince of peace does not divide between the pulpit and the pew. He comes to say, I have brought a sword, and I have come to war against the things in your life that shut God out. This Prince of peace is first the warrior with flaming sword and flashing eyes, and the tremendous word of the ancient prophecy upon His lips, "There is no peace, saith my God, to the wicked." Jesus Christ does not come first with a song and a lullaby and a narcotic. He comes with a sword and a flame and a fire; and there are men and women feeling this, here and now. You know that He will not make peace with the evil thing within you. "First pure." And there are men and women who will yield to Him, and hand over to Him their sword of rebellion, and let Him destroy as with burning the habiliments of their warfare; and to such men and to such women He will bring the peace of God which passeth all understanding.

And He is the Prince of peace socially. What are the

causes of unrest in the social world? Take the word of the inquiry in its most general sense; there is social unrest, and we all know it, we are all talking about it and arguing about it; and all that may be perfectly proper; but what are the causes of it? Caste, and injustice, the failure of men to recognize the absolute oneness of human nature. And so class is set against class, and the dividing lines are being emphasized. Oh the peril of it. And there is injustice in many ways, not only the injustice on the part of those who hold power, but the injustice of misrepresentation on the part of those who lack power; and the injustice as between two men in conflict is that neither of the two will see the standpoint of the other. There are caste differences and injustices.

Or, if you look at the business world, self-seeking is the inspiration of commercial activity, and a vast amount of dishonesty, which has been rechristened business sharpness.

Or, if you look at the Church of God, love of power, and lack of love are the causes of unrest.

What is the way of peace? The Prince comes, first pure; He brings a sword. He is against everything that emphasizes class. He will not enlist as under His banner, even the man who names His name if he bring into the spirit of his conflict that which is against the Spirit of the Lord Himself. He demands that there shall be recognition on the part of all men of the first fundamental necessity of manhood's relationship to God; and then consequently, the great issues and results, of man's true relationship to his brother man. He still comes, and it is not a song merely, it is thunder, saying to men, "Thou shalt love the Lord thy God . . . thou shalt love they neighbour as thyself." On these two commandments hang all the law and the prophets; and He is at war with everything in social life that contradicts the individual right of every man to a relationship with God; and the individual responsibility of every man concerning his brother. He is at war with all the forces of unrest.

Or, if you make a further application, what are the causes of national unrest? And I am not lifting my eyes to gaze any further than the shores of my own land. What are the causes of our own national unrest? Are they two, or is it but one? I leave you to decide. Perhaps one, but it must be stated in two ways. Forgetfulness of God and that which is the result—the enthronement of Mammon. Forgetfulness of God! I wonder if we shall soon hear again in our Houses of Parliament, a man who dare quote his Bible, and do it accurately; and do it, not at the bidding of a party, but at the bidding of God Almighty. I wonder! We have forgotten God. We must not say—as we were told recently—too much about the Congo, lest we disturb the balance of power somewhere. Away with the base thing! Where is God? We have forgotten Him, we are putting Him out of count. If a man says these things, somebody will say he is political. I avow in the presence of God, Whose I am, and Whom I serve, I have nothing to do with the mere paltry tricks of party politicians. I have everything to do with the land I love, with its lack of peace and its restlessness, and I affirm it is because we have forgotten God. Our empty churches, our broken-down family altars, our neglected Bibles, these are the things that matter. And my brethren, the Christ of God is at war with all these disturbing forces. It is the sword that He brings. He has not come this Christmas time to sing a national lullaby. He has come again anew, to declare war against the men who forget God, and against the men who enthrone Mammon in His place. Mammon! Oh what eyes had this Man of Nazareth, what far-seeing vision, what clear and accurate understanding of the constructive and destructive forces of the ages. Listen, You cannot serve God and the devil? Oh no, He did not say that. That is what I should have said. I must have my antithesis perfectly balanced. This is what He said, "Ye cannot serve God and Mammon," for He knew the devil also, and knew that the devil hides himself behind Mammon, behind its gaudiness and its glitter and its ministry to sensuality. The devil keeps out of sight today, he hides behind Mammon. I have said before on one occasion, I fear the thing was printed, but I will say it again, I have stood in amazement in the presence of Watts' great picture of Mammon. You look at it some day; and yet—my apology to his memory—had I to paint Mammon, I should have painted it otherwise, not bloated, satiated, and sensual, but as gaunt and hungry and never satisfied. That is Mammon. Why is wrong forever on the throne? Ask that question when next righteousness is defeated in any locality, or in the nation, why? And the answer will be, Mammon. When a nation forgets God, it always enthrones Mammon.

And so this Prince of peace is against the forces that cause unrest, and that in the interests of peace.

One other word, for even if so far I have only looked at one's own land, if a man be a Christian man, he cannot forget that he belongs to the world. If a man be a Christian man, he has come to a recognition of the unity of the race. And so one other glance, the international unrest, what are the causes of it? I had almost said, and I am perfectly sure you would have been in revolt against if I had said it so bluntly, that the cause of unrest is patriotism. I will qualify my word,—false patriotism, the patriotism that consents, out of a narrow attitude of mind, to use the word foreigner. Is there a more terrible word in existence than the word foreigner? I do not think there is to a Christian man. Foreigner! The patriotism that says, so long as this land, and this country is maintained in peace and prosperity, then it matters nothing what others go down in the struggle; is false, it is of hell!

And the consequent unfairness that grows from it, and the avarice of which it becomes the expression. Would you have an illustration? I will give you one. The fact that at this hour, a paper, standing supposedly for Conservatism—a great word—is consenting to employ the prophet of godless socialism to create strife between this country and Germany. That is what I mean. I will not be silent in the presence of this kind of thing. Silence here would be wicked and evil. Mark well, I pray you the unholy association. A man, brilliant and clever, who has taken stance definitely against revealed religion and the religion of Jesus Christ; and by his own paper is advocating a socialism that is godless in its thinking and godless in its outlook; and yet, this man is to write to show how we are to defeat Germany! And think you, the Christ is in favour of it? I make my solemn protest against it in the name of Christ. What does it mean? It is the outcome of a false patriotism; it is the determined attempt to say that this nation is the only one that really matters. My brethren, here are the causes of unrest. What has Christ to say? He brings the sword, and He is against it. He is against everything that denies the absolute right of all men and all nations, and castes, and rulers, to God, and to the fellowship of their brother man. And there will be long conflict ere peace can be established. A peace based upon unfairness and injustice in thinking and attitude towards other nations is no peace, and cannot live or last.

The supreme passion of the Church of God must be for peace. We must mourn over all war. War in itself is contrary to the ultimate purpose of God. But, we must also remember the refrain of Isaiah, and the declaration of Jesus. "There is no peace . . . to the wicked." "I came not to send peace, but a sword." We must remember that the principle of peace is purity. To make peace with wrong, or to consent to be silent in the presence of the things that are wrong, is to destroy peace.

And yet, let the final word this morning be the personal word. What is the Prince of peace saying to thee, to thee, Oh heart of mine, Oh soul of mine? I feel as though it were almost impossible, and as though it would be almost an impertinence to ask in the case of any other man, and yet let every man ask it. What says the Prince of peace to thee, Oh heart of mine, Oh soul of mine? Does He draw the sword? Then He draws it against some evil thing in thy heart, in thy thinking, in thy outlook, in thy habits; and He will make no peace with it for the sake of ultimate peace. Then do not be at war with Him, but end the war by letting Him win, even though it mean the breaking down of the idol, and the wounding of the spirit; for out of that wounding there will come peace, God's great peace, which is first pure.

CHAPTER II

THINGS NEW AND OLD

Have ye understood all these things? They say unto Him, Yea. And He said unto them, Therefore every scribe who hath been made a disciple to the kingdom of heaven is like unto a man that is a householder, which bringeth forth out of his treasure things new and old.
MATTHEW 13:51, 52

JESUS HAD BEEN INSTRUCTING HIS DISCIPLES IN THE MYSTEries of the Kingdom of heaven; and at the close of His parabolic teaching He declared to them the purpose thereof. He had not been instructing them merely for the satisfaction of their own spiritually intellectual curiosity. There was a practical bearing and value in all that He had been doing. He asked them, "Have ye understood all these things? Do you understand the meaning of the present hour? Have you caught any vision through the pictures which I have presented to your view, of the purpose of God, of His plan?" I am always astonished when I read their answer. "They say unto Him, Yea." I am the more astonished, that He did not rebuke them. He is wonderfully patient with us when we think we understand the things He says. He knew, however, that they had at least seen the broad outline; and He knew that presently, when the Spirit, the Comforter should come He would bring to their remembrance all the things of which He had spoken, and would explain in greater detail and with infinite patience the meaning thereof. Therefore, even though as yet they certainly did not perfectly understand, as their subsequent action demonstrates, He told them the reason of His teaching. "Every scribe," and one is halted by the word, for it is an interesting thing that Jesus uses that word here of His disciples, "Every scribe." What was a scribe? A scribe in the days of our Lord was a moral interpreter. The office of the scribe was created by Ezra, and had continued from his time. The scribes in the days of Jesus were in opposition to Him, but their office was that of moral interpretation, that of exposition of the law, and application of it to the conditions in the midst of which they found themselves. Christ used the word and appropriated the office on behalf of His disciples for all the coming ages. "Every scribe."

Mark the preliminary necessity. "Every scribe who hath been instructed to the Kingdom of the heavens." There can be no doing of His work, no fulfilling of His purpose, no cooperation in His travail, until a man is himself a disciple to the Kingdom of the heavens, and is instructed in the principles of that great and gracious Kingdom.

Let all this be taken for granted, what then? What is the responsibility that rests upon the scribe, the instructed one? "He bringeth forth things new and old."

In these two verses we have one of the smallest, as to number of words, of the parables of Jesus, the parable of the householder; a final picture to teach these men the value of the pictures already given them. The picture is that of a wealthy householder meeting the necessity of all those who are in his household, by scattering to them his treasures.

That is the perpetual responsibility of the Christian Church. Jesus said to the Hebrew people as His ministry was approaching its close, "The Kingdom of God shall be taken away from you, and shall be given to a nation bringing forth the fruits thereof." In that great and remarkable sentence, He transferred the responsibility for certain teaching and certain work, from the Hebrew people who rejected God's King, to a new nation which Peter described in his letter as a holy nation, an elect race. This is the responsibility that is referred to here, as bringing forth things new and old.

"The Kingdom of heaven" is the supreme phrase in this parable. It is not local in its application. We must not narrow that application to Judea. Neither must we narrow it exclusively to the millennium that has not yet arrived. It is not necessary to discuss now the differences between such phrases as "the Kingdom of God," "the Kingdom of heaven," and "the Kingdom." The thing that matters is that we should find the quantity or quality which is common to the whole of them. It is that of the rule of heaven, the mastery of heaven, the establishment of the heavenly order. In preceding parables, Jesus had told the story of the vicissitudes of the Kingdom principle in the present age, showing how sometimes there is victory and sometimes defeat. Through all the parables the phrase, "the Kingdom of heaven," recurs. The word, "Kingdom," does more than mark a realm; it emphasizes a rule. We sometimes speak of the Kingdom of God as though it referred to a place, a time, a convenant, a method. It refers to all of these, but the fact of that Kingdom is greater than all. "The Kingdom of God," suggests the throne of God, the government of God, the reign of God, the sovereignty of God. "The Kingdom of heaven" suggests the supremacy of heaven over the things of the earth. That Kingdom of heaven abides. Take heart, my brethren, do not be constrained to believe that God's throne has trembled, or that the supremacy of heaven has ceased. Every man is in the grip of the Divine government and cannot escape it. The devil does not reign even in hell. God reigns there also. Because the Kingdom of the heavens abides, it has a message to every century, to all conditions of human life, and the responsibility of the disciples of the Kingdom is that of delivering that message.

I think sometimes our phrases mislead us all unconsciously. For what are we labouring? The establishment of the Kingdom? The Kingdom is established. What then is our business? To reveal its bearings upon human life, to dictate its terms to the sons of men; out of the treasure house of the established supremacy of God and of the heavens to cast things new and old upon the earth, and in that sense to establish that which is established, to bring to the consciousness of men the facts from which they can never escape; so to love and help men and the age; that their relation to the Kingdom shall be one that results in blessing upon themselves and upon humanity, rather than in blasting and in cursing.

"Things new and old." What are these? If we can understand this phrase, we are getting to the very heart of the teaching of Jesus here concerning our responsibility. These are one in essence. We are not to understand that Jesus said "things new," and "things old," as though He were speaking of two sets of ideas. There is only one set of ideas suggested; the things are new and old. The new here does not mean fresh in the sense of just about to begin. The old does not mean ancient in the sense of about to pass away. Everything is new and everything is old. The principle is old, the application is new. The root is old, the blossom and the fruit are new. The two are necessary to growth. Destroy the old and you will have no new. Invent a new by the destruction of the old, and that new withers while you look at it. It is equally true that the absence of the new destroys the life of the old. Preserve your old and do not allow it to express itself in the new, and it withers. Some of you have planted bulbs in your gardens, all russet robed and devoid of beauty. Why did you put them in your garden? Why not lay them away on a shelf? Why not preserve them because they are the bulbs out of which flowers sprang two years ago? To preserve them is to destroy them. If you do not allow them to repeat themselves in new blossom and new fruit, they will die. Take the inter-relation of the thoughts of this phrase in another way. New things which contradict old things are not from old things, and therefore they are false; and the old thing which has no new in it is dead and valueless. Was it not this that Russell Lowell meant when he sang:

New occasions teach new duties; Time makes ancient good uncouth;
They must upward still, and onward, who would keep abreast of truth;
Lo, before us gleam her campfires! We ourselves must pilgrims be,
Launch our Mayflower, and steer boldly through the desperate winter sea,
Nor attempt the Future's portal with the Past's blood-rusted key.

But when you recite that, do not forget that if you attempt the future's portal with any other key than that which hangs upon the girdle of the Son of Man you will never unlock it. It must not be a rusty key, but it must be the same true key of David. The Kingdom of the heavens is old, and the application of its principles to our own age is new. Methods, manners, men may change, but this fact of the Kingdom of heaven abideth, rooted in the being of God, and blossoms afresh in every generation among the sons of men.

Let us turn from these generalities. Let me speak of some things new and old, for the bringing forth of which the Church of God is responsible at the present hour.

First the old things. The Church of God exists to affirm unceasingly and without apology the fact of the Divine Kingship; to declare that the throne is occupied and that government is exercised. The oldest of all the old is the fact of God; a fact which we are all so appallingly apt to forget, when we become practical. We remember God when we are poetical; we forget Him as the busy days run on. The Church stands in the midst of the nations, in the midst of the world, wherever her sons and daughters are found, for the old truth. I will use a phrase we are almost afraid of—our fathers loved it, preached it, lived it—the sovereignty of God.

The necessity for righteousness is also old. The fact that apart from righteousness there can be no permanence, no individual life, or social life, or national life. The fact that the wages of sin are still death. You may change your terminology and speak of sin by other words, but the old fact remains.

Or again, the fact that man is a sinner. I am quite willing to postpone discussion for a considerable period as to how he became a sinner. I am interested in the fact. Man today has the same passions, the same heartache, as had his father, and his father's father. We change a man's raiment, but the man abides, the slave of forces that mar, and master, and destroy.

The fact that plenteous redemption is provided is also old. Plenteous redemption for every man, and if not, for no man. Plenteous redemption to satisfy the human conscience; a word of pardon spoken out of the mystery of the bloodshedding of the Cross; and virtue communicated whereby men, gripped, enslaved by the forces that spoil, stand erect.

What of the new things? There is nothing new, save a new statement of the old things. There may be a new interpretation of those things, but in the new interpretation let us be very careful lest we devitalize the old.

There is a new interpretation of Kingship in the terms

of Fatherhood. Do not be afraid of the thought. Do not imagine that Fatherhood merely means tenderness and love. That is weak and false fatherhood. Of all the books written on the atonement through recent years, in this particular respect the one that I think most illuminative is Dr. Scott Lidgett's, in which he shows that in Fatherhood there lie all the facts of God; Kingship is there, Judgeship is there. The King is Father, His law is love. That is not to make law less severe, but more severe. There are no eyes so keen in watching as lovelit eyes. The throne abides, but we have found that the King is Father. The reason of His law is His love. So that today we say to our children not merely, You must because you must, but you must because it is best.

Righteousness abides the old truth; but today we are coming to a new understanding of its reasonableness.

Sin abides, but we are gaining a new understanding of the truth that the essential sin is unbelief. Read the letter to the Hebrews. The master sin with which the writer of that letter deals is the sin of unbelief. What is unbelief? The refusal to obey intellectual conviction. That is the sin of all sins. That is the easily besetting sin. Drink is never an easily besetting sin; men acquire the habit. Lust is not an easily besetting sin. The easily besetting sin, the sin in good standing around, is unbelief, the dishonesty of the man who will not obey the call of truth. There is the new emphasis of sin. That is what we need to say to men today.

What of redemption? The old provision abides. The new emphasis needed is that redemption is necessary, that no man can live the life of his own ideal, the ideal born in the moment of vision, apart from a force that is beyond himself, and outside himself. Harold Begbie, an honest disciple of Professor James, the great psychologist at whose feet we are all glad to sit today, has given the Professor a few additional problems in his book, "Broken Earthenware." What are you going to do with O.B.D.? What are you going to do with the Puncher? Now if Harold Begbie will write another book, and I hope he will, let him not confine himself to slum districts, but let him cross to the West End here, and he will find the same problem. I know the thing of which I speak. I know it better tonight than I did five years ago when I began my ministry here. I know that beneath the veneer, the culture, the refinement, there is the agony of broken hearts, and of conflict with sin. Thank God, I know also that the redemption provided is as powerful in the West End as in the East End. I know that this plenteous redemption is redemption for man as man. What we need is to emphasize its necessity and proclaim its absolute sufficiency.

A new statement of the old things, yes, but more, a new application of the old things is what this age peculiarly needs. It needs a social application based upon a specialized individual application. Here is the trouble with our age. The gleams of light are everywhere, men are seeing visions of an established order, in which man shall be brother to man; yet, the prophets of that new order are principally men who care nothing for their fellow men, but everything for themselves. That is the peculiar trouble of the hour; gleams of light everywhere, and visions of a great brotherhood of man; but how are you going to produce it? It is old, and trite, and commonplace; but it is true that we shall never have a brotherhood apart from a Fatherhood. To attempt the establishment of a social order without the foundation of God is the most fatuous folly. We must begin aright.

The Church of God needs the social application within her own borders. Here is the place where we ought to be in humiliation before God; that we fail within the Church itself; that we have men and women within the Catholic

Church of God suffering alone and unhelped; that it is possible to cross the threshold of the Church of God and carry over with us the wretched, miserable caste conditions which exist outside. That is the paralysis, the devil, that is spoiling our testimony. We need the new application of the old principle of the government of God, in a new social life in the fellowship of the Christian Church. But we must begin aright. The commonwealth is created by the wealth of all. Socialism demands individualism. Individualism creates socialism. Do not be afraid of the word. I said socialism twice and some of you went pale. I decline to hand over any great word to abuse, misrepresentation, and misunderstanding. I make my solemn protest here again that the man is woefully mistaken who says we can have a perfect social order—for the moment whether it be competitive or co-operative is not within my outlook—wherein human wrongs shall be righted, without God. But grant a community of individuals remade by the grace of God, and you have your society. But, ah me, how is it the Church has failed in social realization? Because the children of the Church have held back part of the price. There have been successors to Ananias and Sapphira as well as to the apostles. Because we have not been true to the whole claim of the Divine Kingship in individual lives. Thus we have not been able to realize the meaning of the Divine Kingship in the corporate life of the Church, and reveal it to our own age.

One other word for the purpose of practical and immediate application. The scribes of the Kingdom of heaven are to be the moral interpreters of the law of the Kingdom to their own age. That is our business. In order to do it, we must see and understand our age. How are we to do it? The question is one perhaps more easily asked than answered. We cannot do it by reading newspapers. The whole of our press, with rare exceptions, is touched at the present moment with that sensationalism which destroys truth. The man who is going to see his age will not see it in a newspaper. Sometimes you must read books that do not sell, to see the age. What are the facts of our own age? I can summarize them in three words, Atheism, Animalism, Abjectness. I will grant that there are other things to be said. There is a wistful, longing and looking toward the East for signs of morning. There is an awful hunger after spiritual things which is manifesting itself in trafficking with the occult. There is a new desire everywhere for the heroic.

The secularist halls are closed, you tell me. It is a bad sign. It shows that atheism is more dangerous than it used to be. Atheism is without-Godism. That is very awkward, but it helps me. Without-Godism. One of the supreme evidences is the frivolity of our age. Men have no personal commerce with God, and therefore it is an age of pleasure, of light literature, of frothiness. It is an age of indifference. There is no sense of God, and therefore there are no infidel lecturers. There is no worship, for atheism is the mastery of material ideals.

Animalism is always the sequence of atheism. Men say of the prophet of God, "As for this Moses . . . we know not what is become of him," and the next thing is the making of the golden calf and the worship of it. Although the golden calf is intended to be the representation of Deity, it is in very deed also a representation of animalism. The story of the golden calf is a tragic story. They made a golden calf, and they said, "These be thy gods, O Israel, which brought thee up out of the land of Egypt." Then Aaron built an altar and said, "Tomorrow shall be a feast to Jehovah," mark that I pray you, "a feast to Jehovah." Then they worshipped Jehovah before the golden calf. What is the next thing we read? "The people sat down to eat and to drink, and rose up to play." Now you have the whole tragedy of the situation. That is animalism. "What shall we eat, what shall we drink?" Oh for the return of prophet or apostle who dared to say true things to men even though their sensibilities were hurt. Oh for a Paul to say once more to this age, "whose God is their belly, who mind earthly things"; eating, and drinking and playing.

The consequence is abjectness, submission to forces that are destroying national life, and that without protest. Abjectness is trying to persuade itself that it is of the essence of courage to prepare for war. Abjectness has nightmare if an aeroplane crosses the eastern sky.

What is our duty in the presence of these things? To apply the fact of the Kingdom of God. In face of all the forces of the Kingdom of darkness, what are we to do? Bring forth things new and old, the new application of old principles. New phrasing of old truth, new channels for old streams. Taking the old for granted make appeal for the new.

First, there must be separation of the subjects of the Kingdom of the heavens from all complicity with the kingdom of Satan. That is where we must begin. The Church will have to say, "There is no room within our borders for any man who in his business is identified with the forces that are damning humanity." We must begin there. The Church must be true to the Kingdom of heaven within her own borders. Judgment must begin at the house of the Lord. Let the priests themselves believe and put on salvation. That is the first word.

Then, out of that life of true separation of the members of the Kingdom, the Church may go forth in a new witness to Godliness as against atheism, and spirituality as against animalism, to courage as against abjectness. There must be a new crusade against every form of evil; the Church forevermore manifesting herself as opposed to the things that destroy; the Church against war, and against lust, and against gambling, and against the drink traffic; against all the things that spoil humanity.

I plead today for a new enterprise in the interests of the old and abiding things, to reach the unreached masses of our cities. I am longing for the striking of the hour when it shall be possible for me to stand side by side with Canon Hensley Henson, or Mr. Stuart Holden, or the Bishop of London, somewhere off these ecclesiastical grounds, and preach the gospel to the unreached masses of the city. That hour ought to come. Surely we have some common belief on which we can stand together. My brethren, the concern of the Church ought not to be that of the defence of her own views, but attack upon the strongholds of evil and the proclamation of the evangel to the man who stands outside and with a fair show of reason says, "When you have done your quarrelling inside I will be prepared to listen to you when you talk to me."

I plead for a new enterprise in which we close our ranks, and carry the principles of the Kingdom of heaven to the age in which we live.

In order to close our ranks I think we may do these things. I would first of all, postpone all theological controversy to the calm of eternity. I think we shall be far more likely to come to a correct apprehension of the mystery of the Kenosis in heaven than we ever shall on earth.

I propose that we learn to sympathize with ecclesiastical convictions which we do not share, that we begin to believe that the man in the opposite camp is in heart sincere; that there are things about which we ought to agree to differ, and to cease our controversy in the presence of a common foe and a common God.

THINGS NEW AND OLD

I propose that we abandon once and forever all petty jealousy, and rise into a great and grand conception of the Kingdom of the heavens, that we may speak with no uncertain sound to our own age.

In the name of God and of humanity let us act as though we believed the things we profess to believe.

> Rouse then, soldiers! rally round the banner!
> Ready, steady, pass the word along;
> Onward! Forward! shout aloud Hosanna!
> Christ is Captain of the mighty throng!

CHAPTER III

EXALTATION AND HUMBLING

Everyone that exalteth himself shall be humbled; but he that humbleth himself shall be exalted.
                                          LUKE 18:14

THIS IS CHRIST'S APPLICATION OF HIS OWN PARABLE. Whatever other suggestiveness it may have, it is quite certain that here we are at the heart of the teaching. Most of the local color has faded from the picture; the temple has gone, and therefore prayers therein have ceased; the Pharisee and the publican have changed their names. The principles revealed in the parable abide until this hour; the man who exalts himself is still among us, though the form of his prayer may be altered; the sin-stricken soul still humbles himself and uses the identical prayer, "God be merciful to me a sinner"; and Christ still watches both, and pronounces exactly the same judgment, "Every one that exalteth himself shall be humbled; but he that humbleth himself shall be exalted."

The passion for perfection is in every life. Many men give up the search after it in despair. Many have wrong conceptions of what perfection is. Many others are seeking by false means to attain it. The passion for it, nevertheless, is found in every life.

The more conscious a man is of the strange and subtle forces within his own life; the more conscious he is of the complexity of his own nature; the more he is surprised by the

EXALTATION AND HUMBLING

dawning lights that break out of his own life, or by the shadows which reveal the possibilities of his own evil; the more he is conscious of the conflict within his own personality; the more that man is conscious also of the possibility of some high and noble destiny; the more that man hungers after realization. We all desire exaltation in the true sense of the word. None of us desires to come to the humbling of defeat, disaster, despair.

Listen to the voice within; the voice of your own life. It will startle you. It will inspire you. It will fill you with despair. It will sing the song of your possibilities. It will change the dirge of your helplessness. Such listening will make you desire the fulfilment of your life, the realization of possibilities that are within you. Then, this is the word of Christ to you, "Everyone that exalteth himself shall be humbled; but he that humbleth himself shall be exalted."

Whoso shall take the business of his own life into his own hands, and attempt to realize it according to his own way and his own wisdom, shall ruin it; but whoso shall recognize that his life is so wonderful a thing that he himself cannot know it, cannot legislate for it, cannot realize it, and shall humble himself according to the true law of that life, that man shall find it, that man shall come to life, not foreign to his own nature, but to the realization of what God meant him to be when God made him man.

What then is the supreme sin of all life? It is that of self-exaltation. All the sins of man's life are the issue of this sin; not lust, slavery to drink, or lying, or any of the specific sins which we so often denounce, these are not the sins for which a man is lost. They are the symptoms of a deeper sin, the evidences and activities of a profounder malady. What is that deeper sin, that profounder malady? Self-exaltation. The essence of sin is revealed in this phrase of Jesus; for remember, according to the perpetual teaching of Jesus, according to the whole message of revealed religion, self-exaltation means the exclusion of God; not necessarily intellectually, or not even necessarily emotionally, but volitionally so far as the actualities and activities of life are concerned; self-exaltation means the exiling of God, the dethronement of God, the forgetfulness of God, rebellion against God. That is the root sin. Self-exaltation is manifested in human life in different ways. It manifests itself in self-satisfaction. It manifests itself in a spirit of independence. It manifests itself in an attitude of definite and positive rebellion against religion. It manifests itself in a pride which fears to make confession of Christ and admit obedience to the law of God.

Self-exaltation, as self-satisfaction, is the peculiar sin of moral and respectable people. I do not want to be misunderstood. There is value in what the man of the world calls morality. When presently we have left the Sabbath day, and the sanctuary, and are back again in the market place, we must inevitably recognize the value of that lower level of morality which does not take into account the spirituality of human life, but which does avoid offence against human laws. That morality has its place, it has its value. But now we are in the presence of God; we are attempting to deal with things in the light of eternity; and as in the consciousness of that eternal and awe-inspiring presence we attempt to think of our lives, the moralities and respectabilities of common everyday life are out of sight, nay, they become in thousands of cases a severe and dangerous peril. Self-satisfaction is born of the fact that men have set up a standard of perfection lower than the Divine; and that the standard of perfection they have set up is the result of comparison of themselves with other men, and forgetfulness of the Divine purpose in their human life.

Of that attitude the pharisee is the supreme example. The expression of self-satisfaction is that of despising others, holding in contempt the man who has descended to the depths. You who were never drunk, look with profound contempt upon the man drunk in the gutter. That you would not do if you held the highest standard of morality. That you will never do again when you have seen what is God's purpose in your own life. That you will never do when you have come into living fellowship with the great ideal of life presented to men by this Lord Christ of ours. You hold in contempt the man who has descended to vulgarity because your own standard is a low, base, mean standard.

When we cease comparing ourselves with other men, and compare ourselves with God's meaning when He made us, then we begin to discover the unutterable failure of the life that can be satisfied with such morality, and has never attempted to enter into the spacious inheritance which includes eternity and God, the things that never pass and perish.

Self-exaltation is manifested also as independence. Independence is the peculiar sin of those who are gifted with physical strength and with mental acumen. It is the sin of the man who takes his way from Monday morning to Saturday night, makes his plans, carries them out, accomplishes his purpose and never gets tired. Is that an evil thing? By no means. Let every man remember that is something to be thankful for. Ah, but there is the sin!! The man I am referring to is not thankful. He makes his boast that he has never been helped in his life, that he has had to carve his own way, that he is a self-made man. That attitude is born of that man's failure to recognize that God is the Author of all the possibilities and powers in human nature. That man's attitude is the result of the fact that he has forgotten God. Moses long ago warned the Hebrew people not to forget that the very strength of their right hand, and their wit and wisdom, were gifts bestowed upon them. These men forget that the very substance of their everyday life with which they are doing business and are successful in this world are gifts bestowed upon them from above.

The expression of such independence is the prayerless life. This man never prays. He may bend the knee in the service of the sanctuary, a great many men do that who never pray. There can be bending of the knee but no bowing of the spirit. There can be repetition of words but no prayer. That is a life of self-exaltation.

Again, self-exaltation manifests itself as definite rebellion. This is the peculiar sin of the licentious. It is born of antagonism to Divine interference in human will. It expresses itself in contempt for religion and in attacks made upon religion. I am not speaking of the attitude of the man who has come face to face with the spectres of the mind, who is honestly facing intellectual difficulty in the realm of faith. I am thinking of the man who attacks religion, who laughs at Christianity, who attempts to undermine the faith of other men by his ribaldry. Attacks upon morality are always evidences of immorality in those who make them. A man objects to religion because he is in revolt against restraint, and that because restraint demands that he shall not commit the sin he is committing.

Once again. There is a pride of heart which is of the very essence of self-exaltation. It is the peculiar sin of people who are perfectly familiar with the will of God, perfectly familiar with the requirements of Jesus Christ, who know the evangel and know the terms of human salvation, and not only know them but believe in them. In what sense can these people be charged with pride? In that while the gospel is to them a pleasant song, they have never obeyed its commands, they have never yielded themselves to its truth. Over and over again the reason is to be discovered in a pride of heart which is born of the fear of the opinions of other men; there are hundreds of young people in business houses who would be Christians but they dare not. There are scores of people in this West End who would be Christians, but they dare not. I would like to say in passing that I cannot understand that attitude of mind. I will try to be sympathetic with it. I will do my very best to urge men to abandon it, but I cannot understand it. The air is full of political strife, but there is no man who is a man who is ashamed, on the proper occasion, in the proper circumstances, in private or in public life, to avow his political conviction. In the name of God, what is it that makes a man ashamed to avow in private or in public that he is a Godly man, a Christian man? Wherein lies the explanation of this mystery? It is self-exaltation. To confess Christ is to share the reproach of Christ, for the offence of the Cross still abides. We have gilded the cross, we even wear it as an ornament—alas that we should, but we do—but we have not taken the offence away, the sting is still there. Of that men are afraid, and this pride keeps them from the Christ, and therefore from the fulfilment of the meaning of their own lives.

All such self-exaltation is followed by humbling; and in every case the humbling is the necessary outcome of the exaltation. The humbling is not a capricious act whereby God does punish a man as in any sense apart from the folly of his own choice and activity. The humbling is the necessary outcome of that activity and of that attitude.

The humbling of the self-satisfied will consist in the discovery of self in the light of Divine requirement. The man that is perfectly satisfied with himself because he is no worse than other men comes then, when the light breaks upon him and he sees himself in the light of what God meant him to be, to the experience of humbling. It was Robbie Burns who said—

> Oh wad some power the giftie gie us
> To see oursels as ithers see us.

Oh would some power the giftie gie us, to see ourselves as God sees us. That is far more important. I do not mean now, although that also is true, that we might see our failure as God sees it, but that we might see our possibilities as God sees them. I sometimes feel I would sacrifice life itself if I could but give to my brothers a vision of the glory of their own lives in the purpose and economy of God. There are so many who do not understand the dignity of their own manhood, who never see that it is given to them to enter into fellowship in travail and pain with God for the redemption of the race and the remaking of the world! Oh the tragedy of it! When a man comes to see what God meant him to be, and puts by the side of it the things that have satisfied him, his morality, his respectability by the standards of men, he comes to the most terrible humbling.

The humbling of the independent comes in the discovery of failure resulting from refusal to seek Divine guidance. There are men here who understand that. There are men here who have come to that humbling, but thank God it has been their salvation. Do you remember that hour in which you came to see the unutterable failure of your life simply because you had not sought Divine wisdom? There are tragedies of pain and suffering that come to us mysteriously, and for which we can give no account; we believe these God overrules also; but how much tragedy there is in human life because men do not seek to know the will of God. Oh the tragedies in human lives because men do not ask God what He wants them to do, whether He wants them to be ministers or

EXALTATION AND HUMBLING

carpenters. There are tragedies in the ministry because men choose to enter it as a profession, and then find it to be hell, as every man does who enters for that reason. There are tragedies in the workshop, because men ought to have been preaching, or ought to have been on the distant field, and did not ask God. High dignity and noble fulfilment may be ours in the humblest walk of life. I read a life of Garfield once; a wonderful life, with a wretched title, "From Log Cabin to White House." That title suggested that there was something derogatory in the log cabin, and more of dignity in the White House. That is not so. We can fulfil the function of eternity in a log cabin if God means us to be there, but we cannot if He wants us in the White House. The trouble is we fail in the log cabin or the White House if we forget God. The humbling comes to a man when he says, "I have played the fool" because I forgot God, and thought that by my own wit I could carve out my own career and make a success of my own life.

The humbling of rebellion against God will come in the discovery of the disaster resulting from that rebellion. I need not pause to argue that. You know it. May God make you true to the knowledge. You know perfectly well that the sin which is the real reason of your attack upon religion is unmaking you. It is almost vulgarity to argue it; the hidden sin which makes you laugh at religion, is working paralysis and ruin in your life. You can tear our parable out, fling the New Testament away, shut the Bible, but you cannot escape from that. The humbling of the man who, through continued sin, turns his back upon and opposes religion, comes in the discovery of the disaster that follows upon his own line of conduct. The humbling of pride will come in that dread and yet great hour when the Son of Man shall come in His own glory and in the glory of His Father, and all the holy angels with

Him," and then, in Christ's own words, "Whoso is ashamed of Me, of him will I be ashamed." The Son of Man is coming. I have no anxiety and no care to dispute now with you as to how or when He is coming. He is coming into His Kingdom, He is coming into His glory, He is coming to vindication, He is coming to triumph. If you are ashamed of Him while the conflict is one, He will be ashamed of you in that day. Not that He will indulge in reprisals and say, "Because you treated Me so I will treat you thus," but because your shame and fear of Him today will so undo you that He cannot recognize or receive you in the day of His ultimate triumph. You will be out of place in the society of righteousness and truth and loveliness; for you will be untrue, unrighteous, unlovely, if after having heard the winsome music of His call you decline to crown Him, and for fear and shame turn your back upon His high ideals, and upon the matchless music of His great evangel.

Now turn to the other side of the declaration for a closing word. "He that humbleth himself shall be exalted." What is self-humbling? This is it, "The publican . . . would not lift up so much as his eyes unto heaven, but smote his breast, saying, God be merciful to me a sinner."

That is first a taking of the right place, "God be merciful unto me." I draw your attention not to the petition. "Be merciful," not even to the description "a sinner," but to this revelation of the true relation of human life, God and me. There is no room for a third person there. There is no priest there, thank God. There is no prophet there. The preacher is not there. He is done and out of the way. The real business between the soul and God begins when I have finished; God and me! Every man who will come as far as that tonight will win his own life. That will correct all the false attitudes and outlooks; God and me! Whether you will have it so or not, it is so. You are quite alone with God. How I love to linger on this. I think it is a recent revelation to me, the fact that a man in a crowd is all by himself with God! Oh, the glory of it! I sometimes guess secrets through the windows of your eyes, but at last I cannot tell. Thank God He has secured the loneliness of every man with Himself.

Then follows the necessary confession of truth. I am a sinner. Measure yourself among your fellow men and you will stand erect. Compare yourself with the average man and you will proclaim your morality. But get alone with God, think of God, of His high holiness, His love—and there is nothing that brings conviction of sin to the heart as quickly as the real consciousness of the love of God—and you will say I am a sinner.

Then what? Praying the true prayer, "Be merciful unto me." No demanding from God your rights. I am weary to death of the men who tell me what they would do if they were God, and talk of their rights in the presence of God. What right has the barren fig tree to object if the proprietor should say, Cut it down, why cumbereth it the ground? "Be merciful to me" is the only plea.

One other thing. When a man gets there and is conscious of his sin and breathes that prayer, he is giving expression to faith. No man will ever say that to God, save as there is in his soul the activity of faith in God. You will never ask blind fate to be merciful to you. You will never ask a "double-faced somewhat," consisting of intelligence and power working in co-operation, to be merciful to you! It would be no use. You will never pray to dynamite to be merciful to you. When a man says "Be merciful," he has heard the music of the Divine heart. Such a prayer is the expression of faith. That is the humbling for which Christ calls.

He says that if a man shall so humble himself, he shall

be exalted. What is the exaltation? Christ gives it in the parable, and therefore I need no speculation. "I say unto you, This man," the publican, "went down to his house justified rather than the other." Do you say justification was a Pauline word? I ask you where he learned it. He learned it there. It is Christ's word! What is justification? God's answer to faith. What is that? The outflowing of mercy in reply to the cry of a man who claimed no morality but flung himself upon the compassion of his God. Justification, what is it? The sinner is a sinner no more; he is pardoned, cleansed, reinstated, remade! Justification, what is it? The realization of the position you assumed, God and me. The answer of God is, "Yes, you and I will have fellowship one with another!" Justification is the exaltation; forgiveness of sins, and the consciousness of that forgiveness in the soul, not by argument but by the direct touch of the Saviour God. Do you know it, my brother? If you do, it is a little difficult not to break out into song,

> My God is reconciled,
> His pardoning voice I hear,
> He owns me for His child
> I can no longer fear.

It is possible to stand outside that hymn and criticize it, laugh at it, philosophize concerning it, until you say there is no meaning in it; but you cannot take it out of my heart, out of my consciousness, you cannot take it out of my soul; the forgiveness of sins by the outflowing of infinite mercy, mercy that I know experimentally, and consequent fellowship with God. That is justification.

What then? Then the finding of my own life. When God made me by first creation—for He did make me in my first creation—He made me for some purpose and when I get back to Him He realizes it. "He that loseth his life shall find it."

Shall we not humble ourselves before God? Shall we not isolate ourselves with Him and let Him put upon us His measurement; and then yield ourselves to His mercy, casting ourselves upon His compassion. If we do, then all the strange mystery of our own life will be explained; not immediately, but progressively and gradually; through discipline and by patience, we shall work out our own salvation because it is God that worketh in us both to will and to work of His good pleasure.

May we find our way to Christ in humbling, and so to the crown and throne of realized life.

CHAPTER IV

THE ATONEMENT

You, being in time past alienated and enemies in your mind in your evil works, yet now hath He reconciled in the body of His flesh through death, to present you holy and without blemish and unreproveable before Him.
COLOSSIANS 1:21, 22.

THERE ARE TWO BRIEF DECLARATIONS IN THIS COLOSSIAN LETter which may be said to embody its teaching. The first is that in which the apostle declares, "In Him," that is in the Lord Jesus Christ, "dwelleth all the fulness of the Godhead bodily." The second is that in which he tells those Christians to whom he was writing, the saints at Colosse and the faithful in Christ Jesus, "In Him ye are made full." The theme of the letter is that of the glorious Christ, and of all the glories of the Christ at the disposal of His Church in order that she may fulfil all the good pleasure of the will of God.

In the course of dealing with these great subjects the apostle wrote some of the most wonderful things, if I may suggest such a distinction, that the New Testament contains concerning our Lord and Master. In the passage which we read this evening He deals with the threefold fact of His glory; His glory in relation to His Father in that, He "is the image of the invisible God"; His glory in relation to the whole creation in that, He is "the firstborn of all creation," all things coming by the word of His power, all things moving to the goal of His purpose, all things consisting, or being held together by Him; His glory in relation to the Church, in that, He is the Head of the Church, "the firstborn from the dead"; and, finally, He says of Him "That in all things He might have the pre-eminence."

It is not to be wondered at that in the midst of such spacious and wonderful declarations concerning the glory of Christ, the apostolic reference to the Cross should be equally spacious and equally mysterious. It is in this great passage in which we see Christ in His relation to the whole cosmos, its Originator, its Sustainer, its Goal; that we also see Christ in His relation to the chaos, its Redeemer, its Reconciler, its Restorer. In this passage the apostle declares that through Christ the work of reconciliation is accomplished; not only between individual men and God, not only in the complex mystery of an individual life, not only in this world, but also in the heavens.

Thus the apostle places the Cross of Christ at the very center of everything. As Christ Himself is at the center of all things, and as all things are upheld and made consistent by His power, so also at the center of all is His Cross. The power of the Cross is felt not only in the nearest things but to the utmost bound of creation. The work of the cross must be ultimately measured, not merely by what it does within individual life, but by what it accomplishes in the heavens, among angels, and at last by what it has done in the being and nature of God, because by it righteousness and peace are able to meet together and to kiss each other.

In an atmosphere so full of glory, in the presence of declarations concerning our Lord and His Cross so calculated to fill the soul with awe, we come to this central word, this word that touches us most nearly and most intimately, the word that reveals the way of our reconciliation.

This statement first reveals our need of reconciliation; secondly, declares the provision made by God in Christ, and unveils the method thereof in so far as it can be unveiled for our eyes; and, finally, makes clear to us the purpose of that reconciliation in the economy of God.

The need of reconciliation is made clear in the words, "You, being in time past alienated and enemies in your mind in your evil works." The way of reconciliation is declared in the words "reconciled in the body of His flesh through death." The ultimate purpose of reconciliation in the experience of man is declared in the last words, "to present you holy and without blemish and unreprovable before Him."

The need of reconciliation. Let us at once intepret the meaning of reconciliation by the term atonement, always remembering the true and simple meaning of that word. Our fathers were accustomed to say that the word atonement means at-one-ment. That has been contradicted, but it is a very interesting fact that the very last of our lexicographers, Murray, declares that to be the true meaning of the word. The verb "atone" is not that from which the substantive "atonement" is derived, for the substantive preceded the verb, and at-one-ment was a word used in our language before the verb "atone." The word "atonement" does not actually reveal the method of reconciliation; it rather describes the state of reconciliation. In our theological formulae we use the word as indicating the method which produces the result, and then attempt to explain it. I am not using the word in that way now, but rather in the old and simplest sense, that of being brought into at-one-ment with God.

Is there a need for this? Has man lost his at-one-ment with God? The apostle declares that he has and describes his condition as, "alienated and enemies in your mind in your evil works." This is not mere rhetoric. It is a most careful setting forth of the truth concerning man in his sin, beginning with the profoundest, essential fact in human personality, the spiritual, which is alienated; describing in the next place the mental attitude, the consciousness of human life, "enemies in your mind"; and dealing finally, with that physical side of personality which is the expression of the spiritual, "in your evil works."

Alienated. The force of the word is not, aliens. It is not the fact that they were aliens that was in the mind of the apostle, but the fact that they were alienated, and that suggests activity on the part of God. It presupposes a reason which it does not yet declare, but it declares an action, an action on the part of God. They were alienated, cut off from fellowship with God, and that by the act of God. Just as surely as reconciliation is in one of its profoundest aspects judicial, so also is the alienation that makes reconciliation necessary. Translate the Greek word literally and it reads, "you were made to be strangers," a common word at that time, used of those who had lost their citizenship.

I pause to lay all this stress upon the true meaning and value of this word, because it involves a truth which we are in danger of forgetting. This word recognizes the sovereignty of God. We are very much inclined to speak today as though the fact that we are offspring of God puts us on some equality with God, which gives us warrant to talk to Him about our rights, to make terms with Him as to how He may deal with us, or even to descend low enough in the scale of blasphemy to declare what we would do if we were God. All this is the tendency of the hour.

In the presence of the Cross, making the declaration of the need there is for reconciliation, the apostle declared that man is alienated from God by the act of God, and that in perfect righteousness by reason of man's own sin, the sin of his own will, of his own choice, wherein he has turned away from God. The turning away from God on the part of man, results in the definite act on the part of God by which He shuts man away from fellowship with Himself. "Your sins," said the prophet, "have separated between you and God." That is the Old Testament declaration. It is exactly the same truth. Because of your sins, thundered the prophets to Israel of old, God has cut you off from fellowship.

The sinning man may still pray, may still continue to cross the threshold of the earthly house of God, may still take His name upon his lips, may still sing the songs of the sanctuary, may still intellectually attempt to apprehend the doctrines of Christianity; but he has no personal fellowship with God. God will not admit him to that fellowship. No man can see the Lord without holiness. No man can have fellowship with God while he is still in his sin.

Let us pass to the next phrase and phase. In the deepest fact of human life men because of their sin are alienated from God, cut off from fellowship with him, spiritually dead in trespasses and sins. Therefore, they must be described in the words of the apostle as "Enemies in your mind." That is the consequence of alienation. The consciousness in the soul of man of God's attitude toward him in his sin, creates the attitude of enmity toward God on the part of man. Let me state it thus. God is forever at war with human failure, making no terms with it, making no peace with it, making no excuse for it; therefore, man is forever at war with the will of God which forbids his sin, which would interfere with his sin, which would take from him all the activities wherein he is destroying himself, and perpetuating evil in the universe of God. God is at war with sin in every man, and with every man who is sinning. God is angry with the wicked every day. The wrath of God abideth upon the ungodly. In the strange and mystic consciousness of every man there is the conviction that this is the attitude of holiness toward his impurity, of righteousness toward his wrong, of purity toward his corruption; and he answers it with the attitude of rebellion, and of persistent enmity. Man hates God because God hates man's sin. This is illustrated by the attitudes of men toward God in the world today. I am not speaking merely of blatant and brutal attacks upon the Christian religion. I am thinking also of the objection there is among men everywhere to the mention of the name of God, as though God had some cruel purpose toward man. We may talk of politics, of play, of books, but if we talk about God, we are considered objectionable. Why is it that men will not talk about God? Because they are enemies in their mind against God. Why? Because they know that God is at war with sin, that God excludes the wilfully sinning from fellowship, and will make no terms with their sin. Therefore, men are at enmity against God.

What is the final result? It is expressed in the words, "In your evil works." All the activities of life are evil, when they are activities out of harmony with the will of God. We look upon these activities, and divide between them as between vulgar and respectable, but all life which is godless life is evil life. The man who is alienated from God, and has no direct, immediate contact with Him and fellowship with Him, no conscious fellowship with God, that man is at enmity against God; if he does not blaspheme His name, if he does not write a book to prove He does not exist, nevertheless, he objects to hearing of Him with the result that the physical life is a life of evil, "in your evil works."

Thus, while an initial act of sin called for alienation, continuance in sin results from alienation; and therein is revealed the utter helplessness of man in his sin. The profoundest fact in human life is the spiritual, and if it is excluded from

God, alienated from God, then that spirit life has no right of entry within the veil; it has not ceased to be, but it has no way of appropriating the resources which strengthen it; it is offspring of God, and yet excluded from fellowship with God. Therefore, the mind is at enmity against God, and the works are evil works.

How can there be reconciliation between God and a man in that state? We turn immediately to the next words of our text; words full of sublimity, to be considered with great reverence, "Now hath He reconciled in the body of His flesh through death." In the words, "In the body of His flesh," the apostle refers to the actual human life of Jesus of Nazareth. Behold it for a moment, and think of it, as it stands in vivid, startling, almost appalling contrast to the picture of humanity which we have been considering. Man is alienated from God. This Man lived the life of perfect fellowship with God. Man because of his alienation in spirit from God, and the consequent enmity of mind against God, is in his bodily life performing evil works. This Man, because of His friendship with God, went about doing good, good works instead of evil works. This Man is of my humanity; but by this contrast He is seen to be entirely different from that which I am. We know the meaning of Paul's words, alienated, enemies in your mind, in evil works. We know every phase of the description experimentally. We know their inter-relation; that because we were away from God, our minds were at enmity against God, and the works of our lives were works of evil. Knowing these things, we come into the presence of this Man in the body of His flesh. Everything is of our nature, but is not of the nature of our living. We were alienated! He lived in perfect fellowship! Our mind was enmity! He was the Friend of God, the One in Whom alone that phrase has ever been perfectly fulfilled and manifested in meaning to the sons of men. Our works were evil. He did only good works.

Now, let us understand this. We have not yet reached the realm of reconciliation. Not by what He was in the body of His flesh can He reconcile me to God. The whole stupendous truth is declared in the next two words, "through death."

The incarnation is not reconciliation. In its very nature it cannot be, for God in Christ, in the perfection of the life of Jesus, is the sternest foe of sinning man. That fair and beautiful life condemns my faulty and sinning life.

The teaching that fell from His lips, the ethic He revealed as being the will of God for man, simply brings me to a consciousness of my humiliation. It is impossible for me to realize that high ideal.

All His deeds were deeds directed against the evil works in which I live. If I have nothing in Jesus other than that unveiling of Divine purpose, and that picture of a Man Who is of my nature but lived in other relationships, then there is still no reconciliation. I am still at war with God in Him. If Jesus Christ were merely a Teacher, a Social Reformer, He could win this country and all civilized countries within six months. But it is because He still stands for heart purity, for rectitude of spirit with God, for the fundamental things of holiness and righteousness and truth, that men are against Him. Not in the body of His flesh with its revelation of the true meaning of every human life and the divine intention for human life, is there reconciliation, nor can there be.

This Man died. Now, if our reconciliation could have been by incarnation, then that death was the most awful reflection on the power and wisdom of God that has occurred in all human history. Unless there be some profound meaning; unless it be, as Peter said it was, of "the determinate counsel and foreknowledge of God," unless there be something infinitely more than the capture of a victim by brutal humanity and his murder, then the permission of that murder undermines my faith in the goodness of God and in His righteousness, for the problem of evil is focused here. Sigh as you will over the sorrows and sighings of humanity, over the problem of evil, there is no problem of evil in London slum or suburb, in China, Africa, or India, comparable to that of the Cross. What is the meaning of that death, the death of One Who in the body of His flesh lived a life of perfect harmony with God, realizing the Divine purpose, illumining the Divine meaning, and satisfying the Divine requirements?

"You . . . hath He reconciled in the body of His flesh through death." This declaration does not attempt to tell all the secrets. The New Testament never has made that attempt, and those men who have made the attempt have proved their inability.

"Through death"; and if we would interpret the meaning of the word "death" there, we must do so by remembering the Person referred to. The image of the invisible God; the first-born of all creation; the Origin and Sustainer and Goal of the cosmos; in a mystery entirely baffling my poor finite mind, He came into flesh, and He died. That is the one death. There is no other death by the side of that. The death is infinite because the Person is infinite. In the body of His flesh "through death." Here is the manifestation, the unveiling. Just as in His life, the grace and glory of the Father are unveiled by their veiling in flesh; so that death, of infinite passion and pain, is an unveiling. We must interpret the death by the One Who died. There is no analysis of this, no plumbing of its depths, no possibility of satisfactory theorizing!

"Through death." What is death? Death is the penalty of

sin. We cannot escape that word penalty. Death is the penalty of sin, not merely its issue, its outcome; that also for the method of God's penalty is always poetic. Penalty is the fruitage of sin necessarily. Then here is the mystery, that the Sinless died.

May God help us to remember this that before that Cross of Calvary we never can see everything. These are some of the things we may see. In the mystery of that Cross, this One upon Whom our eyes have been resting is not in conflict with God. He is working together with God. "God was in Christ reconciling the world unto Himself"; not merely in the days of public teaching, not merely in the days of miracle and wonder-working, not merely in the subsequent days of resurrection light, but surely also in the Cross, "God was in Christ reconciling." "You . . . now hath He reconciled in the body of His flesh through death." That act of death no man can fathom. It excludes me forevermore as I try to understand its deepest meaning. So far as I am allowed to say this let me say it, I have never read a book on the atonement that has quite satisfied me, but every one has given me some new and true view of it. Still, I have never read a book that has satisfied me. There are quantities and elements that defy analysis and elude comprehension. That death, at the heart of the universe, is felt to its remotest bound, for He reconciles all things in the earth and in the heavens to Himself, and in that great reconciliation, great because of the Person and the death, I find my possibility of reconciliation. By that death is created the greatest possibility for the man who is alienated, that he may come into fellowship with God; for the man who is at enmity against God, that he may come into friendship with God; for the man whose works are evil, that he may come to fruitfulness in all good works before God.

Now, I am certainly touching things we are all familiar

with, for I am touching the realm of the experience of the saints. There are men and women, thank God, many of them in this house who know I am speaking the language of their own experience, men and women who can say, "Our fellowship is with the Father and with His Son Jesus Christ," by which they mean God speaks to them and they speak to Him. They call to God and He hears them. Men may indulge in all the speculative arguments against prayer that they please, but they will never disturb the certain confidence of these people. They know, they hear the voice amid the roar of the city, they hear the voice in the silence of their own heart. God speaks to us, we speak to God. We are no longer alienated, made to be strangers; we are made fellow-citizens with the saints, and fellow-citizenship with the saints means right of access to God. We know that God is, not because you have argued for Him, or demonstrated Him by syllogism, but because He speaks and we hear, we speak and He answers. That possibility was created through this death. It is by what that death has done for us in our own moral consciousness that we have found our way to God. It is out of that consciousness of sin forgiven, which in this same chapter the apostle speaks of as "our redemption the forgiveness of sins," that we have come to fellowship with Him. That fellowship means friendship, we love to speak of Him and all His wondrous ways. In the days of formalism, when Malachi delivered His message, he declared, "Then they that feared the Lord spake one with another and the Lord hearkened and heard." God is still hearkening and hearing men and women who love Him, as they speak of His name out of friendship with Him, and love of Him.

    This fellowship and friendship issues in the possibility of fruitfulness in goodness. Very slowly does the full fruit come! We know that all too well; but thank God, He is patient with us. It is first the blade, then the ear, then the full corn in the ear, and He with patience waits for the final fruitage.

The ultimate purpose is that we should be holy, that is, no longer alienated but in fellowship with life, holy in character as He is; without blemish, that is, no longer enemies, but by love satisfying love; and unreprovable, that is, no longer evil workers, but pleasing Him in all things.

Let this last matter be most carefully observed. The work of reconciliation which He did is necessary to a reconciled life. Concerning this there is very much false thinking today. The atonement is too often spoken of as though it afforded a mere provision of pardon. It does that; but infinitely more. Its results are judicial, necessary to experience. It is judicial, but it is radical; it touches character.

Atonement was necessary. Until alienation, and enmity, and evil works are dealt with there can be no reconciliation. God cannot be reconciled to man in his sin. Man must be reconciled to God in His holiness. The possibility of holiness is the true gospel hope for those who know their alienation, and who in response to the constraint of the Holy Spirit enter into fellowship by the way of the Cross. We may find our way back into intimate personal fellowship with God; "Nothing in my hand I bring Simply to Thy Cross I cling."

If we so come, we shall know the reconciliation; and it will be reconciliation that begins with the consciousness of God and issues in love of God, and finds its crown in the works that are pleasing to God.

CHAPTER V

FELLOWSHIP WITH GOD

Our fellowship is with the Father, and with His Son Jesus Christ.
I JOHN 1:3.

THE GREAT WORD OF THIS PASSAGE, WHICH AT ONCE ARrests our attention, is the word "fellowship." While not exclusively so, it is peculiarly the word of John; and as I find it in this letter, and in the two brief ones which follow, I am always impressed with the thought that these letters are the result of that wonderful thing Jesus said to His disciples in the farewell discourses, part of which we read this evening, "Henceforth, I call you not servants, but friends." It ever seems to me that the word fellowship, as John makes use of it, is the peculiar and particular word of friendship.

It is an interesting fact, which some of you have doubtless noticed, that in these three letters John never speaks of Jesus as Lord, and never speaks of the disciples of Jesus—believers in Him—as servants. I do not mean to suggest that John forgets the relationship which he and his fellow-disciples bore to Jesus as His bond-servants; or that John ever forgets the supremacy and sovereignty of Christ, that He was, indeed, the Lord; but it is an interesting fact that he does not speak of Him as Lord. These are peculiarly the letters of a close, and intimate, and personal friendship with Jesus.

This word "fellowship," therefore, is an illuminating word concerning our friendship with God and our friendship with Christ; our friendship with God through Christ.

I have already said that the word is not exclusively used by John; Paul uses it, it occurs in the fundamental proposition of his first letter to the Corinthian Church, "God is faithful, through whom ye were called into the fellowship of His Son Jesus Christ our Lord." The word thrills us, with all the deepest, and the sublimest, and the tenderest things of our relationship to Christ, and in Him to God.

It is a rich and spacious word, full of suggestiveness, almost impossible of full and final translation. That is borne out by this fact; the word which is here translated "fellowship" is translated in many ways in the New Testament—"fellowship, contribution, distribution, communication, communion." Or, if we turn from this actual word, which is an abstract noun, to the common noun, it is translated "partakers, partners, companions."

I believe that all these are needed in our language if we are to have any idea of the richness of this one great word; the word which is descriptive of the great and gracious fact of our friendship with God and with Jesus Christ.

If we tarry for a moment longer with the word, it is only that we may inquire if there be any illustration of its simplest meaning. I think we can find one in the Acts of the Apostles. It is declared that in those early days of apostolic love and fervour, the disciples had all things in common. The word so translated is the root from which the other word is derived, and in that translation we get nearer the heart of its suggestive meaning than in any other word in the New Testament.

What is fellowship? Having all things in common. What is it to have fellowship amongst men? To have all things in common with them. What is it to have fellowship with God? Although the statement is a stupendous and amazing one, I am constrained to make it—it is to have all things in common with Him. That word is the one that indicates the perfection of our friendship with God, and my desire this evening is to lead you along a line of quiet meditation as to what our fellowship with God is, for the sake of encouragement for those who are the Lord's, and, perhaps, to win, and woo, and allure those who lack this friendship; that before this service ends they also may become the friends of Jesus, the friends of God, henceforth to know what fellowship with God does really mean.

I shall, therefore, select from these different words two, which mark two phases of the one great fact. I will take that rich word of the Church "communion"—fellowship is communion—and I will take one of those common nouns, rendering it in its abstract fashion, and say the word means partnership. Why make the difference, for they signify the same thing? Because in our use of these words we use them in different relations. We use the word communion in the realm of friendship; we use the word partnership in the realm of business; and for that reason I select these two words, because by so doing we shall come to a better understanding of what this fellowship with God means. Fellowship with God, then, as to privilege, is communion with Him; the actuality of friendship and fellowship with God, as to responsibility, is partnership with Him. I almost hesitate to say this because it is so incomplete and unworthy a method of presentation; but for the purpose of arresting thought and fixing it here, I will say that fellowship with God means we have gone into business with God, that His enterprises are to be our enterprises.

FELLOWSHIP WITH GOD

Let us first dwell on our fellowship with God as communion; our fellowship with God as friendship.

I will take three simple illustrations of what friendship is on the earthly level, in order that we may climb to the higher height, and understand what is meant by our fellowship, our friendship, with God.

I propose to give three quotations, which have appealed to me personally, as setting forth most perfectly the ideal of human friendship. I begin with these words from Mrs. Craik's *Life for a Life*.

> Oh, the comfort, the inexpressible comfort, of feeling safe with a person; having neither to weigh thoughts nor measure words, but pour them all right out just as they are, chaff and grain together, knowing that a faithful hand will take and sift them, keep what is worth keeping, and with the breath of kindness blow the rest away.

Is not that a perfect description of friendship? How many people are there in company with whom you can pour out everything in your heart, say everything, say anything? Very, very few; for God does not give us many friends in this world; many acquaintances, and we value them all. But that is a perfect description of friendship. With your friend you think aloud, there is no restraint; there is no need to keep up an appearance—the blunter thing would be to say, there is no need to play the hypocrite. You pour everything out, knowing this—your friend will sift between the chaff and the grain, and with the breath of kindness will blow the chaff away, and keep only the grain. That is friendship on the human level. And it described what true friendship with God is—that is on my side of the fellowship. With God it is my privilege to pour out everything that is in my heart, chaff and grain together, saying anything, saying everything I am thinking. But have we learned that lesson? Do not we think altogether too often our conversation with God must be that of carefully prepared and often stilted phrasing? I think we never so grieve His heart as when we attempt to speak thus with Him. Conversing with God reaches its highest level when, alone with Him, I pour out in His listening ear everything in my heart; and the manner in which I have learned that secret, and live in the power of it, is the measure of the joy and strength of my friendship with God.

It is perfectly true, it may be done. I can say, and I do say, when alone with God things I dare not say in the hearing of other men. I tell Him all my griefs, and doubts, and fears; and if we have not learned to do so, we have never entered into the meaning of this great truth concerning fellowship. He will take out the grain, and with the breath of friendship blow the chaff away, only we must be honest when we are dealing with Him. I believe that if your heart is hot and restless about the way God is dealing with you, and you force yourself to the singing of a hymn of resignation, He spurns it; but if you pour out your anger as Martha did when she said, "I know he shall rise in the last day," then He will be patient, and loving, and gentle; and out of the infinite love and gentleness of His heart He will speak some quiet word of comfort.

How much do we know of this fellowship? How much have we practiced talking to God of everything in our souls?

Or take another illustration. Goethe speaking of his friendship for one with whom he held conversation, said this:

> For the first time I carried on a conversation; for the first time was the inmost sense of my words returned to me more rich, more full, more comprehensive from another mouth. What I had been groping for was returned clear to me. What I had been thinking I have been taught to see.

Is not that even a more subtle and delicate definition of friendship? Not only can I pour out all the things in my heart; but my friend will say yes, and repeat the thing I have said, and repeat it definitely better than I could ever have hoped to say it.

Here again is the revelation of what friendship with God means to those who know and practice it; and even though this may be a more delicate and wonderful definition, I think we all understand it perhaps a little better, for there have been moments when we have struggled to say things to God, and have heard Him saying them again to us better than we could have said them. Is not that what Paul meant when he said: "We know not what to pray for as we ought"? Is not that the supreme inspiration for high and prevailing prayer—the consciousness of inability to make prevailing prayer? But Paul added: "The Spirit maketh intercession for us with groanings which cannot be uttered," that is, He says the things for us, and we know that God is praying prayers we fain would pray, and answering our imperfect articulation with the perfect words that prove His perfect comprehension.

Or once again, Dryden, describing his friendship for his truest friend, said:

> We were so mixed up as meeting streams, both to ourselves were lost. We were one mass. We could not give or take but for the same, for he was I, I he.

What is that but Dryden's method of declaring that he and his friend had all things in common? And dare we take that last illustration and use it of friendship with God? Without a doubt. Here we touch the real meaning of fellowship; here we are at the heart and center of the great idea.

Let us now consider the other aspect of fellowship as

partnership; mutual interests, mutual devotion, mutual activity.

Fellowship with God means mutual interests: God interested in me, and I interested in God. The overwhelming sense of the heart, as these things are uttered, is that of the inequality of the friendship. That I may be interested in God is understandable; the infinite marvel at first sight is that God can be interested in me. "What is man that Thou art mindful of him? Or the Son of Man, that Thou visitest Him." Fellowship with God means that God is interested in my being, is all its parts; in my spiritual life, in my mental ability, in my physical need. Be not anxious about what you shall eat, or drink, or put on, for your Heavenly Father knoweth you have need of these things.

Now, would to God, brethren, I knew how to say this thing as it ought to be said. Presently, the evening service will be over and the day of worship and rest done, and most of you will be back in the midst of all the everyday things we speak of as the daily task, the common round. But fellowship means that God is as profoundly interested in a man on Monday in his office and store as when in the sanctuary; that there is no part of the life in which God is not interested. I only pause for lack of words to express a thing so sublime and yet so simple. The difficulty in business, the perplexity that burdens the mind—all these things He is interested in. God is interested in me, and in my development! Oh! let us begin where it is always best to begin—interested in the growth of the child. Just as interested as you are, infinitely more, in the physical development. Are you interested in the manifestations of your child's opening mind; in the questions and problems of your child? God is also interested.

I shall not be misunderstood when I say this: that while I personally differ profoundly with what is known as Unitarian theology, I am conscious we owe a good deal to Unitarians if it only be that they have brought us back to the consciousness of the nearness of God to human life, as revealed in the perfect manhood of Jesus. And do not let us forget it for our own comfort, our own strength. Brethren, we do not leave our God here when the Benediction is pronounced. Are you dreading tomorrow? Remember, God will be with you there, as profoundly interested in the piece of work your hands have to do, in the problem your mind has to face, as in the sanctuary at this hour.

Yes, but it is equally true I am to be interested in the things of God, in His ultimate ends and His present enterprises; that as His heart and mind are set upon my perfection, upon that ultimate realization when I shall be presented perfect before His throne; so also this fellowship demands that my eyes are to be forevermore upon that goal. If God will find His rest in me when I am perfectly conformed to His will, I should never find my perfect rest until His kingdom is established and His glory perfectly come.

Partnership also means mutual devotion. God's resources are all at my disposal. And now I must speak, I fear, in the language that indicates duty—my resources ought all to be at His disposal. His resources are all at my disposal; His knowledge, His wisdom, His power, are all at my disposal. How small a demand we make of Him! How often we settle down in our own wisdom and neglect asking for aught, while He is waiting to give! How constantly we dishonour Him because we do not appropriate all He has put at our disposal! All His resources at our disposal!

But have we responded to the other fact that all our resources are to be at His disposal? All of them, not a tithe, not a tenth. Oh! tithe your possessions if you will, but let your tithing be the evidence that the nine-tenths are also His. The man who takes his income and says, One-tenth is God's and nine-tenths are mine, is a bad Jew, and certainly not a good Christian. All belongs to Jehovah, just as the one day in seven is the symbol of the fact that the seven days belong to Him. All our resources at His disposal. That is the law of friendship, and if He put all His at my disposal, and I keep back part of the price, how unworthy I am of this great fact of fellowship with God.

But partnership means also mutual activity. God accommodating Himself to my weakness and I rising by that accommodation into co-operation with His mind and with His strength. Of these two things, the one to emphasize is that of God bringing Himself to my weakness. "Thy gentleness hath made me great." Do you remember George Matthieson's description of gentleness? He declared that when you speak of a brook running down the hillside, and away through the meadows, as a gentle brook, you are using a false term. He says there is no gentleness in a brook, but that if you watch the mighty ocean when it kisses the golden sands, and does not harm the child at play, then you may speak of gentleness. Gentleness is strength held in reserve, and placed at the service of weakness—"Thy gentleness hath made me great." Why does not God move more quickly? Why does not God accomplish His purpose in the world, and put an end to all the things that fret and puzzle us? Count that the long-suffering of God is His patience. Remember, that it would be possible, as we believe in God, for Him to end everything with a crash. But where would some of us be if He did so? Vulgarity is in a hurry; omnipotence is never in a hurry. All His processes are slow, as they appear to us, because of the gentleness of God. He waits for men. If it be a marvelous thing that Enoch walked with God, it is a more marvelous thing that God walked with Enoch, waiting for him as for a weak little child along the way. Just as you, father—strong man, equal to great speed—walk by the side of your little child that is just beginning to walk, accommodating your strength to the child's weakness, your speed to the child's slowness; so God forever accommodates Himself to our halting pace.

I wonder if that brings to your heart the comfort it brings to mine! I look back over my own life tonight, and see how wonderfully it is true; He is waiting, always waiting. Ah, I have kept Him waiting when I ought not, but He has waited even then. Always waiting—so patient with my foolishness, my weakness, my fear. Our fellowship is with God, and fellowship is friendship, and friendship means that partnership which, on His part, is the accommodation of His strength to my weakness.

But the gentleness does make us great, and by comparison with the pace we once had, how much quicker the pace is today; and by comparison with what we once were able to do, how much more we are able to do today! Let us not be afraid of boasting in the Lord, but say: "I can do all things through Christ who strengtheneth me." He leadeth us everywhere in triumph. When you think of the "all things," and the triumph, in comparison with God's ability, then you will remember again the slowness and weakness; but when you think of what He enables us to do in comparison with what we would have done without Him, then we marvel at the victories and accomplishments, for He is enabling us.

If God accommodates Himself to us in gentleness, He enables us to rise to new activity with Him, in almost overwhelming power.

Our fellowship is with the Father. The fellowship of the friendship that says everything, knowing that He will listen and blow the chaff away; the fellowship that says its best, and hears repeated by the friend the inner meaning of the best; the fellowship that merges into such identity of interest that we discover that God and we are in every deed in partnership with each other. He is committed to all the things that pertain to the fulfilment of my life, while I am committed to all the things that pertain to the fulfilment of His purpose and of His glory.

And yet, brethren, there is another test of friendship which goes beyond these, a more severe test of friendship than the ability to talk and be listened to, than speaking the innermost thought that the friend may repeat it better, than the merging of lives. The supreme test is the ability to say nothing, and be content when nothing is said. Silence is the final proof of friendship, and contentment in silence. When I want a holiday and a true rest, I want a true friend, and the true friend is the one I can sit with in the railway train and say nothing. When I am introduced by courtesy, and acquaintanceship results, and I must always be saying something to my host, that is not friendship. Very valuable for a little while; but in the home of my friend I sit down, and stare at him, and say nothing. He looks right back at me, and says nothing.

My true friend meets me some morning, and there is not the old smile, there is not the cheery word. Now if there be true friendship, I am not disturbed by these things. I am quite sure that this attitude is on the surface, that there is a reason for it. I prove my friendship by respecting his silence, and not seeking for explanation. I think that is the final proof of friendship. The moment you ask your friend to declare his friendship, you reveal your doubt of his friendship. Well, I am afraid we shall have to look to heaven for this friendship, but we have it in God if we will, and it is here we fail.

Is there an hour when you can no longer pray? Then do

not pray; and know this—God knows. Of course, if the reason of your inability to pray is that you have violated the laws of friendship, that you have sinned against it, then speak with repentance and with tears, until you be restored to joy and salvation. But if there be no conscious reason in your own life, let me quote from the ancient prophecy—"Who is among you that feareth the Lord, that obeyeth the voice of His servant? He that walketh in darkness, and hath no light."

Well, now what are we to do, prophet, because we are often there? Let him compel himself to sing? Nothing of the kind. What then? Let him trust in the name of the Lord, and stay upon the Lord without speaking. God is equal in His love to the strain of a silence that is born of honesty. Are we? Nay, nay; am I? And I shall not answer with public confession, but I do want the thing to search me. That is where I break down. If God does not speak, and there is no light and no revelation, I begin to wonder if He loves me. Oh, cultivate heart-silence.

And, my brethren, God's truest friends are those to whom God is most often silent. Would to God I could comfort some heart with that. The light has gone out, and you are obeying Him, walking in darkness. Do not imagine that is because He cannot trust you; it is a supreme proof of His trust; silence is the last test. Our fellowship is with the Father, so that if we are driven to silence we need not be afraid; so that if He is silent we ought not to be afraid.

It was a great hymn to which Bliss was writing the music when he was suddenly taken from life in a railway accident. They found in his writing-case the music, half-written, to that hymn:

> I know not what awaits me;
> God kindly veils mine eyes,

> I'd rather walk in the dark with God,
> Than go alone in the light;
> I'd rather walk by faith with Him,
> Than go alone by sight.

We often sing it. May God make it true to us. That is the final proof of friendship.

"My soul, wait thou upon God." "Oh, yes," we say, "we will do that; it is the easiest thing to do." Nay, it is the hardest thing to do! It is much easier to work for God than to wait for God. It is the waiting that tells and wears the heart. It is suspense that kills. There is relief in the hour of catastrophe, if there has been long waiting. Remember how often He has had to wait for thee. Let us be ashamed that we are keeping Him waiting, and yet let us know that His friendship will bear the test. If in our deepest heart, when there is no song, no psalm, no ecstasy; no joy, we are true; His friendship will bear the strain. And He wants us to be such friends that we can bear the strain of silence and the great test of quietness.

But, my brethren, we need to practice our fellowship. He wants to talk to me of His own secrets, of the meaning of my life, and the way He would have me go; and I believe, brethren, one of the greatest lacks in the present day is that we do not take time to listen. "Oh," you say, "God does not speak to men now as He spoke to Abraham." I do not believe it. I think the true thing to say is that men do not listen as Abraham listened. We do not give God the chance to speak. The practice of fellowship.

> I am listening, Lord, for Thee,
> What hast Thou to say to me?

Quite easy to sing in a crowd; but we want to learn to practice it in our own individual life; and the practice means that we must take time to speak to Him of our work and His work; of our need and responsibility; of our sorrows and of our joys; of our defeats and of our victories. That is the practice of this fellowship, and we need to take time for these things.

Brethren, in closing, has it ever occurred to you that God is often disappointed that we are so busy doing things for Him, that we have not time to talk to Him? I feel that is true of my own life. I feel increasingly that I have to guard against being so busy for God that I have no time for God Himself; and God created man for His glory. For what is man to be? What is the ideal of human life? That he may enter into the secrets of God, and be the friend of God; and if God's friends never visit Him, never talk to Him, even though they are busily occupied in His work, they are robbing Him. Let us see to it that we take this great word and attempt to enter into the fulness of its suggestion.

Oh, presently we shall be back again facing the problems and perplexities, and doing that piece of work we laid down yesterday, glad to be away from it for very weariness. But now, when we take it up tomorrow, let us remember God is as interested in it as in the song with which we close the Sabbath. And if we will, brethren, that very piece of work—so poor, so commonplace that we desire not to do it —will become transfigured; and we shall find that the least thing of every day is part of God's method for building the city, and winning the world, and bringing in His kingdom.

May it be ours, therefore, not only to hold the doctrine of fellowship with God, but to practice it, and enter into all the fulness of the blessing, for His name's sake.

CHAPTER VI

THE PASSION-BAPTISM

I came to cast fire upon the earth; and what do I desire, if it is already kindled? But I have a baptism to be baptised with; and how am I straitened till it be accomplished.
LUKE 12:49, 50.

IN THE CALENDAR OF THE CHRISTIAN CHURCH THIS IS spoken of as Passion Sunday. The day has been devoted to the Church's contemplation of those sorrows of our Lord which, in human history and to human observation, culminated in the Cross.

I propose to ask you to meditate with me through the medium of these words of Jesus, on our Lord's thought of his Cross, in those days when His face was stedfastly set toward Jerusalem.

Perhaps there is no passage in the gospel narratives which has suffered more difficulty of translation than this. It is one in which absolutely literal translation would almost result in misinterpretation. A reverent translation into our more modern speech, greatly helps us. In Weymouth's Testament the text reads thus:

> I came to throw fire upon the earth, and what is My desire? Oh that it were even now kindled! But I have a baptism to undergo; and how am I pent up till it is accomplished!

These words constitute what I venture to describe as a soliloquy of Jesus. By that I mean they were not addressed directly to the crowd; nor directly, even to His own disciples. They occur in the midst of a set discourse, but they stand alone. You can omit them entirely, and that particular discourse is not interfered with, its meaning is not hampered, it abides. In the midst of it He broke out into these words. I would venture, very reverently, to describe this soliloquy of Jesus as a heartburst.

Let us look at the chapter. It opens thus, "In the meantime, when the many thousands of the multitude were gathered together. . . . He began to say unto His disciples first of all." He was speaking in the presence of the multitudes, but first of all to His disciples. The discourse runs quietly on until we come to the thirteenth verse where we find the first interruption, "One of the multitude said unto Him, Master, bid my brother divide the inheritance with me." The Lord answered with a parable. At verse twenty-two He resumes the discourse to His disciples, "And He said unto His disciples . . ."; and proceeds quietly, until He is again disturbed, not this time by one of the multitude, but by one of the disciples, "Peter said, Lord, speakest thou this parable unto us, or even unto all?" The Lord answered Peter with a parable. Now let us link verse forty-eight with verse fifty-one, and by so doing we find the true connection of the discourse. Between those two verses lie the words of my text.

If all this is somewhat tedious, it is absolutely important. It is only as we can get back into the very atmosphere of the occasion upon which our Lord uttered these words that we can hope to come into full sympathy with them, or into anything like intelligent understanding of their meaning.

Earlier in the gospel story it is declared that He set His face stedfastly to go to Jerusalem. He is on His way to the Cross. He is traversing the Via Dolorosa. His own soul is filled with sorrow, and He is talking to His disciples. A man in the multitude interrupts Him, "Master, bid my brother divide the inheritance with me." He rebukes him for his sordidness and resumes His discourse. Peter interrupts Him. He answers Peter in a parable; and there breaks in upon His soul anew His perpetual consciousness of how dull His disciples and the multitudes are. The man who said "Bid my brother divide the inheritance with me" is typical of the crowd, and they do not understand Him at all. They imagine He is there to be a divider of property, a mere social reformer. His own disciples did not understand. Peter said, "Is this parable for us, or for the rest? Is there no difference between us?" While patiently instructing their dullness, the abiding sense of their dullness and of His own limitation, finds expression in a great heartburst; "I came to cast fire upon the earth; and what do I desire, if it is already kindled? But I have a baptism to be baptized with; and how am I straitened till it be accomplished."

Jesus was straitened, so straitened that the disciples could not understand Him; so straitened that the jostling crowd misinterpreted Him. Reverently, let me say the whole thing. He was eager for His Cross, because He knew that apart from that He could not fulfil His mission.

Mark the opening words of this soliloquy. "I came to cast fire upon the earth." In the third chapter of this gospel, Luke tells us how His forerunner, John the Baptist, had declared to the multitudes who listened to him, "I indeed baptize you with water; but there cometh He that is mightier than I, the latchet of Whose shoes I am not worthy to unloose: He shall baptize you with the Holy Ghost and with fire." I turn to the second treatise of Luke, which we call the Acts of the Apostles, and I listen to Jesus now on the other side of His Cross and resurrection, and He says, referring to the very words of the forerunner, "John indeed

THE PASSION-BAPTISM

baptized with water; but ye shall be baptized with the Holy Ghost not many days hence." I turn over the page and come to the second chapter, "And when the day of Pentecost was now come, they were all together in one place. And suddenly, there came from heaven a sound as of the rushing of a mighty wind, and it filled all the house where they were sitting. And there appeared unto them tongues parting asunder, like as of fire; and it sat upon each one of them. And they were all filled with the Holy Ghost, and began to speak with other tongues, as the Spirit gave them utterance." That was the historic fulfilment of the prediction of John; the Holy Ghost came and they were baptized, and the symbol of His coming was fire.

Between the prophecy of the forerunner and the historic fulfilment occurred the soliloquy of Jesus, in which in effect He said, "I cannot fulfil John's prediction, I cannot cast the fire that purifies, energizes, and remakes; that enlightens the darkened intellect, enkindles the deadened emotion, energizes the degraded will, until I have been baptized with My own baptism." Pentecost cannot precede the Cross. That is the theme of the soliloquy.

Let us reverently tarry in the presence of the great words, conscious in every word that I utter, and to which you in your reverent patience will listen, that the last things can never be said about that baptism. Yet, let us listen to these words of Jesus because in them there is an unfolding of truth about the passion and the Cross which is full of value.

This fact of the coming Cross was perpetually present to the mind of Christ. He never told His disciples about His Cross until after Peter's great confession; but there are evidences in the early story that He knew of it, and that He was moving toward it, not as a victim, but as a Victor; not yielding Himself to an ultimate disaster because He was helpless, but moving with determination toward the ultimate process, and the final victory.

John tells us that at the commencement of His public ministry He entered the temple and cleansed it. They challenged Him; "What sign shewest Thou unto us, seeing that Thou doest these things?" His answer was strange and mysterious. He said, "Destroy this temple, and in three days I will raise it up." They, materialized as they were, imagined that He was speaking of the temple in the midst of which men were still worshipping. In the days of Pentecostal illumination that speech of Jesus was understood by His disciples, and writing long afterwards in the light of the spiritual interpretation, John declared "He spake of the temple of His body." I look back at that scene and I see Him cleansing the temple; and find that when men asked Him what was His authority for so doing, He answered, not so that they could then understand, but out of His own consciousness, My authority for cleansing the temple, and restoring it to its true purpose is the authority of My coming Cross and My ultimate resurrection.

Again, sitting in the quietness of a starlit night upon the roof of an Eastern house, He conversed with Nicodemus. In honest and splendid perplexity, the inquirer asked, "How can these things be? How can a man be born when he is old?" Jesus, borrowing an illustration from the ancient literature of the religion to which this man belonged, said, "As Moses lifted up the serpent in the wilderness, even so must the Son of man be lifted up: that whosoever believeth may in Him have eternal life." Nicodemus could not understand the answer then, but in effect the Master said, "You as Me, how a man can be born again, how he can receive new life which shall master and negative all his old life, and My reply is that only by the way of My death, only by My lifting up on the Cross shall I ever be able to communicate My life. You cannot see My life, without My dying. In its truth and grace and glory you never can share it save as I die." The Cross was in His heart when He talked with Nicodemus.

Passing over the earlier days, we come to the glorious scene on the mount of transfiguration; and the theme of His conversation with the heavenly visitors, Moses and Elijah, was that of the exodus which He should accomplish, His Cross and His resurrection.

When the Greeks found Him, and the disciples told Him, "The Greeks desire to see Thee," He said this strange and startling thing, "Except a grain of wheat fall into the earth and die, it abideth by itself alone; but if it die, it bareth much fruit. He that loveth His life loseth it; and he that hateth his life in this world shall keep it unto life eternal." That is to say, He had declared that if the Greeks desired to see Him and enter into understanding of what He was they could never do so until He was dead and risen. In newness of life won out of death would they behold Him.

These are illustrations taken almost at haphazard from the ministry of Jesus showing that the Cross was ever present in His mind.

In this soliloquy He tells us why it was ever present, as He reveals His own estimate, first as to its necessity; and secondly, insofar as we are able to grasp it, as to its nature.

Let us notice first then the teaching of this word of Jesus concerning the necessity for His Cross. "I am straitened." The difficulty here is lest, in attempting exposition, by multiplicity of words one should darken counsel. I find many expositors teach that our Lord was here speaking of His own sorrows. The word "straitened," however, reveals the reason of the sorrows, which is infinitely more than a declaration of the fact. "I am straitened"; that is I am confined, imprisoned, shut up, limited; or as Dr. Weymouth has it "pent up."

It was a remarkable thing for Him to say. There He stood amid His disciples, a fair and perfect Example; there He stood, the final moral Teacher of all the centuries, and yet He said, "I am straitened"; I cannot do My work, I cannot complete My work; I am unable to communicate My life, the dynamic force that will enable men to obey the teaching, and to imitate the Example.

He was straitened in His teaching. "I have many things to say unto you, but ye cannot bear them yet." He was straitened in His work. "Greater works than these shall ye do, because I go to My Father." There He stood in the midst of a world full of sorrow and sighing and sin, longing to cast that fire on the earth which should purify and energize and remake, yet unable to do it; quite able to teach, to present the ideal, but these were not the things for which He had finally come, for these are quite useless alone.

If I am told today that it is my business to preach the ethic of Jesus, and that is enough; if I am told that all the Christian preacher ought to do is to call men to imitation of the great Example, and that is sufficient; my reply can only be that such opinion is out of harmony with the opinion of Jesus Himself. He did here clearly affirm, that while He was a Teacher and an Example, and only these, He was straitened, unable to do the ultimate thing for which He had come, unable to accomplish the great work upon which His heart was set. He came, not merely to give men an example, not merely to enunciate an ethic, but to cast fire, the symbol of purity, the symbol of power; fire for cleansing, for energy; but He could not do so until He was baptized with His baptism. When He uttered these words, He was waiting for, setting His face stedfastly toward, that whelming in darkness, the inner and deepest mystery of which none of us can ever fathom or understand; and He said, "I cannot complete My work, cannot scatter this purifying, energizing fire, cannot open these blind eyes, touch these cold hearts, and remake these shrivelled powers, save by the way of My Cross." In these words we have revealed our Lord's sense of the necessity for the Cross.

More reverently still, and with softer footfall, let us examine the light which this soliloquy throws on the nature of the Cross. The passion baptism was to be a baptism through which it should be possible for Him to open those blind eyes, and unstop those deaf ears, to make these men understand the things He could not now make them understand. The word itself is suggestive, "I have a baptism." There is only one meaning for the word, and that is immersion or whelming. That toward which He was going was not an experience in which He would stand by the awful silence of a dead sea, and taste its brackish waters. That to which He was going was an hour in which He would fathom its depths, and enter into spiritual and profound fulfilment of that which had been written long before, "All thy waves and thy billows are gone over me." Apart from that whelming in death and in darkness, He could not complete His work; but by that way, He was able to scatter fire, and fulfil His purpose.

If, then, by way of that whelming He was able to fulfil His purpose, we know this much at least, that it was a baptism in which He was able, in some mystic mystery of Divine wisdom and power, to deal with the forces that spoil humanity, to deal with that which, in the spiritual life of man, has produced blindness and inability.

There they stood about Him; His disciples looking at Him with wide open eyes of loving human affection, yet never seeing Him; listening to the words He said with reverent attention, and yet never hearing! The multitudes day by day listened to His teaching, watched Him healing, and imagined He had come to divide property! He said, "Only by the way of the Cross can I fulfil My mission, but by way of the Cross I will open these eyes that they may see, open these ears that they may hear, touch these hearts that they may understand the deep spiritual meaning of My mission. I have come for the remaking, not of accidentals, but of essentials; and through the remaking of the essentials for the remaking of the accidentals. I have not come to divide as between human inheritances, but to put men right with God, and right with each other, that so they may divide their inheritances upon a spiritual basis."

It was only by the way of the Cross, according to His own estimate, that He could accomplish that work. Fire, illuminative, energizing; clarifying the vision, making the pulses of the soul beat, and making eternity a reality; could only be given, said Christ, by the way of His Cross. Whatever we may think about the Cross, that is what He thought about it. It was only by His Cross; by His whelming in death; by His immersion in immeasurable and unutterable anguish and sorrow; that He could take hold of the poison which had spoiled humanity, and negate it, make it not to be, cancel it, destroy it, and so liberate the fire and remake humanity.

We cannot end with the text. Our Lord and Master is no longer saying in the midst of human history, "I came to cast fire upon the earth; and what do I desire? Would that it were already kindled? But I have a baptism to be baptized with; and how am I straitened till it be accomplished."

These are not the words of Jesus here and now. In reverence I change his words, as in His presence I utter them. He is saying now, "I came to cast fire upon the earth, and lo, it is kindled! I have cast it because I have been baptized with My baptism; and therefore, I am no longer straitened." We have not to do with the straitened Christ, but with the unstraitened Christ. We are not listening to the teaching of Christ under circumstances of limitation because the Cross was not accomplished. The teaching is the same; but we are dealing with Christ on the other side of the Cross, so that He is able not only to teach but to give power to obey. We have not to deal with a Christ, upon the wonder of Whose pure and strong and glorious life we look with amazement and then become conscious of our own inability to copy Him or be like Him. We have to do with a Christ Who brings to us an ideal that captures our admiration; and Who then touches us with power so that each of us says, "I can do all things through Christ which strengtheneth me."

Let us ever bring into our religious thinking the historic sense, and let us remember that our Lord passed to the passion baptism, was whelmed beneath the infinite mystery of those dark waters; and that He emerged from them in Resurrection, ascended on high, and led captivity captive, and received gifts for men, and scattered the fire; and therefore, we may share that gift immediately, and so enter into all the fulness of the meaning of His mission. He is straitened no longer.

"He Who spared not His own Son, but delivered Him up for us all, how shall He not also with Him freely give us all things?"

"All things are yours; whether Paul, or Apollos, or Cephas, or the world, or life, or death, or things present, or things to come; all are yours; and ye are Christ's; and Christ is God's."

He "giveth us richly all things to enjoy."

All that is the result of His passion-baptism. Christianity is not one perpetual agony of sorrow. Your Christianity is not witnessed to by the misery of your countenance. God has freely given us all things, and that to enjoy. All things are ours to enjoy because He went to His Cross. It is by way of the tree that the leaves of healing come. It is by the way of the Cross that the crown is placed upon our brows. It is by the way of passion-whelming, that the baptism comes to us which is the baptism of fire, of purity, and of energy.

Now let me make the final application. There is a sense in which this soliloquy of Jesus is one which we must make our own. If we would enter into life, we also have to say—and yet I pause again to interpolate this warning, let us be very careful of the sense in which this thing is said—"I have a baptism to be baptized with, and how am I straitened till it be accomplished."

I take you back to the chapter we read in Mark. Jesus had His face set toward Jerusalem, toward the Cross and the suffering. He was telling His disciples that He must go to suffering, that He must be killed and the third day rise again, when there came to Him James and John—Matthew says their mother spoke for them—and asked Him to grant them whatever they wished. And He answered, "What is it that you would ask of Me?" Then they said this, "Grant unto us that we may sit, one on Thy right hand, and one on Thy left, in Thy glory." He replied, "Ye know not what ye ask. Are ye able to drink the cup that I drink? or to be baptized with the baptism that I am baptized with?" They said, "We are able." Is not that the profoundest proof of the fact that Jesus was straitened and unable to make men understand? Think of that answer of James and John, "We are able."

Yet, what did He say? "The cup that I drink ye shall drink; and with the baptism that I am baptized withal shall ye be baptized." What did He mean? If what we have been saying is true, that He drank of the cup in unutterable loneliness, that His great passion-baptism was isolated and alone, a whelming in which none could possibly share, then what did He mean when He said this to these two men? It was the word of His Grace. It was the declaration that while He would tread the winepress alone, He would carry them with Him into the midst of the sorrow vicariously, and bring them into new life by standing in their place in death. Paul said, "We have been crucified with Him." Historically Paul's hands were not nailed to the Cross; but His hands were nailed to the Cross. Essentially, Paul never went out into the infinite and awful mystery of atoning death, nor could he, nor can I, nor can you; but Paul was crucified with Him. He had gathered Paul into His own personality and heart. He was infinitely more than Man in Himself, He was the sum total of the people He had gathered into His own personality, the sum total of humanity, and in that strange hour of His baptism there also was I baptized. In that strange hour in which He drank the cup, there also I, in Him, drank the cup. You shall drink of My cup, you shall be baptized with My baptism. You cannot drink the cup alone, you cannot be baptized alone or independently or separated from Me, but in Me you shall drink the cup and be baptized with the baptism.

It is as though He had said, "I am going into this baptism not for Myself but for you." The old terms of the theologians must be retained. His death was vicarious.

That is where you and I must begin to live if we would live at all in spiritual fulness. If I declare that there are senses in which we can and must say, "I have a baptism to be baptized with, and how am I straitened till it be accomplished," I do not mean that by my identification with His Cross in self-surrender I find my way into life. There is a very subtle peril abroad in much of the finest devotional literature of the day; I hear men talking about their identification with Christ as though there were some value in it. There is no value in it. Everything must be of grace. I shall have to come on the last day of life to His Cross, saying, "Nothing in my hand I bring." Because I bear in my body brands that speak of suffering for Him, I am no more worthy of His salvation. Neither the brands I bear, nor the suffering I share, bring me nearer to God. When at last I lay my head on the pillow at the close of the one short day of work I can render to God, I shall die a sinner saved by grace, and in no other way shall I enter into life. Not by the merit of my service, not by self-denials, not by the cross I carry shall I ever enter heaven; but by His baptism and by His cup of sorrow drunk to the dregs. So only shall I ever come into life beyond, and so only can I ever enter into life here.

Those powers of which you boast yourself, those splendid capacities of your magnificent humanity—the anthems of them are being sung in every magazine today; but know this, that the dawning will darken to midnight unless you enter into life by the way of Christ's Cross.

There it stands in the midst of the centuries, the one and only hope of humanity, and only by taking my life from Him as a gift purchased in the mystery of His passion-whelming, can I ever find its fulfilment according to the purpose of God.

But this is the last word of all. The passion is accomplished, the victory is won, the fire is scattered. This is the day of Pentecost. Every man in this house can leave the sanctuary with fire which will enable him to say, to do, to be, to the glory of His name.

CHAPTER VII

THE TRIUMPHAL ENTRY

On the morrow a great multitude that had come to the feast, when they heard that Jesus was coming to Jerusalem, took the branches of the palm trees, and went forth to meet Him, and cried out, Hosanna: Blessed is He that cometh in the name of the Lord, even the King of Israel.

JOHN 12:12, 13.

IN THE CALENDAR OF THE CHRISTIAN CHURCH THIS IS known as Palm Sunday. On Sunday last we considered our Lord's interpretation of His passion-baptism as indicated in words chronicled only by Luke, "I came to cast fire upon the earth; and what do I desire, if it is already kindled? But I have a baptism to be baptized with; and how am I straitened till it be accomplished."

Now amid the Lenten shadows there breaks a ray of brightness, and flashes a touch of color. We are accustomed to speak of our Lord's entry into Jerusalem as a triumphal entry. There are certain senses in which that description is warranted; yet, it may be a misleading description. The picture is one of ineffable sadness. Contemplated in the light of the ministry of Jesus; considered in relation to all the surrounding circumstances, it was a very, very sad entry. It is a picture of great sadness, merging into gladness; of ineffable sorrow, preparing the way for unutterable and final joy.

It was the first day of the week. In the calendar of the

Hebrew people it was the day on which the sacrificial lamb for the Passover was secluded. The Master had spent the Sabbath in quietness among His friends. The day of rest over, He is seen passing to Jerusalem amid the thronging and surging multitudes. It is a little difficult, I sometimes think, for us to comprehend the vastness of the crowds that gathered in Jerusalem at the Passover feast. Josephus sets the number at three million. In all probability we are correct if we say that at that great Passover feast, half, or even more, of the population scattered around Jerusalem gathered to the city. Jerusalem was quite unable to entertain them, even the surrounding villages were overcrowded, and thousands lived in booths and tents erected that they might be able to be present at the Passover feast.

The fame of Jesus had, of course, spread through all the countryside. His name had become a household word. The three years of His public ministry, the wonder of His works, and the more matchless wonder of His words had carried His fame everywhere. The people were eager and anxious to see Him, many who had never seen Him, and others, many who had often see Him, were desirous of seeing Him again. There was the added wonder of the raising of Lazarus as we are told by the evangelists. The last great public sign in demonstration of His power had been that of the raising of Lazarus. Then the news spread that He was actually coming to Jerusalem, was to enter Jerusalem that day; and so He came, passing through vast multitudes lining the way, thronging the streets.

Now the remarkable thing about this story is that He chose to enter publicly, and deliberately arranged for His entry in such a way as to provoke demonstration. You will remember another occasion where there was a feast in Jerusalem and His brethren after the flesh tried to persuade Him to come up and do this very thing; to present Himself publicly in the midst of the crowds and proclaim His Kingship; and He had said to them with a touch of tender sarcasm, "My time is not yet come; but your time is always ready." He eventually went to that feast, but He went quietly, unobserved, finding His way in all probability over some of the mountain paths and through their passes, and it was not known He was coming until suddenly He was found in the temple teaching. How different this entry. He chose now to enter publicly, evoking demonstration. It was by His own arrangement that He went riding upon the colt, the foal of an ass, surrounded by the little band of His own disciples; and by those vast Galilean crowds who had always more sympathy with Him than the crowds of Judaea; the crowds from Galilee of the Gentiles, as the Judaens termed them with contempt; Galilee, the country merging on Gentile land and which had passed under Gentile influence, and in that way had become contaminated.

This entry of our Lord was part of the Divine program; that is made most clear in the Gospel of Matthew, which reveals Him in His kingly character. After He had been rejected by the rulers, He departed from Jerusalem and for a period following Caesarea Philippi, the period during which He was instructing His disciples in the necessity for His coming Cross, He had not been near the city. He is now seen going back to the city for a definite purpose, in awe-inspiring solemnity to challenge those rulers, to compel them by parabolic method to find a verdict against themselves, and then at last to pronounce the doom of the city.

I draw your attention to that only in passing, and yet, we must not lose sight of it. I feel personally that it cannot be too often emphasized that the whole movement of the ministry of Jesus in the latter days, was under His own government and by His own arranging. If we look at Him during those passion days as a victim of circumstances, we miss the vision entirely. Not as a victim did He take His way to Jerusalem and to the Cross, but as a Victor. This entry into Jerusalem was for the specific purpose of uttering its final doom, rejecting the Hebrew people from their position in the economy of God. It was during this final visit to Jerusalem that He uttered the words so full of awful solemnity, "The kingdom of God shall be taken away from you, and shall be given to a nation bringing forth the fruits thereof." This was a Kingly entrance. He was going deliberately and with determination, for the awe-inspiring and solemn work of pronouncing doom on the city. Yet, He was going to break a way through the doom toward the ultimate victory, going—to use the descriptive phrase of the conversation with the heavenly visitors on the mount of transfiguration—to accomplish an exodus.

Our attention then is to be fixed upon this actual entry; and we will observe it first as to the event itself; secondly, briefly as to the sequel; and finally as to the lessons it has still to teach.

Look for a moment at this entry of Jesus as a patrician Roman would have looked at it. If you do that, your heart will be filled with contempt for the whole movement. I make that suggestion in order that we may see this thing as it really appeared. Has it ever occurred to you that it was a very remarkable thing that the Roman officials did not interfere with this demonstration? They were there to quell insurrection, to hold in check the hot, turbulent Jews, and yet, there was no interference on their part! They were accustomed to see these vast multitudes gathered for religious exercises at Jerusalem; but they were perfectly aware of this strange movement and this unusual excitement manifest. They knew of the prophet of Nazareth, but they did not inter-

THE TRIUMPHAL ENTRY

fere. Why not? Because the whole thing was so utterly and absolutely contemptible. I put it more strongly still and say that which we describe as a triumphal entry would have been in the eyes of the Roman a laughing stock; the Roman who perchance had seen in the eternal city sitting on its seven hills, the triumphal return of a conqueror! I need not stop to describe in detail those triumphal entries, in which the conqueror, drawn in triumphal car, with kings whom he had overcome in war chained to his chariot wheels, amid the plaudits of the assembled multitudes, entered the city in military magnificence. Some old soldier who had seen such an entry into Rome, would look at this entry characterized by old clothes, broken trees, unarmed peasant folk, and would have held it in supreme contempt, in the kind of contempt that the West End still feels for any procession out of the East End at any hour of any day. It was just a mob; unorganized, shouting, tearing branches from trees and casting them in the way, taking their garments off and putting them across the back of the colt upon which a man rode. A man riding upon old clothes, in the midst of broken trees, surrounded by a shouting mob. That would have been the Roman outlook upon the whole scene. Grotesque!

Yet look again, for it was a most impressive procession. Forget the accidentals of the old clothes and the broken trees, and the patrician contempt for peasant folk; and see humanity thronging, pressing, jostling, around one central Man. I have seen many impressive congregations gathered in Westminster Chapel, but one abides in my memory with more impressiveness than any other. Several years ago, there was a procession of unemployed to the House of Commons, and we opened these doors simply to shelter the women while the men went on to the House. I saw this building filled from floor to ceiling with women of the East End, and never was I more impressed by any gathering in all my public ministry. The very fact that they were out of their usual place, and that there were upon them the marks that would have caused them to be held in contempt by patricians, was impressive. There was eagerness and anxiety in all their faces. Their singing of "The Marseillaise" I shall never forget; nor when asked what hymn they would like to sing they replied, "Count your blessings," and they sang it. It was a vast mass of human beings, eager, intent, wondering, ready for anything. That is the grandeur of the crowd that surrounded Jesus as He rode that day.

Look once more upon this gathering and see, so far as it is possible to see, the great spiritual truth, the thing the multitude did not see, the thing that His own disciples did not understand, the thing which at the moment He alone perfectly understood; He was taking His way to the goal which the people desired, but in a way they did not understand. They crowd around Him, these Galilean peasants, and the children of Jerusalem, crying, "Hosanna—Save now: blessed is He that cometh in the name of the Lord," were crying out for the establishment of a Kingdom, for the authority of a King, for deliverance from the yoke of bondage which rested upon them, for the dawning of a new day of light and life and peace. He was riding through the midst of that clamour toward that very goal. He was going by a way that they knew not of, a way that they so little understood that, presently, they turned the cry of Hosanna into the hiss of crucify.

He was moving through the worthless present, transmuting it into the triumphant future. If we fix our eyes upon Him alone, the other things which the patrician Roman would hold in contempt become transfigured and they become beautiful. The old clothes marked sacrificial loyalty on the part of the men who flung them upon the colt. Nothing else

THE TRIUMPHAL ENTRY

was at hand, therefore they brought their garments and spread them upon the colt that He might ride upon them. The old clothes of the disciples were more beautiful than the purple of patrician Romans. The very tree branches were in fact more beautiful than any human work of art could possibly be. Unarmed men have always been His army, for conducting His warfare and bringing in His victory.

The very things upon which I gaze and hold in contempt when measured by human standards have suddenly cast upon them a light and glory, that transmutes them into fine gold; and there is suggestiveness and beauty about this entrance from which one cannot escape.

Look for a moment at the crowds. The disciples, passionately eager for His crowning. This is what they so often hoped He would do. This is the kind of demonstration to which they have been attempting to urge Him. At last He is riding in, fulfilling prophecy, to proclaim Himself the King of Israel. In their gladness, in their shouting, and in the manifestation of loyalty, there was a strange yet natural reaction from the sadness of those days since Caesarea Philippi. In our Lord's contemplation of His passion, these men could not understand or follow Him; they shrank from the Cross; but this is what they had hoped for. At last, it appeared to them, that He had abandoned those words He had been uttering about the necessity for buffeting, bruising and dying in Jerusalem. At last He was going to Jerusalem, not to yield Himself to the hostility of His foes, but to proclaim His Kingship. They were filled with zeal for Him; but it was zeal without knowledge. He will teach these men, in preparation for the days to come, in the only way in which they can understand His teaching; that the Kingdom cannot come as they expect. Even though He provoke sentiment, and compel demonstration; even though the crowds are ready to shout

His name and proclaim Him King; He cannot escape from that determinate counsel and foreknowledge of God which is for Him the way of the Cross.

Turn from that inner circle and observe the multitude; seeking a King, and now crowding around Him. I have often wondered what they meant when they shouted "Hosanna," and I am not quite sure until this moment. Hosanna is a combination of two words in the Hebrew tongue, the one meaning *save*, the other being always an exclamation, sometimes "Ho," sometimes "Now," but always exclamatory. Look at these people round about Jesus. Look at the children as they take up the song and make it ring in the temple courts. What is the thing they sing? "Hosanna, Blessed is He that cometh in the name of the Lord, even the King of Israel." It is an appeal. I think we are perfectly safe in saying it means *save now*. You discovered from the reading of the paragraph in Psalm 118 that this was a quotation from the ancient psalmody. What did they mean? Were these Galilean peasants appealing to Him, or were they appealing to Jerusalem? Did Hosanna mean they were crying to Him to "Save now," or were they appealing to Jerusalem to receive the King? I leave it as a question, please understand that. If for the moment, I only give you my own conviction you will receive it as such and not as dogmatic or final. I think they were appealing for Him, even though as I have already said, the "Hosanna" presently merged into "Crucify"; but remember, they were two different crowds that cried, "Hosanna" and "Crucify." They were the Galilean crowds that cried, "Hosanna," and the Judaean crowds that presently cried, "Crucify." I believe that day the Galilean multitudes appealed in their song that He might be received. It was the Galilean appeal to Jerusalem to receive Him. Who answered? Not the city, not the rulers, not the publicans, but the children. For a mo-

THE TRIUMPHAL ENTRY

ment there is the most perfect picture of the temple in all the ministry of Jesus. Again He cleansed it, driving out the traffickers. Then He stood in the midst surrounded by children and cripples; children singing the Galilean song, and the sick being brought to Him for healing. This for a brief hour ere He doomed the city and said, "Your house is left unto you desolate," notice "Your house," which at the beginning of His ministry He had called "My Father's house."

Whether the multitudes were appealing to Him to save, or to Jerusalem to receive, the fundamental truth is the same; they were seeking for His authority. Yet, the basis of their desire was wholly wrong. The basis of their desire was selfish, they would crown Him, as they had attempted to do again and again, because they believed that if He were King they would be fed with material food, healed of physical disorder, brought into the place of material blessing. There is no spiritual passion in the cry, no deep sense of sin underlying it. So He rode in with disciples mistaking His meaning, glad because He is abandoning, as they think, at the last moment, His purpose of the Cross; surrounded by the multitudes seeking authority, appealing to Him to save, or to Jerusalem to receive, as the case may be, in order that the Kingdom may be established upon a material basis.

Now look once more. The only consistent people in the crowd apart from the King, are the Pharisees; hostile, fearful, rebellious, determined; consistent with themselves. Remember, a man may be consistent and that may be the most terrible indictment you can bring against him. John was beheaded that Herod might be consistent; "I have given my word to the wanton and I will behead the prophet"; so spake Herod. Let us beware of being consistent if consistent means persistent in a thing which is evil.

So the procession moved on, and the King moved in.

Though the disciples and the multitudes alike saw the glitter of a crowning, He saw the blood of the Cross. They imagined He was now coming to establish His throne, and break the yoke of Rome and set His people free; He knew that He was moving toward His final baptism, and so He knew that He was moving toward the glory of the crowning and toward the victory that lay beyond.

What of the sequel of this entry? The tears of Jesus. As He observed the city, He wept over it. The temple cleansed by Jesus and restored for a brief hour to its own true use. The accursed tree to which the King went of His own choice and of His own will; the tree which He made the throne of empire, the great center of that government which shall at last build the city of God and establish His order in the world.

The sequel! The disciples all forsook Him and fled. The multitudes of Galileans left and hurried away. The Judaean crowd took up the cry, "Away with Him, Crucify Him." The Pharisees remained consistent, and murdered Him. Jerusalem was destroyed.

Looking back upon that scene, these are the things that it seems to say to my heart and soul. I hear the King saying in the midst of all that multitude, "My Kingdom is not of this world," which does not mean that His Kingdom is not to be set up in this world, but that the Kingdom of the King can never come according to worldly ideals, by worldly methods, or result in the glamour and glory which is entirely and absolutely of the world.

I say this with all carefulness and all reverence; let us be careful lest we desire to crown Him still upon the worldly foundation, and by earthly method, and only for material glory. The peril has run through the centuries and today desires to make Jesus King because He can feed the multitude.

THE TRIUMPHAL ENTRY

He will have no throne upon that basis. He will never allow Himself to be crowned in that way. He will build God's city in the world. He will revolutionize the social order. He will bring, ere His work be done, the true brotherhood growing out of the recognition of the Fatherhood of God. But He must begin at the center, at the spiritual center, and in no other way will He ever do His work. His Kingdom is not of this world as to ideal, or method, or ultimate glory. His Kingdom is over the world, over all its necessities, the clothes that He sat upon; over all its beauties, the trees with which they strewed the way of His entry; over its finality, men, for whom all things were made, and who constitute the crowning glory of the creation of God. His Kingdom is over the world, and it will be established over the world and all the facts and forces of the material will also be under His dominion. But these He will remake, renew, render finally beautiful by dealing with the spiritual center, and from that spiritual center He will change the material circumference. Do not let us be led astray by any demonstration that seeks to put Him on the throne in any other way than that of His own appointment.

What is the nature of our joy in the presence of the King? The question appeals to me as being full of searching power. Is our joy that of these multitudes? Is our joy that of these disciples? Or is our joy that which was the inspiration of the King Himself? What was the joy of the multitudes in that brief hour of acclamation? The joy of believing that the King would provide peace and power and plenty. Peace interpreted as quietness to dwell under their own vine and fig tree in comfort. Power, as ability to break the yoke of Rome by their own hand. Plenty, as freedom from all material poverty. This is what they were looking for. This is the joy that was in the heart of the multitude. What was the joy in the heart of the King? The vision of the purity of the redeemed earth, of the peace that would issue from that purity, of the power that would come to men by the way of that purity, and of the plenty which would result. His joy was that of the certainty that by the way of His coming Cross and passion, He could remake men at the center of their being, so that they should be pure, clean, holy, and conformed to the character of God; and the certainty that out of the remaking of the spiritual life there must inevitably come the renewal of everything related thereto. The passion and joy of the fickle crowd was that for material comfort. The passion and joy of the Lord, which was His comfort and strength as He walked the way of the Cross and endured it, was that for the holiness which was within the will and nature of God, and that of His certainty that out of such conformity to the will and nature of God, there must come the final result of peace and good-will among the sons of men.

Therefore, what is my joy in the presence of this Christ? Is it that of my conviction that He will establish an order that shall be materially perfect; or is it the deeper joy of the assurance that He will glorify God in human history by holiness and purity? The first which is selfish will make me cowardly and unfaithful, and may change my singing of "Hosanna" into my crying "Crucify." The second, which is Godly, will enable me to suffer, to dare all things, if necessary to die; but it will make me victor in fellowship with the triumphant King.

So our last glance at this picture is in the presence of that question. See the disciples and the multitudes; full of expectation, joy and singing; but wholly selfish, wholly of the earth, utterly out of harmony with the deep spiritual purpose of the One around Whom they lift their acclamation.

Behold the King! What is His passion? It is the passion

THE TRIUMPHAL ENTRY

for purity, and the passion for holiness, the passion for the victory of God.

May it be given to us to share that passion and that vision, that so we may be prepared to share the travail that makes His Kingdom come.

CHAPTER VIII

DEATH ABOLISHED

Our Saviour Jesus Christ, Who abolished death.
2 TIMOTHY 1:10.

WE COME TO EASTER MORNING WITH JOY AND GLADNESS, and with a great sense of triumph filling our hearts. We have been treading the shadowed way that led to Calvary, and standing in awe and amazement in the presence of the infinite mystery of the passion of our Lord. This morning in our hearts there is the assurance that the winter is over and gone, and the time of the singing of birds is come. The storm has spent itself, the great Master Mariner is triumphant, and the Ark rides upon the waves of a sunlit sea. Egypt is behind, the exodus is accomplished. Death is abolished, life and incorruption are brought to light.

It was the brilliant German critic of Christianity, Strauss, who declared that of the Christian faith the resurrection is the center of the center, and that is true. "If Christ hath not been raised, then is our preaching vain, your faith also is vain . . . ye are yet in your sins . . . if in this life only we have hoped in Christ, we are of all men most pitiable," for our hope has been the greatest of hopes, and our despair must be the most unutterable of despairs.

Christ is risen; and His resurrection was first of all, as to His own mission, perfect vindication of Himself, the proof, in the cosmic order, of His sinlessness. It was also the vindication of all His teaching; He had affirmed through the days of His public ministry—and men had listened to the affirmation and had refused to believe it and had crucified Him eventually for making it—that the supreme thing in human life is the spirit, "Be not afraid of them which kill the body, and have no more than they can do"; speaking out of His own essential spirit life He said, "I lay down My life, that I may take it again," "I will go up to that which men call death, and you shall see Me die, but I, the essential spirit will take hold of My body, and bring it back again that you may behold it." When He was laid by loving hands in the grave, His enemies said, "We remember that that deceiver said, while He was yet alive, 'After three days I rise again' "—and if He never rose they were quite right, He was a deceiver; but the resurrection demonstrates the truth of His own teaching, that in the economy of God the spirit life is independent of the body, is able again at the time appointed to reclothe itself with the body, because it is the dominant factor in personality. The value of the resurrection in the mission of Christ is that of its perfect vindication of Himself, of His teaching, of His power.

The value of the resurrection to the sons of men is, therefore, necessarily that of demonstration. By that resurrection I know that my sins are forgiven. Blot out that historic resurrection and the doctrine of the forgiveness of sins is a sigh of hope without foundation in fact upon which faith can fasten. By that resurrection I know that the Cross is the means by which my sins may be forgiven. That resurrection is the demonstration of the possibility of a holy life, for He Who said, "I lay down My life, that I may take it again," said "I lay down My life for the sheep." In the energy of that communicated life we live that we may become holy. If He rose not, it is a false dream. By that resurrection there is assurance of the life beyond, and illumination thereof for all time. It is to that last thought that we turn this morning.

The text appears in a paragraph, the burden of which is Paul's appeal to Timothy to be brave and true in the testimony of the gospel of the Lord Jesus Christ. The whole paragraph makes perfectly clear that the central fact of the gospel, that which indeed is the gospel, is the fact of the appearing, or the epiphany of our Lord and Saviour Jesus Christ. That is the gospel which Paul preached, the gospel committed to Timothy, the gospel of the Church.

The central fact of that manifestation or appearing is that of the resurrection. Here the apostle describes the resurrection as the abolition of death, victory over death. He moreover declares that, by the way of the resurrection, life and incorruption were brought to light in the gospel.

Death is abolished by that illumination. That illumination results from that abolition.

Let us remind ourselves briefly, and with all patience and sympathy, of the fact that the fear of death is not only widespread but it may be described as universal. Man does fear death. You remember the words in which Shakespeare describes death:

> Death is a fearful thing.
> The weariest and most loathed earthly life,
> That age, ache, penury and imprisonment
> Can lay on nature, is a paradise
> To what men fear of death.

Or the words in which Young describes it,

> The Vale of Death! that hushed Cimmerian vale,
> Where darkness, brooding o'er unfinished fates
> With raven wing incumbent, waits the day,
> (Dread day!) that interdicts all future change.

DEATH ABOLISHED

Or to go back to literature more ancient than either, more sublime than either, the literature of our own Bible. Listen to the voice of perhaps the oldest book in the Bible, and hear how Job in the midst of his agony thus describes death:

> ... The land of darkness, and of the shadow of death;
> A land of thick darkness, as darkness itself;
> A land of the shadow of death without any order,
> And where the light is as darkness.

I quote these not as illustrating the lower manifestations of fear, but the higher; they are records of this universal fear, from the highest of men.

This fear of death still abides very largely, even among the children of God, the children of light. Perchance it is the last fear to be overcome in the heart of the trusting saint, as death is the last enemy to be overcome. We are conscious of the chill of it even though we live in the warmth of the risen Sun of righteousness. There is a sense in which this fear haunts us and abides even after we have seen life and immortality brought to light in the gospel.

May we reverently ask the reasons of the fear? What fills the heart with fear in the presence of death, either our own death or that of our loved ones? First of all, let us remember that even if we believe man is immortal, it is still true that death is the passage from the familiar into the unfamiliar. We do not know what lies beyond; it is the bourn whence no traveler returneth. We have all felt the terror of that as we have stood by the side of the loved one about to cross over. It is the leaving of the familiar and the reaching of the unfamiliar. It is the severing of associations, and the ending of fellowships. It is the interruption of plans and purposes. and the cessation of endeavor. These are things against which men find themselves in revolt. These are the things which make men afraid. These are the reasons why man does so perpetually and so persistently fight against death.

What is the reason of these reasons? What lies behind all this? How are we to account for it? This same apostle in his Corinthian letter dealing with the subject of resurrection, makes this affirmation, "the sting of death is sin." The fear of death is the last activity of conscience. Conscience, deadened, hardened, seared, acts in the presence of death. Conscience asserts continuity, and in a moment fear takes possession of the soul. Do not misunderstand me at this point. I do not say that fear of death is the fear of punishment for sin in the next world. That is not my argument now. Conscience asserts continuity, and when the spirit contemplates continuity after this strange dividing line of death, and believes that death is but the passing on from the familiar into the unfamiliar, the severing of old associations, the ending of old fellowships, the interruption of plans and purposes, the cessation of endeavor, then the soul is in revolt, the emotions are stirred with fear, but why? Because through sin man has lost his vision of himself, of the meaning of his life, and of the things that lie beyond; because man looking out at death is blind and cannot see death as it really is in the economy and purpose of God. All the reasons which I have assigned for fear, which are true reasons, are, nevertheless, false as in themselves. Death need not be, nor ought to be, the passage from the familiar to the unfamiliar; Death is not the severing of association, the ending of fellowship; it is not the interruption of plan and purpose, and the cessation of endeavor; unless all these things are out of harmony with the ages and with the God of the ages, and the purpose of the ages. If a man shall live out his life of three-score years and ten simply in the realm of the dust, or even if a child, or a youth shall so live, as the result of faulty teaching of fathers, mothers, teachers, all these reasons for fear are there.

Now the declaration of this text is not that Christ destroyed death, but that He abolished it. The declaration is that He made death idle by bringing life and incorruption to light through the gospel. This Greek word is translated in other places in the New Testament, "made of no effect." That is the true thought here. He has made death of no effect. He has made death void, empty. He has emptied death of all that which filled the heart with fear.

Let us see how this has been done. What was the way of His victory? First of all, in His own personal resurrection He abolished death. I am not dealing at all with that infinite mystery of the Cross which preceded resurrection. It was not in the hour of resurrection that He made atonement. It was in the act and article of death that He atoned. In His resurrection, He, the permanent, the continuous, the spirit, the essential, took His body out of the tomb, leaving the graveclothes absolutely undisturbed, and leaving the stone still in its place. The graveclothes were not, as we have sometimes interpreted the story, folded up tidily in one place; they were in the actual wrappings in which they had been about His body; the napkin was not with the graveclothes, but in a place by itself, apart, exactly where it had been about His sacred head. He had left the graveclothes unmoved, every fold as it was around His body; and the stone still there. It was when John and Peter saw those undisturbed graveclothes that they believed He had risen. If they had seen the graveclothes carefully folded and smoothed, they would have thought someone had stolen the body; but when they saw them wrapped as they had been about the body, still there and the body gone, they believed. An angel rolled back that revolving stone that men might see that He was not there. In that article of resurrection He, the permanent, persistent spirit, the essential Jesus as Man, took again that body, and by the touch of His spirit so transformed it that it was no longer subject to the laws which are only of the material, but became the spiritual body of which Paul speaks in his great Corinthian letter. Thus in resurrection He abolished death, made it null and void, made it of no effect. He demonstrated for all time the fact that there is a life than can and will master death eventually, even on the physical plane.

He tarried for forty days, showing Himself as alive from the dead. Have you studied the brief story of those forty days? It is a wonderful unveiling of life and incorruption. He merged the familiar and the unfamiliar. We are afraid of death because we are leaving familiar things and going to unfamiliar; and for forty days He merged them in each other, perpetually comforting, startling, satisfying, and surprising. The doors are locked for fear of the Jews, no bolt is shot back, and He is there, and you can put your finger in the print of the nails. He merged the familiar with the unfamiliar.

He demonstrated identity, continuity, mastery over death. They had seen Him die, they knew He was dead upon the Cross, but He is alive. There He is, and in His feet and hands are woundprints, and His side; but doors cannot retain Him. He can walk by their side, so close to them that they can listen to Him but do not know Him, all the way to Emmaus; then He will break bread and they will see Him, and just as they would hold Him, He is gone. Do not try to get rid of these last two chapters of John. The light is never clearer than in these two chapters. He is merging the familiar with the unfamiliar. He is saying to us, "You speak of going to unfamiliar things, just over the line they are there, all the old things, but there are other things you cannot quite understand, I will give you glimpses of them that you will never forget when your loved ones go; strange mysteries of being you cannot understand, but they are the same; even the woundprints are there."

He demonstrated the continuity of association and fellowship: There are things I dare not try to say, as I think He said them; I have to say them roughly, for imitation would be sacrilege. I can always hear how He uttered that woman's name that morning, "Mary." She knew Him then. "Rabboni, Master, it is Thou! Yes, you have not lost Me." She would have clutched Him, but He said, "No, Mary, you will have to learn to depend not upon the touch of flesh, but upon communion of spirit. The associations are not broken, My Father and your Father, My God and your God. You will have to learn to do without the touch of the flesh, Mary; that is all."

He revealed the unity of plan and purpose here and beyond. What was the passion of His heart while here? The Kingdom of God, the salvation of men. "The Son of man came to seek and to save that which was lost." He stayed long enough to say to His disciples, The plan is the same, the purpose is the same, the endeavor is the same; I out of sight, you in sight, are going into partnership. "Ye shall be My witnesses . . . to the uttermost part of the earth."

If that was the personal action in the abolition of death, what was the relative action? Again I quote from the Corinthian letter, for in these words the whole argument is stated more briefly and forcefully than I can hope to state it, "The sting of death is sin; and the power of sin is the law: but thanks be to God, which giveth us the victory through our Lord Jesus Christ." In the darkness and mystery of His Cross He so dealt with sin as to be able to whisper to my sinful soul the word of absolution and the word of peace, so as to give me a conscience void of offence toward God. Directly, you have a conscience void of offence toward God; you have a new vision of God, a new vision of yourself and a new vision of the hereafter; and death who had stood before you stern, hard, iron, brutal, cold, is as you look transfigured into an angel of mercy whose kiss is the kiss of love, the porter forevermore at the gate of life, "Thanks be to God, which giveth us the victory."

What is this victory in our outlook on death? Christ put Himself where death had been standing. This is His word to the Christian, "Till I come." This is His word to the Christian through His servant and by inspiration, "Absent from the body, at home with the Lord." We looked for death, but we are not looking for death today, we are looking for Him, and even if, presently, by the weakening of this mortal tent in which I dwell, the loosening of its bands, my body becomes, to use the magnificent description of Longfellow when he wrote of the slave, "the worn-out fetter which the soul had broken and flung away," I shall meet my Lord. Never was finer thing written about death than that. The spirit conscious of the worn-out fetter, breaks it, flings it away, and then is at home with the Lord. So Christ stands there, where, I know not and care not, whether near or far, just over the border-line of this service, perhaps ere it is done the flaming glory of His advent feet, or perchance after a long, hard day's work, there stands, not death, king of terrors, but Christ, the King of love, and He has abolished death. Death is unemployed, idle. Christ has taken his place.

Mark the effect of this upon fear. Again you may express it in words not usually used in this connection, but I think accurately used in this connection, "Perfect love casteth our fear." The reason of the reasons of fear is gone.

DEATH ABOLISHED

My sin, oh the bliss of this glorious thought,
  My sin, not in part, but the whole,
Was nailed to His Cross, and I bear it no more,
  Praise the Lord, Praise the Lord, Oh my soul.

"The sting of death is sin; and the power of sin is the law: but thanks be to God, which giveth us the victory through our Lord Jesus Christ."

With the passing of the reason of the reasons, the reasons also go. Men fear death because the beyond is unfamiliar; but the beyond is not unfamiliar to us. We know the country well to which the loved ones go. But you say, that is the difficulty, we do not. Think again. I am afraid the Church of God is losing that great and gracious art of contemplating the country beyond. I know that it is out of fashion to teach even children to sing about a heaven beyond the blue. It is certainly quite out of fashion for Christian people to talk about heaven. We are told to make heaven here. I believe that with all my heart. We need have no anxiety about the heaven beyond, but it is good sometimes to contemplate it. As the saintly Rutherford said, "it is good to climb and look in advance upon the home of the soul forever; to observe its buildings, its furnishings; the country, the hills and valleys." We do it all too little. This is the thing I want to say. We know the country for we argue of the country from the country's King. If you really want to know what heaven is like, get any little bit of earth where Jesus is King, and you will see it. Do not be afraid of your imagination. Flowers? Oh yes, immortals, Asphodel, never fading. Birds and animals? Surely yes; armies of white horses for the saints to ride upon. You say, "You are talking figures of speech." Quite probably so, but figures are used to help people to see facts that are too brilliant for their seeing. Facts are always finer than figures. I argue the country from the country's King. No, the country beyond is not unfamiliar. I not only know it, I am learning its language, I am gradually coming to understand its very accent. I know men and women, saints of God, who have walked and talked with Him for fifty years or more, and their accent is so much the accent of the other side that men call them foreigners. We know the country to which the loved ones have gone because we know the country's King.

We were afraid of death because death meant severing of associations and the ending of fellowships. I bring you back to this great word of the catholic Church, and I use the word in its true sense, the universal Church, the peculiar word of an older day, the communion of saints, which does not merely include the fellowship of the saints who are in the Church on earth, but the communion of all saints who have entered into rest and are beyond the vision of the senses. The communion abides; we are not divided. We are waiting, so are they. We are not yet perfected, neither are they. They are in the Paradise of God where the vision is clearer and temptations are over, and the battle is won, but they are not yet perfected. "God having provided some better thing concerning us, that apart from us they should not be made perfect." We are united in our waiting. They are waiting for that for which I am waiting, the resurrection. We cannot visit them. They cannot talk to us, and we violate the whole order of revelation when we try to do it. They cannot revisit us, I do not know that they can watch us, except perchance now and then by some special permission of heaven. There is a unity and affinity which defies and laughs at absence of articulate speech and the vision of the senses. I pass no day that I am not conscious of the nearness of at least one who entered within the veil sixteen years ago, my first lassie; but I never try to bring her up to mutter to me. I never insult the high and holy revelation of God by making use of some fleshly medium that I may hear a whisper that is from hell and not from heaven. But I know the touch of her spirit upon mine, for the spirit life cannot be measured by the dimensions of the material. I know though she cannot come to me, I shall go to her.

> Not as a child shall we again behold her;
>   For when with raptures wild
> In our embraces we again enfold her,
>   She will not be a child;
> But a fair maiden in her Father's mansion,
>   Clothed in celestial grace;
> And beautiful with all the soul's expansion
>   Shall we behold her face.

I have not lost my child, she is mine as she never was before.

Did we say that death interferes with plans and purposes, and endeavor? No, there is continuity of service. They are not idle. It is death that is idle. What are they doing? I only know one thing, they are praying; what else I do not know, I will not pretend to say. This I know, They rest from their labours, but their works have gone out with them; and while the heart of their Lord is restless because His work is not completed, their hearts are restless with His restlessness. They are in perfect fellowship with Him. They have not grown callous about this world of ours, they pray. Oh, it is a great theme, I cannot exhaust it. The Lord is risen indeed, Hallelujah.

This is not the gospel of callousness. We still miss our loved ones, and we still shed tears. Our sense of loss is the result of what God made us emotionally, and we should be less like God if we did not miss them. Our tears He never rebukes. I miss the loved one who is leaving my home and crossing the ocean for a little while, and I have even known tears shed on such occasions. The sense of loss is not wrong when the loved one passes on, and I know I shall never again touch that dear hand until the morning of resurrection. This is not the gospel of callousness. Christ does not rebuke your tears. It is the gospel of comfort. The boy you have let go far away across the ocean, you miss him yet, but he is not as safe as the child Jesus took to be with Himself, not nearly as safe. Tears there are, but the rain of our tears in the light of the resurrection creates the rainbow which arches all the sky and is the perpetual witness to the ultimate victory.

But if Christ did not rise, all this is unutterable nonsense. Do not imagine you can retain this verse if you deny the historic Christ and the historic resurrection. It is a miracle in the midst of the ages, not natural evolution. That is not resurrection. It was triumph over tragedy, mastery over death by life in the supreme act of God for man. Deny it and you have no comfort—the thud of the clod upon the coffin and that is all. But blessed be God, He is risen, we know He is risen.

There is no song before Calvary. That is, there is no Easter song for me without Calvary. "How am I straitened till it be accomplished," that is before Calvary. Let me say this other thing. There is always the Easter song after Calvary. You cannot prevent it. You may have Pilate's mandate, and Herod's soldiers, and all hell's opposition; but the song will laugh at your opposition.

What was true in history is true of your life. You will never sing the resurrection song until you know Calvary; but to know Calvary is to know resurrection and the Easter song.

May God, the God of all comfort, send you home, especially you my beloved who are bereaved, not to be callous or indifferent, but to know that He gilds the teardrop with His smile and makes the desert garden bloom awhile; to know that He has your loved ones safe, and that when God comes, He will bring them with Him.

CHAPTER IX

THE TEACHING OF THE RESURRECTION

This Jesus did God raise up.

ACTS 2:32.

"THIS JESUS"! THAT OPENING WORD FASTENS ATTENTION upon a particular Person, and compels us to consider Him, even before we pay attention to the declaration of the apostle.

The lesson we read constitutes the second part of the first message delivered by an apostle of Jesus Christ after the Pentecostal effusion. Having claimed that this outpouring of the Spirit was in fulfilment of prophecy, Peter proceeded to declare that this fulfilment was the result of the mission of Jesus of Nazareth. Commencing with words intended to arrest anew the attention of his hearers, he said, "Ye men of Israel, hear these words," and his discourse then became descriptive of this Person and His work, up to the statement of our text, "This Jesus did God raise up." Thus, between the opening words of the paragraph which we read for lesson and those of our text, we have the picture of the Person to Whom reference is made by the text.

This description was first historic. Peter drew the attention of these people to One Whom they knew. "Jesus of Nazareth" was the name by which He was well known through all that region.

He reminded them next that the Person of Whom he was

speaking was a Man separate and distinct from all other men in the perfections of His humanity, that having been evidenced by the wonders he had wrought, or more accurately, as the apostle put it, by the wonders God had wrought through Him. Finally, he further reminded them that they, the men of Israel, had delivered this Man over to the Gentiles, men without law, who crucified and slew Him. Of Him Peter declared, "This Jesus hath God raised up."

In the course of that description of the Person, the apostle claimed that He was in very deed that Messiah for Whom they had been looking, citing from their own psalms the words of David, and showing that the words David uttered could not have been fulfilled in the experience of David.

This Jesus Whom ye knew; this Jesus Whom ye slew; this Jesus Who is the Messiah for Whom you so long have been waiting; "This Jesus did God raise up."

Let us now consider what this act of God in the case of this Man really meant. Once in the history of the human race, a Man murdered by His enemies was raised from the dead, and exalted by God to the place of universal power. What is the significance of this fact?

Let me at once summarize the things I desire to say. The fact that God raised Jesus of Nazareth from among the dead signifies first, His absolute approbation of Him. It signifies secondly, His rejection of all other men. It signifies finally, the Divine appointment of the approved One to the right of restoring the rejected many.

Take the first of these facts, the Divine approbation of Jesus of Nazareth. I am constrained to say that this particular phase of our consideration needs emphasizing. Has it occurred to you, or am I wrong in my suspicion, that we are a little in danger of asking too constantly today whether Jesus satisfies us? Thank God for every man and woman in

THE TEACHING OF THE RESURRECTION

this house who can say, "Thou, O Christ, art all I want"; but that is not the profoundest question. If this Jesus is to be to me anything other than One Whom I admire, if He is to be to me the central force and fact of my religious life, the profounder question is, "What is God's estimate of Him?"

The whole story of Jesus presents constant and cumulative evidence of the Divine approbation of Jesus. There were remarkable signs of this at His birth. We very often speak of the humility of His coming, but that coming was accompanied by many wonderful signs. All the worlds known to men were moved there at. Angels broke silence and sang over Bethlehem's plain. Kings from afar were moved to follow the guidance of a star and to bring gold, frankincense and myrrh. The underworld of evil was shaken to its very center, and found earthly manifestation in the malice of a king and the murder of innocents. The world was not ready to receive Him, but the Divine approbation of the holy child was manifested by external and material signs of the most surprising nature.

Through the years of His public ministry that approbation was thrice declared. On the day of baptism a voice declared, "Thou art My beloved Son; in Thee I am well pleased." On the holy mount the voice declared, "This is My beloved Son, in Whom I am well pleased; hear ye Him." A little nearer to the darkness of Calvary, when the Greeks were asking to see Him, out of His sorrowing soul there came the wail, "Now is My soul troubled; and what shall I say? Father, save Me from this hour. But for this cause came I unto this hour. Father, glorify Thy name." The Heaven's silence was again broken, "I have both glorified it, and will glorify it again."

The Divine approbation was marked in all the miracles of Jesus. That to me is a subject full of fascination. The miracles do not prove His Deity, but the perfection of His humanity. Mark the carefulness of the apostle here when he said, "Jesus of Nazareth, a man approved of God unto you by mighty works and wonders and signs, which God did by Him in the midst of you." The doing of the wonders and signs was the evidence of the perfection of His humanity, not of His Deity. It was through the absolutely perfect Man that God was able to do works which were wonders and signs to imperfect men, because they were operations in realms higher than fallen man had yet discovered, but which were perfectly familiar to the perfect Man. In all these things, we have manifestations of the Divine approbation.

At His death supernatural seals were set upon Him, giving evidence of God's approbation. The quaking earth, the darkened sun, the yawning graves; these were all God's evidences that the thing being done was a thing of sin against the cosmic order.

But the supreme sign, the final manifestation, the ultimate seal was this, that He did raise Him from the dead, and we must always add, what Peter immediately added, "Being therefore by the right hand of God exalted." Not merely resurrection from among the dead, but resurrection immediately followed by exaltation. Easter must be linked to Ascension before we understand perfectly the values of this demonstration. Others were brought back from death in the economy of God for purposes of His own, but only to pass back into death. Lazarus was raised by Jesus, but only to pass back into death and through death to the life beyond. The child of Jairus was raised from the dead, but to pass back into death again. This Man; raised in actual bodily life, not the same as that laid down, but different; exactly the same, but transformed; this Man never saw death again. He tasted death for every man. "Death no more hath dominion over

Him." So we must ever add to the resurrection the fact of Ascension when we think of the Divine demonstration.

What then is this demonstration? The resurrection first attests to the perfection of the life of this Man. The resurrection declares in human history that this Man, rejected of men, is accepted of God; that this type of human life, for which the world cannot find any room, is God's type of human life.

What is the type? I can only state the great subject in phrases. God-centered; self-emptying; man-serving. That is the whole story of the life of Jesus. If as rapidly as memory can do its work, you will think of that story from beginning to end, you will find these things include all the facts; and the resurrection declared in the midst of human history, This is the Man of God's right hand. This is the Man of God's pattern, of God's purpose. This is the type of human life that satisfies God.

The resurrection further demonstrates the fact that in this Man the type was triumphant. There was never a single moment in His life when He moved from the true center of His life, which center was God Himself, He never became eccentric. I pause a moment because the worldly man calls the Christian man eccentric; while in reality it is he who is eccentric, away from the true center, not the Christian man. His life then was not eccentric; but always God-centered, though all the forces of the world, the flesh and the devil sought to draw Him aside, out of the true orbit of His life, or in the words of the writer of the New Testament concerning the angels, sought to make Him move out of His proper habitation. This Man was not only the type in the sense of being an idealist in His teaching, He was in His own life triumphant, and the resurrection is the great demonstration of God's approbation of that type of life.

The resurrection attests also to His accomplishment of purpose. Not only personal victory, but relative accomplishment. His purpose in the world according to His own teaching had been that of revelation and of mediation. He was in the world to reveal the Father, to bring men to the Father.

Did He succeed? Was the presentation of God which He made in life true? Was the unveiling of God which He suggested in death true? Has He mediated by true speech, and has He mediated in the mystery of that passion baptism prior to which He declared Himself straitened? Has He been successful? How shall I know? I stand in imagination on the eve of Easter day outside the tomb. I want to know whether He has succeeded in the purposes of revelation and mediation.

Angel hands roll back the stone, and I look in and see those graveclothes, and know that He is risen, and know not only that this is the perfect Man, but that this Man has fulfilled His purposes of revelation and of mediation.

Consequently, the resurrection attests to the completeness of His victory. It was a victory over death, and in this selfsame sermon Peter said, "It was not possible that He should be holden of it." This is one of the passages in God's word which I always wish I could recite with the emphasis which would express the emotion the words create in my own heart. I think there was a touch of contempt when Peter said "it" in reference to death; and infinitely more than a touch of reverence and of worship when He said "He," with reference to the Risen Lord. "It was not possible that He should be holden of it." Why not? Because He had dealt with sin, which is the sting of death. In some unutterable, unfathomable mystery in the darkness, He had taken its power out of death; by dealing with sin, He had robbed it of its sting, and made it forever more a porter at the gate of life. When

THE TEACHING OF THE RESURRECTION

I see Him raised, exalted, I know that He has won the final, perfect victory over sin, over sorrow, over Satan; and I know it, because I see His victory over death.

All that involves the second matter which I suggested. If God raised Jesus, He did by that act show His rejection of all other men. This is an aspect of the truth which we are in danger of overlooking. We cannot believe in the resurrection without, upon consideration, seeing how true this is. In accepting the perfect One, God rejected all imperfection. Imperfection is to be known by perfection. What is the perfect type? Life God-centered, self-emptying, man-serving. The imperfect type is life, self-centered, self-seeing, and self-serving. God rejects that type of humanity forever. I do not pause to describe the more vulgar manifestations of human sin. Let us keep on levels admittedly somewhat higher. Humanity may be cultured with the culture of the schools, refined with the refinement of aestheticism, but absolutely self-centered; and God rejects that humanity. Morality in the sanctuary is a thing of the spirit. Morality in the economy of God is conformity to the type of humanity revealed in Jesus. We are in danger of being satisfied with something that does not satisfy God in ourselves and in our fellowmen. By that resurrection of Jesus; by that stretching out of the right hand of the Almighty power, and the taking of this Man out of the grave, this Man Who was crucified because of the type He had revealed; by God's taking Him out of death and setting Him at His own right hand; He said to humanity: "This is the one and only type acceptable with God, this is the one and only type of human life that can find entrance into fellowship with God, here or hereafter." The resurrection of Jesus is the severest condemnation of everything else than that which He revealed to men as the true ideal of human life. So that when I am testing my own life, I do so, not by my neighbor, by my friend, or by the averages of failing humanity, but by the one and only Man upon Whom God has set His seal of resurrection.

That is human life. There is a side, in this matter, full of comfort and encouragement, for when by that resurrection, God set His seal upon the type of human life revealed in Jesus, He revealed to every human being the true meaning of human life. When I look upon this Son of man, risen from the dead, and when I contemplate His life in its beauties and perfections and glories, in those glories of grace and truth which John referred to, in all the rich and beautiful character of absolutely unselfish living, I not only know what God's ideal is, but I know of what I am capable by Divine creation. For that life God made me, not for a life of human refinement and human morality which is careless of the woes and wounds and weariness of humanity; not for that self-centered life which is of the very essence of devilism; but for fellowship with Himself and for service of my fellowmen; for that self-emptying which pours out life in order to help others. That is God's humanity, and He rejects every other type. For that He has made every one of us; however hard the heart may be, however blind the eyes in the presence of humanity's woes, however perverse the will that refuses to serve; the heart is made for compassion, the eyes are made for seeing, the will is made to be the driving power of sacrifice. So the resurrection, while it is condemnation of all failure, is the repetition of the fact that God made man for Himself, to be like Himself, in self-emptying love and in sacrificial service.

Finally, in accepting the work of Jesus, God refused all other methods of salvation. He said by the resurrection, "Neither is there any other name under heaven, that is given among men, wherein we must be saved." But we would prefer to work out our own salvation. We would prefer to accept the great Ideal and see if it be not possible, without reference to the death and resurrection of Jesus, to work out our own salvation. God declares by resurrection that this is impossible, for every method of salvation attempted by man is doomed to failure and disaster.

By this resurrection God crowns Him Victor, and reveals the ultimate defeat of everything that is opposed to Him. Take one brief glance at the Cross in the light of resurrection. There, worldly power has won its victory over Him; there, worldly culture laughs at His folly, the Cross is foolishness to the Greek—and the Greeks are with us yet; there, ritualistic religion has put an end to the voice that spoke only of the spiritual, and to the Man who violated the traditions of men. Yet, in that Cross God has revealed to men that not by might of human effort, not by the culture of the human mind, not by religious observance of human invention can man come to victory, because these things have in themselves the elements of their own destruction.

The Resurrection is God's attestation of the perfect victory of His Son; His rejection of every other type, and of every other method of salvation.

The resurrection is the revelation of human failure, when we look back at the historic facts. When they nailed Him to the Cross, they did their last with Him. God never allowed another rude hand to touch the dead body of Jesus; only loving hands touched Him after He was dead, only the hands of loving disciples—secret disciples by the way, for in the day of unutterable tragedy all the confessors were gone—two secret disciples, Joseph of Arimathaea, and Nicodemus, took His body, and with loving touch laid it to rest in the tomb. This is a very gracious and blessed fact to my own heart. Man had done his worst, and his best; not even the disciples witnessed the resurrection. The resurrection was God's act, and in the very blindness which came to the disciples I have a revelation of God's rejection of humanity; they were not permitted to see Him rise.

Then notice how in that resurrection there was rejection of everything that rejected Him. The priests; if the matter were not altogether too sacred one could indulge in satire at the expense of the priests! They went to Pilate and said, "We remember that that deceiver said, while He was yet alive, After three days I rise again," and they asked for soldiers to watch the body of a dead Man! Was there ever such confession of impotence? Yet, in spite of their shrewdness, that He be not stolen, He went; went without the unwrapping of the graveclothes, without the rolling away of the stone, without the breaking of Pilate's seal! Wrapped in graveclothes, shut in by a rolling stone, sealed with the Roman governor's authority, watched by soldiers under the inspiration of the priests; but He rose! Therein was demonstrated the truth that God rejects Roman power, Hebrew priestism, Greek culture, and even disciples who were unable to follow. They were all rejected in that great hour of resurrection.

But there is infinite compassion in the story. There, is the unveiling of the Divine love. If God by that resurrection rejects men, why does He do so? Because they are failing to fulfil the meaning of their own lies, as well as failing to satisfy the intention of His will. He only rejects the failure in order that He may make again the marred vessels, restore the years that the cankerworm hath eaten, make the desert blossom as the rose! By way of rejecting me, a failure, He makes possible my remaking, in His own image and likeness.

That resurrection is the Divine ratification of the new and living way. It is the acceptance of the Man Christ Jesus in a representative capacity. That resurrection said to these disciples, and says to us today: "There was more in the Cross than you thought." The Cross; how they had shunned it; how they had been afraid of it from the first mention of it at Caesarea Philippi; through all those weeks how they had shrunk from it! The Cross scattered them, drove them away from Christ. Yet, by the way of resurrection they saw that there was profounder meaning in that Cross than they had known. By the way of resurrection the Cross was seen as something sufficient for rejected men. Take up the New Testament and read the epistles, and see what these writers say of the Cross. What gave them their belief in the Cross? The resurrection. There is no more remarkable word in the whole of them than that of Peter who preached this sermon on the day of Pentecost, when in his letter he declared that they were begotten again unto a living hope by the resurrection of Jesus Christ from the dead. The Cross was their despair; it became their hope when they saw it in the light of resurrection; the Cross was the place of defeat, but when they saw Him alive they knew that the Cross was the place of victory.

By resurrection God declares that the Cross has within it healing for all wounds. The risen Man is accepted as the Head of a new race; and the life which He liberated through the mystery of the Cross is accepted in Him as Firstborn, and in all the newborn who enter into life by the touch of this risen Christ. By the resurrection God declares that He accepts man in Christ, and in Christ alone. Crucified with Christ, risen with Christ, seated in the heavens in Christ; these are the apostolic words unveiling the true meaning and value and issue of resurrection.

By this resurrection then God declares to all men everywhere that the humanity for which He looks is the humanity of Jesus. Let us make this thing personal and immediate. Is my humanity His humanity? Are my motives His, my impulses His? If not, then know that this day of resurrection and light and glory is a day that declares my condemnation.

Tear up the New Testament, deny the resurrection, and I have nothing to say; but if this be the central, established fact of Christianity—I am not arguing it, I am accepting it, preaching upon the basis of its actuality—then know this, the resurrection is not merely a song in the night, it is the thunder of an awful severity, forevermore declaring that God will not be satisfied with imperfection or with any type of human life save that which approximates to the type revealed in Jesus.

But know this also, weary heart and disappointed man, confessing your sin; saying, as in the presence of the resurrection glory, "If that be God's accepted type then am I rejected, for I am unlike that"; know this, that resurrection declares to you that the Lord in the very mystery of His dying did make provision for your living. In the cosmic order He never ought to have died. Unless there be this profounder explanation of His dying which the New Testament offers, His dying is the most terrible reflection upon the government of the universe. When these things are seen in the light of the resurrection and we are able to say, "He loved me and gave Himself for me"; then the resurrection is a song and an evangel; the bedrock of my confidence, the refuge of my soul, the assurance in my heart that I am not deceived and that God can, and will, have compassion upon me, and receive me in Christ; and through Christ communicate to me the dynamic force I need for the Christly life.

The resurrection was the end of the first man, the first Adam, and the doom of all the race that sprang from Him. The resurrection was the acceptance of the second Man, the last Adam, and the birth of a new race. As we believe in Him, we receive His life and we are accepted in the Beloved.

The final note of the resurrection is that of hope for every man however bruised, however spoiled; however in the grip of vice, lust, passion, and sin; however disappointed with himself as he stands in the light of the revelation which Jesus has given to him of the meaning of his own life; for it declares that he can be remade. The resurrection is the proof of the evangel.

CHAPTER X

WAS THOMAS MISTAKEN?

Thomas answered and said unto Him, My Lord and my God.

JOHN 20:28.

IN THE BIBLICAL ORDER THIS IS THE EIGHTH DAY AFTER Easter, and consequently, the anniversary of the day on which Thomas uttered his great confession; and our Lord, His final beatitude. The confession of Thomas was the greatest of the confessions which fell from the lips of disciples of Jesus during the period of His presence among them in manifest and bodily form. The final beatitude of Jesus, the beatitude meant not for Thomas, not for the other apostles, but for us who name His name, and, believing thereinto, have received that gift of abounding life which comes in answer to such faith.

This confession of Thomas was without ambiguity in its terms. The evangelist was, moreover, most careful to state that the words were not in the nature of a declaration which might have been addressed to the Almighty Father, but that they were addressed to the Lord Himself. Notice the carefulness of the words, "Thomas answered and said unto Him, My Lord and my God."

Was Thomas mistaken? That is a serious question; and upon our answer to it must depend our intellectual, emotional and volitional attitude toward Christ Himself. If

WAS THOMAS MISTAKEN?

Thomas was mistaken, then our attitude toward Christ cannot be that of Thomas. If Thomas was right our attitude must be that of his great confession.

Let us first consider the confession of Thomas as to its nature and as to its reason; and, secondly, inquire the bearing of this confession upon our attitude toward the Lord Jesus Christ.

I need hardly tarry above a few moments with the first suggested matter—that, namely, of the nature of the confession. As I have already said, it was a confession without ambiguity, perfectly clear and simple, from which there can be no possible escape. Thomas, looking into the face of his Lord, said to Him, "My Lord and my God." "My Lord," which was a confession of the absolute sovereignty of Jesus, and therefore a confession of absolute submission to Him. Yet, had there been no other word spoken, it would not have arrested our attention, or perhaps demanded so serious consideration. The disciples had called Him Lord so often; and, indeed, it may be said that the title as it was then used was not as significant as I have indicated in my present definition of its meaning. The title "Lord" as used at the time had in some cases very little more significance than the title "Sir" as we use it in addressing men today. As it fell from the lips of this man, however, I think I am warranted in saying it came with full and rich and spacious meaning. I do not think for a moment that you will differ with me when I say that Thomas, saying to Christ upon that occasion "My Lord," did in that word recognize the sovereignty of Christ over his own life, and did by that word yield himself in willing submission to that sovereignty.

The second word of the great confession is even more arresting, and, indeed, it is by the second that I interpret the value of the first. Not only "My Lord," not only the One

Who is sovereign over my life and to Whom I am prepared to render whole-hearted submission, but "My God." The word stands without exception for absolute Deity; and therefore indicated, on the part of the man who employed it, that he bowed before the One so addressed not only in submission but in worship. "My Lord," the confession of sovereignty and of submission; "My God," the confession of Deity and of worship.

Let us inquire into the reason why Thomas made the confession. Let us first of all look at the man. We did not see very much of him in the New Testament. Matthew, Mark and Luke all name him, simply placing him among the number of the first twelve disciples who subsequently became apostles. Luke also tells us that he was with the twelve in the upper room on the day of Pentecost. These are the only references which the evangelists Matthew, Mark and Luke make to him. It was reserved for John to give us pictures of him; and these are few, but they are full. We see him first in the eleventh chapter on the occasion when the Lord was turning His face toward Jerusalem, with the intention of bringing back Lazarus out from among the dead. It was Thomas who said in heroic despair, "Let us also go, that we may die with Him." The next picture of him is in the upper room, when the Lord was delivering His final discourses, which we call the paschal discourse. Thomas was the second to interrupt the conversation. Christ was talking about His own going away, and it was Peter who first interrupted Him. As our Lord answered Peter, He said, "Whither I go, ye know the way." Thomas, who would never pretend to believe anything of which he was not sure, said: "Lord, we know not whither Thou goest; how know we the way?" Jesus answered Him: "I am the Way, and the Truth, and the Life; no one cometh unto the Father but by Me." Then Philip interrupted:

WAS THOMAS MISTAKEN?

"Lord, show us the Father, and it sufficeth us." The answer came tenderly and quickly: "Have I been so long time with you, and dost thou not know Me, Philip? He that hath seen Me hath seen the Father." Thomas was listening. The next time we see Thomas is in this chapter twenty. Once again and only once again. He was one of the seven who stood on the shores of the lake when Jesus restored Peter to service. These are all the pictures we have of the man, but they are certainly enough to enable us to say two things concerning him. He was a man at once cautious and courageous. We speak of Thomas as a sceptic. Yes, but let the word be redeemed from our abuse of it. He was a sceptic. He was a man who was compelled to investigate, to inquire, a man who "would not make his judgment blind," a man who would "face the spectres of the mind," and would make no confession of faith, of hope, of confidence, unless it were a confesson absolutely honest, true to the profoundest convictions of his mind. He was cautious; he was courageous. This is the man from whose lips the greatest confession fell that was ever uttered in the listening ear of Jesus during the time He was present among His disciples in bodily manifestation.

The confession was the result of a triumph over difficulty. Wherein lay his difficulty? He knew perfectly well that his Lord was dead, dead as both Thomas and all the disciples expected He would be if He persisted, in spite of all their warnings, in going up to Jerusalem. I believe that Thomas had either watched the crucifixion from a distance, or else that he had taken one last agonized look at the dead body of the Lord. I think when the disciples told him that they had seen the Lord, in his answer there is a revelation, not of hard, cynical scepticism, but of a broken heart: "Except I shall see in His hands the print of the nails, and put my finger into the print of the nails, and put my hand into His side, I will not believe." The impression of the wounds was upon the spirit of the man. Perchance that was why he was not present on that Easter morning when the Lord was manifested. No hint is given as to the reason of the absence; only the fact is chronicled.

Thomas said, "Unless I see what you saw, I will not believe." He did not ask for something other than they had received. He did not ask for some special revelation, denied to the rest. He asked for the same proof, and for that alone. Jesus was dead; Thomas saw the wounds, and knew that He was dead. Eight days passed away. Thomas was now in the upper room with the rest. Suddenly Christ stood in the midst. Now what were the evidences that produced this confession? First, the things he saw. He saw Jesus, and he knew perfectly that it was the very Lord and Master he had seen nailed to the Cross, and Whose wounds had been apparent to him. There He stood, wounded, dead, alive with the very scars displayed. He was alive out of death. Then Thomas believed.

What did he believe? Not that Jesus was alive. Do not let us read these stories carelessly, or we miss our way in the very heart of the confession. When Jesus said to Him, "Because thou hast seen Me thou hast believed," He did not mean he believed He was alive; that required no exercise of faith. The fact that Jesus Who had been dead was alive was demonstrated by sight. Then he believed. What did he believe? Not that Jesus was alive. That, he saw and knew. Of that, vision was proof. It is not true, even though we still repeat it, that seeing is believing. "Because thou hast seen Me, thou hast believed." There are two separate statements; seeing first, believing followed. Seeing that He was the living Christ, what did he believe? He believed what he confessed, "My Lord, and my God." He believed that the One Whom he had seen

WAS THOMAS MISTAKEN?

die, and known dead, but Whom he now saw risen and alive, was the Lord, that He was God.

So far I am not arguing as to whether he was justified in his belief. I am only trying to show the process by which he came to that belief. Thomas—cautious, courageous—had seen his Master die, had seen His wounding; knew He was dead. Then he saw Him alive, confronting him; and as a result he believed, first, that the risen One was his Lord, and, secondly, that He was his God.

The inquiry of supreme importance is this: Was that conclusion justified? Though I weary you with repetition of the circumstances, I want us to get back into the naturalness of the scene. Thomas saw Him dying, saw Him dead, saw the gaping wounds. Was he justified in saying "My Lord, and my God"? Was that conclusion justified upon the basis of that evidence? That is the heart of the inquiry.

If the conclusion that Jesus was God was based merely upon the fact of resurrection, I declare it was not justified. The resurrection did not demonstrate Deity. The Hebrew Scriptures told of the actual raising of certain men from the dead. This man Thomas had seen three dead ones come to life during the ministry of Jesus. He had seen the child of Jairus after resurrection. He had seen the son of the widow of Nain, lying dead upon the bier, carried out to burial, raised to life. The very last sign of the Lord had been that of the raising of Lazarus, and he did not say, "My God," because Lazarus was alive from the dead. If the confession was merely the result of the resurrection, then I declare it was not justified, that the fact that Christ was risen from among the dead is not enough upon which to base a doctrine of His Deity; but if he believed on the basis of that resurrection as the sequence of all that had preceded it, then I claim that he was justified.

In that hour when Thomas became convinced that the One he had seen dead was alive from among the dead, there came back again to him with gathered force, focused into one clear, bright light, all the facts in the life and ministry of Jesus which had preceded that resurrection. All the way from Caesarea Philippi to Calvary, Jesus had told Thomas and the rest He was going to die and rise again, but they had never believed Him. Now Thomas looked at Him and saw Him alive: He had said He would come back from the dead so repeatedly that you cannot find me a single instance when Jesus foretold His coming Cross, that He did not also predict His resurrection. No one had believed Him. I do not mean to suggest that their unbelief was malicious or unkind, or that they questioned His sincerity, but they thought He was mistaken. Had they believed what He told them, that He would rise again, they would not have been scattered at the crucifixion, or they would have gathered back again into Joseph's garden, waiting to see if He would come; but they never believed. Thomas, now looking into His face, remembered all that He had said as He stood confronting Him. In that moment all the predictions of Jesus were fulfilled by His standing there alive, and He was vindicated in those claims He had made. In that, His resurrection was differentiated from that of all others; it was part of a fore-ordained purpose.

Yet, more than that contributed to produce the conviction which made Thomas add "My God." Let me rapidly group what Thomas had seen before the Resurrection. I am simply trying to interpret by looking through the lattice windows of the pictures already referred to. What had Thomas seen in Jesus? First of all, he had undoubtedly been captured by the charm of His personality. Then he had been impressed with the splendor of His ideals. Still later, he had been amazed at the foolhardiness of His heroism. I am trying to speak out of Thomas's experience. There had entered into the mind of the Master the conviction that He was bound to go to Jerusalem, when every sane man knew perfectly well that His enemies were waiting to kill Him; and He Himself knew it, yet with splendid heroism but awful foolhardiness He would go. That is what Thomas felt. What next? Thomas had seen an exhibition of His power more wonderful than he had ever seen before, when He called Lazarus out of the grave. Then what? Arrived at Jerusalem, Thomas had been impressed by the mysticism of His teaching in those paschal discourses in which He talked so strangely. We really do need to get back into the atmosphere to understand how these men must have felt as He uttered His last words to them. We read them over and over again in the light of the Spirit's interpretation until their great teaching flames and flashes in eternal value; but these men did not understand these things as we understand them. They had heard Him say, I am going away, and where I am going you can come. None of you ask Me where I am going; I am going to the Father, and if I go, I will come again to you. I came from the Father. I have been in the earth. I am going again to the Father. Put yourself in the place of Thomas, and listen to such words; they must have sounded mystical, mysterious, the words of a Dreamer, with no logical sequence or connection. When He said, "Where I am going you know the way," Thomas could bear it no longer, and he blurted out: "We do not know where You are going; how can we know the way?" Finally there had been the tragedy of the Cross, the horror of it, the shame of it, the brutality of it, the devilishness of it!

All these things were in the past, separated from each other, with no relation to each other, separated because seeming to contradict each other. The irresistible charm of His personality, the splendor of His great ideals for humanity, the apparent foolhardiness of heroism that marched straight toward murder; the wonderful power that tarried on the march to bring back out of death a man, while He Himself was going straight into death; the strange mysticism of His teaching about going to the Father when they knew there were those in the city that would murder Him; and the end of it all when they arrested Him, and swore His dear life away, nailed His kind hands to the Cross, plunged a spear into His side. Thomas turned away, and there was no Easter Sunday for him. Do you wonder at it?

He was there the next Sunday, the next first day of the week, and there stood his Master, the same; the same charm of personality, the same light flashing from His eye, undimmed even though He had been through death; His heroism vindicated, for He had been to death and had mastered it; the wonder of His power greater than ever, for He had not been raised by another—He had come back Himself; more mystical than ever, for no door had opened to admit Him; and, finally, the Cross of shame was seen shining in the light of resurrection. In that moment Thomas said: "It is my Lord; it is my God!" The isolated, separated incidents merged into a great whole and captured the man, so that he bent in worship. I, perhaps, should not have had clarity of vision enough to come so quickly to conclusion, but I must eventually have made the same confession had I had such experience of this One, infinitely more than man, "My Lord, and my God."

Take any one of those impressions alone, and you can nearly account for it, but never quite. Take them all and merge them in the mystery of resurrection, and you cannot account for them. Yes, we have known people with great charm of personality. We have known people with great ideals. We have seen foolhardiness in heroism, but there we must halt. We have not seen men raise the dead, although we may be able nearly to account for that. We have heard great mystic words from others. That day, in the upper room, the whole of these impressions came back surging upon Thomas, light meeting light, tone merging into tone, until harmony from the heart of the universe swept through him, and he said, not "My Lord" alone, but also "My God."

When he made the great confession, Jesus looked at him and said: "Because thou hast seen Me, thou hast believed." He did not deny its declaration; He did not refuse its implication; He did not say to Thomas, "This is a mistake."

Can we believe that Jesus is Lord and God? Can we say of Him "My Lord, and my God"? We have not seen; can we believe? What evidence have we? John writes: "Many other signs, therefore, did Jesus in the presence of the disciples, which are not written in this book: but these are written, that ye may believe." John said: "I have grouped together here words and works of this self-same One, crowning all my story with this story of the resurrection; I have put before you in the writings the things that Thomas had before him, that though you have not seen Him you may also believe." All the evidences Thomas had we have in these writings. What is this Gospel of John—a biography of Jesus? Certainly not. Some of you have often heard me say it; forgive me if I repeat it. Arrange this book chronologically, and you have not the happenings of twenty days. It is a document of signs, words uttered and works done, and the whole of them interpreted finally by the resurrection. In the presence of this writing, if Thomas was justified in saying "My Lord, and my God," I am also justified in saying it.

Yes, but you say: "Are you sure of the writing? Are you sure it is a true story?" You must let me answer that after my own fashion. If it be not true, I still earnestly desire to find the men who invented it. There is nothing in literature like it, no dream like it in all your dreamings, oh masters mine!

But we have more than the writings; we have the witnesses. We have the witness of those who have had life in His name. John said, "These are written that ye may believe." Can you find any people who have read the writings, and have believed what Thomas believed, and who as the result have had life in His name? The question is an absurd one. That is the history of nineteen centuries of Christian effort; the writings, men believing, men receiving life, men sealing the accuracy of the writings by the witness of their own victories won. Life, what kind of life? Life that masters sin, that realizes holiness, that is growingly conformed to the image and likeness of God. These are the victories of the writings through nineteen centuries. I need not go back to apostolic times. All this host, not one or two, not occasional individuals, but tens, twenties, hundreds, thousands, millions who have believed in the Christ of these writings and have received life; and I know they have received life not because they say so, but because I have seen it working dynamically in them until the evil things that mastered them have dropped off like leaves from a tree smitten by the lightning of God, and fresh, beautiful things have been manifested in their lives. The witnesses to the accuracy of the writings compel me to say: "Seeing that I have in the writings all that Thomas had, and I have in the witnesses those who seal the writings, then also in the presence of this Christ who has been winning these victories, the Christ of these writings, I must say, and I can no other, so help me God, He is my Lord and my God."

What is faith? Mark Rutherford says: "Faith is not belief in fact, demonstration, or promise. It is sensibility to the due influence of the fact, something which enables us to act upon it, the susceptibility to all the strength there is in the fact, so that we are controlled by it. Nobody can precisely define it. . . . All we can say about it is that it comes by the grace of God, and that failure to see the truth is not so lamentable as failure to be moved by it." Thomas was convinced of truth when he saw the risen Christ. That was not faith or belief. He felt the whole fact of the truth and its appeal, and he answered it when he said, "My Lord, and my God." That was belief. I may or may not be able by my argument concerning the writings or the witnesses to bring you into intellectual conviction of the truth; but if I do it is quite useless. It is not by conviction that man receives this life. It is by answer to it, by uttering that voluntary confession.

"Blessed are they that have not seen, and yet have believed." The experience growing out of faith is an experience of blessedness, and it seals the act of faith which at the beginning is a venture in response to conviction; and no man has ever made that act of faith in the presence of this Lord Christ, but that there has been such answering experience.

Our decision as to whether Thomas was right or wrong will make a very great difference. Supposing Thomas was wrong, what then? Supposing it was a mistake, that this Jesus risen from among the dead was not God, absolute God, very God, what then? On highest levels let me state it. Our intellectual conception of Christ is one which makes trust impossible. I may be able to have confidence in His ideal and in His endeavor, I may admire it and even seek to imitate it; but trust him—no. No man of my own nature can command my perfect trust. I cannot trust Him. Why not? He is as finite as I am. He cannot see any further beyond the horizon than I can see, or if He can see further than I can, there is yet more beyond His seeing, and I must have a guide who can lead me there. I cannot trust Him if He be only man.

Our emotional attitude must be changed. If Thomas was wrong, our emotional attitude toward Him is one of sympathy and nothing more. I can sympathize with His great ideals, I can wish He had been able to establish that Kingdom that men thought He was going to establish. I can sympathize with the tragedy of His death, and say He is Brother to all suffering souls who have walked such ways of darkness. I can enter into sympathy with Him, but that is all.

If He be not very God, my volitional relation to Him is immediately changed, and I speak on the highest level only. What is my volitional attitude to Christ if Thomas was wrong? It is one of friendship, which takes His advice, but is able to better it, friendship which gives as well as takes advice. If He was not very God, then indeed He was a child of His own age, and today we know infinitely more than He did. I catch gleams of truth, but I can better them from later teachers. That is the consistent attitude, if Thomas was wrong.

If Thomas was right, then I worship. Then, though I say I love Him, I am almost afraid to sing it glibly, for my love is reverent, adoring love, which, while I touch the warm flesh of His condescending humanity, is conscious of the splendors of Deity; not the love of friendship, which takes and betters advice, but the love of worship which when He speaks asks no question; when He seals truth concerning my own life, concerning God or the Holy Scriptures, know that truth is final. That is my Christ. I do most definitely and solemnly affirm that the confession of Thomas is my confession, "My Lord, and my God."

We must understand that those two attitudes, both of them honest, cannot merge, cannot mix, cannot walk together. They must in honesty stand apart, for if the thing I believe of this Christ is true, then those who rob Him—for me, at least—are degrading Him. Whereas I may respect them, I cannot work with them. If the thing they say is true, then I am an idolator, for I am worshipping a man.

The question is a supreme question, and it is one we are bound to ask, and we are compelled to answer; and upon our answer must depend the whole of our attitude both toward the Christian religion and all those who bear His name. The hour is an hour in which loyalty demands that if we believe Him to be very God, we reaffirm the truth with lip and life.

CHAPTER XI

CHRISTIAN CITIZENSHIP: NO ABIDING CITY

For we have not here an abiding city.
                                        HEBREWS 13:14.

IT IS REPORTED THAT THE GREAT GERMAN CHANCELLOR, Bismarck, declared on one occasion that great cities are great sores upon the body politic. I do not suppose any of us who are at all familiar, experimentally with the cities of today, or from our reading, with the history of the cities of the world, will be inclined to differ from that opinion. The history of cities has through all time been the history of the gathering together of men, and the presence among them of forces which destroy. We are perpetually confronted in our dealing with human nature with two apparently contradictory impulses. The first is that of the gathering together of men into the life of the city; and the second is that of the ceaseless and almost restless desire to be away from the city.

"We have not here an abiding city," wrote this teacher of the Hebrew people, and the words, as you will remember, occur in the midst of the great argument concerning faith; its nature, its operation, its rewards; and the postponement of its final victory. The words of my text are taken from that chapter in the letter which is, as to the argument, the continuation of the teaching commenced at the close of the tenth chapter, running through the eleventh, and continuing until the close of the treatise. If we remind ourselves of the underlying teaching of that entire paragraph, we shall come to a better understanding of the meaning of our text.

The letter to the Hebrews is a letter written in order to warn men against the specific sin of unbelief. It illuminates for us, therefore, as perhaps no other writing in the Bible does, the true meaning of faith. It reveals the fact that faith is not merely intellectual apprehension and conviction of truth; and shows that faith is the assent of the will, and the yielding of the life, to the claim of the truth of which the mind is convinced. It is the letter, if I may say so, which more than any other writing of the Bible gives Biblical force and warrant to the suggestion of the title of Professor James's essay, "The Will to Believe"; showing forevermore that belief in its profoundest sense is not conviction merely, but conduct proceeding out of conviction, and harmonizing with the conviction. From beginning to end the writer has but one sin in mind, the sin of unbelief; that is, the sin of refusing to yield obedience to the claim of the truth, when the truth has brought conviction to the mind.

The positive teaching of the letter is that of the superiority of the Christian economy to all that had preceded it; the superiority of the revelation by the Son, to the ministration of angels; the superiority of the leadership of the Son, to that of Moses who led the people out but could not lead them in, and to that of Joshua who led the people in but could not give them rest; the superiority of the priesthood of the Son, to that of Aaron who perpetually repeated sacrifices which brought no peace to the conscience. After these arguments we have the illustrations of those who by faith, that is, by yielding to the claim of the truth, wrought righteousness, subdued kingdoms, stopped the mouths of lions, quenched the power of fire; and marched through seas of blood and through ever darkening perils to victory; and who by their activities of faith laid all the ages under debt to them for their triumphs. In the course of that great illustrative chapter, the central thought is that these pilgrims of faith, warriors of faith, builders of faith, were forever moving forward toward the establishment of a city. Abraham left Ur of the Chaldees because in it he could find no rest, and he left it seeking a city whose Builder and Maker is God. That chapter is gathered carefully around that central word of revelation; and thus we discover that the march of these men, their pilgrimage, their warfare, their constructive passion, were inspired by the vision of a city, a city established, a city of perfect order, a city Whose Builder and Framer is God.

The eleventh chapter of the letter closes with this very significant declaration, that while these men of faith of bygone days saw the city afar off, set their faces toward it, made persistent pilgrimage to reach it, fought opposing forces on their way, yet they never reached the goal toward which they ran, or saw the city built. "These all, having had witness borne to them through their faith, received not the promise, God having provided some better thing concerning us, that apart from us they should not be made perfect."

It would be possible to write a continuation of the eleventh chapter of Hebrews; we could gather the names of apostles, confessors, martyrs, reformers, statesmen, prophets, preachers; and if we did so, thus completing the list of the pilgrims, warriors, builders of faith; then of all those who have crossed the borderline and are out of our sight, we should still have to say, the goal is not yet reached, "these all, having had witness borne to them through their faith, received not the promise."

Now in order that we may take this first part of the larger text and understand it, I must tarry a moment longer to add something to that already said concerning this pilgrimage, this warfare, this passion of the men of faith. What, according to this whole contextual teaching really is the goal toward which these men ran; and toward which men of faith have ever been moving through the centuries? The hymn we sang together will mislead us unless we are careful.

I am not saying we should not sing it; there are values in the hymn and we shall continue to use it; but the idea of our hymn was that the pilgrim hosts are moving toward the heaven that lies beyond.

> We are travelling home to God,
> In the way the Fathers trod.
> They are happy now, and we
> Soon their happiness shall see.

That is not the teaching of this letter. I am not denying the reality of the heaven that lies beyond. Some day by God's good grace and by the merit of the Saviour I hope to reach it. But that is not the pilgrimage, that is not the warfare. We are not fighting to build heaven. The living Lord passed out of sight saying in infinite tenderness and pity and love and compassion to His fearful followers, "I go to prepare a place for you"; and that He will assuredly do.

What then is this pilgrimage, what is this warfare? What is the consuming passion of the men of faith? I answer that inquiry superlatively, that I may state it briefly. He has gone to prepare a place for us beyond; our business is to prepare this place for Him. The city which Abraham went to seek was not a city postponed beyond this world; but the city of God established on the earth; the city of God, the symbol of the whole wide world subdued to the Kingship of God. Toward that the men of faith have ever moved. Toward that the men of faith are moving still today. The supreme passion of faith is not the selfish desire to win heaven, but the self-emptying desire and devotion to win the earth for God.

It is not my intention now, or indeed on the three subsequent Sunday evenings in which I propose to tarry with this line of consideration, to deal with dispensations and methods; all these are interesting and valuable, but they are not within the province of the present consideration. We are looking at the ultimate desire, the ultimate passion, of the men of faith. It is a passion for the establishment of the Divine order, or in figurative language, for the building of the city of God. To this the whole Bible bears witness. You open it, and you are introduced quite quickly to a garden scene. You read through it, and you journey in spirit along the way of the wilderness, over which there is a highway, a way of battle and of turmoil and of strife. You come to the closing book; and you find the city of God, the heavenly Jerusalem; not heaven, but a city descending out of heaven; and while you look, you hear the all-inclusive anthem, "Behold the tabernacle of God is with men, and He shall dwell with them, and they shall be His peoples, and God Himself shall be with them, and be their God." The Bible is a mirror giving us human history from the Divine standpoint, and revealing those methods of God with men, and those methods of men with God, whereby from the garden man comes ultimately to the city.

In every human being there is a sense of the city, and the desire for the city. However much we would if we could—and let me say it quite bluntly, we would if we could—keep our young people away from great cities, and let them live in the country; we cannot keep them away, the lure of the city is in the heart of the young, they crowd toward the city. I am not discussing the question from the economic standpoint, but from the human standpoint. The underlying passion for the city is according to the Divine purpose, according to the Divine will; one of the primal forces of life, one of the elemental things of human nature, from which there can be no escape.

Whether you count the Scripture lesson of this evening as poetry or history, for the moment I care nothing, I am after its central lesson. The first city the Bible names was built by Cain, a murderer, a self-centered man, whose offering was refused because he was refused. That is the first city to which the Bible refers. The naming of names will be enough to help us to see the history of cities since; Sodom, Babylon, Nineveh, Carthage, Rome, Paris, London, New York; a long, continuous succession, and always the same thing, the city expressing human failure as nothing else can; startling the ages, and inevitably passing and perishing; in the time of their existence places where evil gathers, and where Satan's seat is; then crumbling to decay.

Man is always attempting to build a city; he has never yet built a city. Why? Because man has been attempting to construct a city out of a garden, in forgetfulness of the God of the garden, and the laws of his own life in relationship to that God.

"We have not here an abiding city." Why not? Let us answer that question first, by reminding ourselves of what the Christian character really is, and what it therefore demands.

The first essential element of the Christian character is the death of self—so easily said, so imperfectly understood, so little realized—the death of self; not the destruction of self, but the death of self, so far as self is a separate personality thinking only of itself and making all outside forces minister to its own well-being and advancement. The Lord Christ begins by saying to men, "If any man will come after Me, let him deny himself . . . and follow Me." That is the central fact of Christian experience, denial of self.

The result in the economy of grace is holiness of character; purity of motive; holiness and righteousness, the two sides of the one great pure Christly character; holiness, rectitude of character; righteousness, rectitude of conduct springing out of rectitude of character. Add to these two things that one inclusive word which has in it the fire of holiness and the passion of self-denial, the great word love. These are the distinctive elements of Christian character.

What is the result wherever these things are realized? A new refinement; life finding self realization according to the original purpose of God through self denial; life set free from all the vulgarities that spoil, and coming into realization of all the refinement and beauty of character which once had its manifestation in human history in the Person of our Lord Christ, the Man of Nazareth. And not refinement only; but that permanence which defies decay, which realizes that the things of past failure are things of no moment; which enables a man to think of death as transition merely, and to challenge the rider upon the pale horse, "O death, where is thy victory? O death, where is thy sting?"

What are the resultant needs of the people who share this character? A dwelling place in harmony; the congregating together of like characters; enterprise inspired only by such motives; the City of God. The presence and work of our Lord in the world was for the creation of these characteristics, and of this character. I go further, and say that the presence and work of our Lord in the world has resulted in the creation of these characteristics and of this character. Dealing with individual men, He communicates the dynamic force which produces the change; and those who are so converted, turned back again to the Divine ideal for humanity, born again, find their life centered no longer in self but in God, and are conscious of the passion for holiness without which no man can see the Lord, and feel within them the thrill and throb and driving of this great eternal life. Those who partake of these characteristics become men and women who are constrained to say, "We have not here an abiding city." The men of faith are homeless in this world, having no place where they can perfectly rest; having no place where the surroundings are in harmony with the mysterious and mighty forces of their own life, as created by their contact with this Lord Christ Himself.

Turn from that first consideration, and think of earthly cities. We have already glanced at them in general outline, having named several. Plato declared that the origin of the city was the desire of man to protect himself against marauding and wild beasts. Aristotle declared—and came far nearer to the deepest truth—that the city was the outcome of the social instinct in individual life. Moses, in the chapter I read, does not attempt to give us a philosophy; but tells the story of the building of a city; it was an attempt to make out of a garden a city, and an attempt to do it without God. Cain went out from the presence of the Lord, by which the writer did not at all attempt to suggest a localized Deity, but in figurative language spoke of a man who turned his back upon God and chose his own way, determined to carve his own fortune, and be independent of the Divine government and instruction. He went out from the presence of the Lord and built a city. In that case the city was the outcome of social instincts on the lowest levels; and men still look upon cities as opportunities for self-aggrandizement, and for ministering to covetousness. What is the history of London at this moment? Write it in one brief and burning word, the survival of the strongest—not the survival of the fittest, the fittest is not always the strongest. If you doubt it, stand any Saturday night upon the Embankment with our men who are doing work which is perhaps the most sacred of any we are trying to do, touching the flotsam and jetsam of the city, unemployable men, many of them; but mostly men unemployed as the result of the grind of brute strength flinging out weakness. If you could be divested of your accidental—or if you prefer the word providential—resources, and put down here in this great city with its tides of life and its abundant wealth, what would you do? In spite of all your education and ability, you would be ground with the rest. London is selfish to its heart and core. It is not peculiar in that. That is true of every city in the world today.

Perhaps, after all, there is no city more eloquent to the man of faith than Rome, the eternal city—oh, the irony of it! Those who have stood in Rome will understand what I mean. Rome is in three layers, pagan, ecclesiastical, modern; and the weakest of these is the modern. I am speaking materially of course. There was a strength in pagan Rome which abides until this day in spite of the overlaying of ecclesiastical Rome. There was the strength of awful cunning in ecclesiastical Rome, that abides in hoary magnificence in spite of the newer Rome that is arising. Three layers of failure; perpetual memorials of man's inability to build an eternal city without God.

Whatever city you come into, throughout the world, you will find the same thing. Why? Because of the man who builds; because the man attempting to build is self-centered and not God-centered; because at the heart of city life, varying its expression, changing its garments, altering its methods, there always sits enthroned the individualism of selfishness. Look at the advertisements on the hoardings or in the newspapers, and listen to the song of self! The Greatest Boon ever offered to the Public! The Greatest Discovery on Earth! The Largest Retail—something—in the World! Buy of Me: Take My Wares: They are the Best! What does that mean? Make me rich, whatever other man may suffer. Selfishness is everywhere.

If these are the incidental symptoms, the essential malady is godlessness, forgetfulness of God. Have you given up the story of Babel? Restore it to your Bible for it is the veritable truth. Let us make us a name! Let us be a confederacy independent of all men, and of God Himself! That is the ancient story of the Bible; but you can find it in tomorrow's newspaper in the last Trust formed, the newest monopoly cursing the earth: Selfishness! That is the history of the city. Self in its lowest forms, the lust of the flesh, the lust of the eyes, the pride of life; with a neglect of all those who are unequal to the strife and the struggle. Great cities are great sores upon the body politic.

"We have not here an abiding city." And again, why not? Because there can be no harmony between the principle of self-death and the principle of selfishness; between the method of sacrificial service and the mastery of covetousness; between the determined proclamation of the evangel that declares salvation for the lost, and the determined propagation of the philosophy which is expressed in the words, the survival of the strongest. The two things contradict each other necessarily and perpetually. We have here no continuing city for we are men of faith; men who believe in God and in holiness and in love. The cities of earth are built by men of sight, attempting to do without God; who speak of sin as though it were an infirmity which does not very much matter: who prate of love but never practice it in commerce, statesmanship, or social life.

Here we have no continuing city. The conserving elements are lacking, and the corrupting elements are regnant. "Change and decay in all around I see." How often we glibly sing it; it is true also in this wider sense. We might write it over cities everywhere, over the cities of today. We may pull down our barns and build greater; but if God only comes into the life by an after-thought, by the use of the disjunctive conjunction "but," of what use are the barns and the produce laid within them, and the things in which we make our boast?

Here we have no continuing city, because the men of faith are a continuing people, those who are to put on incorruption, which cannot dwell in corruption. It is only when the elements of corruption are eliminated, and the leprosy of sin is dealt with in human life, that the city of God will be built. "Here we have not an abiding city."

What one would like to do is to preach next Sunday evening's sermon at once, for all this is preliminary. I would not like anyone to go away saying that the preacher has declared the aloofness of the men of faith; that they have no continuing city, and therefore, that they have nothing whatever to do with the cities in which they live; that they have no responsibilities concerning the cities of today. That is not the teaching of the passage, and I pray you listen to the rest of the verse, the sermon will matter little, "we seek after the city which is to come." Not we seek one that lies beyond, but we, the men of faith, discontented with things as they are, seek the city of God, moving ever towards it.

Whatever the future may have in store for us, today we have no home on earth as a people. I am convinced that the first lesson of powerful service is that of the separation indicated by the Abrahamic indices of tent and altar. There, at the center of the Hebrew line of worthies rises the great figure of Abraham who left Ur of the Chaldees and went forth to seek a city. What were the signs of his attitude? The tent and altar. The tent; easily struck, easily carried, easily pitched, and as easily struck again. The altar, wherever there is a tent, a place of worship, a place of recognition of God, a place to which to come for the renewing of vision and the communication of virtue. These two things are the symbols of the life which leads on to victory.

The measure of the separation of Christian men from the maxims and methods and motives of the cities of men is the measure in which they are able to correct the things that are wrong; to destroy the forces that destroy; to construct the city of God. We men of faith make no greater mistake than when we take up our abode in any city of earth saying: "Here are we, and of this city we are citizens"; saying in contradiction to the great word of the letter, Here we have found our abiding city! No, the tent is the symbol of the life of the man of faith; always ready to be disturbed by the Divine government, always ready to respond to the command to move away to bear witness somewhere else. That is the first lesson, but not the last, not the final one.

There is much to be done while we sojourn in the tent. We shall have to pray for Lot and for Sodom; we must go out and fight for the rescue of Lot; but there will always be Melchisedek, the Priest to meet us on our way, and minister to our needs. The first lesson is that of the tent, side by side with the altar.

The Church of God—speaking now in more general terms—can only help the nation, as she is composed of pilgrims, warriors, builders of faith who dwell in tents, and erect altars, and work with sword and with trowel for the building of the city of God.

Our only true content should be in our abiding discontent with everything unlike God. That is but another way of saying all I have been trying to say. The measure in which we sit down in the city, and are content with it, and rejoice over it, and are satisfied with it as it is, is the measure in which we have lost our vision of the City of God, and personal fellowship with the God of the city.

Out of our supreme content and rest in God and in His will, arises the restlessness of perpetual protest against everything that is unlike God. That is the driving force which will enable us to destroy the destructive, and to help in the building of the city of God. Pilgrims, warriors, builders, "We have not here an abiding city"!

CHAPTER XII

CHRISTIAN CITIZENSHIP: THE SEARCH FOR THE CITY

For we have not here an abiding city, but we seek after the city which is to come.

HEBREWS 13:14.

ON SUNDAY EVENING LAST WE TOOK THE FIRST PART OF THIS verse, "We have not here an abiding city." This evening our subject is the second part, "We seek after the city which is to come."

The "We" of the writer refers to the men of faith, those who live by faith in God, those who share the vision of the ultimate victory of God in human history.

The declaration occurs in the letter which is pre-eminently intended to warn the men of faith against the perils of apostasy; the letter in which no specific sin is dealt with, but from the beginning to the end of which the one all-inclusive sin of unbelief is the only sin in the mind of the writer; the letter that perhaps in some ways more wonderfully than any other writing in the Bible sets before us the movements of the Divine economy, and shows how they all center in the Son of God; the letter which opens with the magnificent thunder that announces the fact of God, and proceeds immediately to the all-inclusive declaration that the God of the universe has not left men without witness and without testimony, "God, having of old time spoken unto the fathers in the prophets by divers portions and in divers manners, hath at the end of these days spoken unto us in His Son"; the letter that from that first and wonderful declaration proceeds to show that the speech of the Son is superior to all preceding it and absolutely final; superior to that ministry of angels whereby the ancient economy was initiated; superior to the great leaders of men, to Moses who led the people out and could not lead them in, to Joshua, who led them in but could not give them rest; superior as Priest, abiding forever, Priest in the power of an endless life; superior as the File-leader of the men of faith, going first in the great procession, taking precedence over all others by reason of the clearness of His vision of the ultimate issue, and by reason of the splendor of His devotion to the process of travail and pain by which the triumph will come.

It is in this letter that the writer says, speaking of faithful souls, adventurers upon the great highway, those who have seen the promise but never yet have realized it, "We have not here an abiding city, but we seek after the city which is to come."

Our Bible opens with a garden; it closes with a city; and the garden and the city are alike of earth. The final vision is that of Jerusalem—not heaven, but coming down out of heaven to earth, as a bride adorned for her husband; and the great anthem that celebrates the coming of the City is "Behold the tabernacle of God is with men and He shall dwell with them." Between the garden and the ultimate city, we find all the tragedy of human sin, human failure, human inability; and all the magnificent processes of God's government, forever moving, to our seeming with great slowness, but with infinite sureness, toward the ultimate goal of the establishment in this world of His own Kingdom, and the realization of His own purpose among the sons of men. Between that garden and that city, there is a long succession of pilgrims of faith, visionary souls, fanatics in the thinking of the men among whom they lived, leaving earthly cities to seek one they saw, but no other saw; abandoning the values of the passing and perishing, because convinced of the values of the eternal and permanent. Abraham leaving Ur of the Chaldees to seek a city of heaven that lies beyond, to establish a heavenly order in the world, until at last in those wonderful hours when the seer of blue Galilee beheld the ultimate things of the processes of God in the affairs of men, he saw Jerusalem from on high coming out of heaven, and the mystic glory of the established Kingdom flamed before him. If we are of the number of those who see that vision, and hope for that result, who believe that the victory must be won, then we are of the number of those who have to say, "We have not here an abiding city."

What then shall we do? We are men and women who by God's good grace are men and women of vision, who see the ultimate; and understand that the supreme words descriptive of the ultimate are words made precious to us by the ministry of our Lord; men and women who understand, that at last, in the established Kingdom of God and city of God, love will be the all-inclusive reason for activity, light the sufficient intelligence that men may not stumble, and life the energy equal to obedience to love in the power of light.

What shall we do? Shall we wait for the city that is to be, in the sense of selfishly desiring it? That were to deny our Christianity. Then shall we have conventions and conferences and gather ourselves together for the deepening of our own spiritual life, and in order to sing about the heaven to which we shall go when we have done with the bearing of burdens? That were to unfit us for heaven, and demonstrate our unworthiness to enter in. Shall we retire from all the busy activities of the great cities of the world, and shut ourselves within stone walls, and give ourselves to meditation and prayer? That were to miss the very purpose of our life in Christ; that were to cut the nerve of prayer, for men can only pray for the world's woe and wounds as they live near to them, and enter into constant comradeship with them. What then shall we do, for here we have no continuing city?

"We seek after the city which is to come." "We seek!" If I could only fasten that one word, so old and so familiar that it has almost lost its power of appeal, upon mind and heart and conscience, I should thank God for the opportunity given me. Seek! Did the writer of this letter mean that we are to be looking for the heaven that lies beyond? Surely not; for death is the way to that, unless our Lord shall come to gather us to that great and spacious life which lies beyond. That is not the thought at all. That is not the argument of the writer. That is not the master passion that moved pilgrims of faith in the past. Reverently, let me declare it, knowing I am touching upon supreme and superlative things, that was not the master passion that sent our Lord with face set toward Jerusalem, the faltering, falling city. What then does the writer mean? Does he suggest that we should look for some unknown earthly land where we may build this city; that we are to seek some Eldorado? That, my brethren, were in itself of the essence of selfishness. Wherever men have attempted to find some tract of country hitherto unoccupied, in order there to build a new state, a new city, the result has been the condemnation of the method, for the impulse behind such activity is merely that of finding a safe city into which the privileged may gather, and be free from the stress and strain of all the things of conflict. You cannot find me any settlement of men which has attempted to escape from the burden and battle of the actuality of life in city, village, or town, that has ever justified its own aim or object or been a success; for God lays upon all selfish endeavor the paralysis of His disapproving touch.

The word "seek" has occurred before in our hour of worship. We heard it from the lips of our Lord in the midst of that great Manifesto of the King, wherein everything as I full well know and would perpetually enforce, was spoken to His own disciples and not to the mixed multitudes. To them He said, "Seek ye first His Kingdom and His righteousness, and all these things shall be added unto you." In that wonderful passage, in which He revealed to men so much of the Father heart of God, showing that God cares for the flowers and the birds that have no ability to think and plan and arrange, and argues that He will therefore much more clothe and feed those to whom He has given the ability to think and plan and arrange; that passage in which He shows the unutterable folly of the man who sets his heart wholly upon treasures that are of the dust, and with a fine touch of sarcasm, mingled with pity, reminds men that moth and rust consume, and thieves break through and steal; that wonderful passage in which He puts into contrast in a way that surprises us the more, the more we study it, with its revelation of His perfect understanding of human nature and the tragedy of human sin, "Ye cannot serve God and mammon"; in that passage we hear Him say, "Seek ye first His Kingdom and His righteousness."

The particular word made use of by the writer of the letter to the Hebrews is an emphasized form of this word which our Lord used. It suggests strong passionate desire, accompanied by earnest effort in the direction of the desire.

Seek; not merely gazing, in the hope that we may see; not merely superficially looking for, and expecting; but seek. "We seek after the city which is to come."

The thought suggested is not merely that of looking to see if we can find a city built; it is that of fellowship in the process of building the city. We do not merely turn our back upon Ur of the Chaldees, and go wandering forth in the hope that somewhere, sometime, we may discover a city in which the principles of righteousness and truth may obtain; but we turn our back upon Ur of the Chaldees, in order to seek the righteousness of God and His Kingdom, in the establishment of that Kingdom, and the building of that city.

I am not now entering into any discussion as to whether or not there may not be an opening heaven, and the actual descending of a city. I am not Sadducean enough to deny these things. I believe there will be startling surprises when at the crisis of His Advent our Lord will bring all things into subjection to Himself.

I am speaking now, however, of the present responsibility of pilgrims who have no continuing city. As we look back over the long line of heroes and heroines of faith described for us in this letter; or as coming away from them, we track the footway of others through the centuries since the time of our Lord Himself, we find that these men of the pilgrim character, these men and women who found in the cities of earth no permanent resting place, became pilgrims with tent and altar, and sought a city of God by exerting in the cities of men those influences which were possible to them by their comradeship with Christ Himself.

The nature of the seeking is suggested by the words, "The city which is to come." Not the city to which we go, but the city which God is building, and between the building of which by God and the seeking for which by His people, there is the most intimate relationship.

From these most general statements as to the meaning of the text, let us turn to practical application. How can we help toward the establishment of this Kingdom and the building of this city of God? First, by inward and personal realization of the principles of this Kingdom. The citizen of London, who is a Christian man, will help toward the building of the city of God, first by absolute personal abandonment of himself to the Lordship of Christ, by recognizing that Christ is infinitely more to him than an ethical teacher, infinitely more than a great pattern of human life, infinitely more than a Saviour from the punishment of sin and from sin itself.

All this is He, this Lord Christ of ours; ethical Teacher, speaking as men never spake, with a severity so terrible that even today I cannot read the words of His ethical requirement without trembling; perfect Pattern for human life, so that the nearer I come to Him the more I recognize the distance between Himself and myself, perfect Saviour, so that I know in the deepest of me that He has pardoned my sin.

But He must be more than all this to us; He must be Lord and Master of our lives. If I have received from Him the gifts that He bestows, and render to Him absolute obedience, I can co-operate with Him in the building of the city of God, in the bringing in of the Kingdom of God into the world. Everything else will follow when that first principle is realized and yielded to; but nothing else will follow until it is so. There can be no larger seeking for the Kingdom of God until the Kingdom of God has come in our own lives. In other words, we cannot divorce private and public life, and declare that a man can be an influence and instrument for the establishment of the Kingdom of God, if in his own life he is impure. I can strike no blow against the powers of darkness which will tell, if I am allowing them to hold high revel within the citadel of my own personality. In beginning to build the city of God, I make my contribution, first and fundamentally, when I see to it that all my own life is under the Lordship of God's anointed and appointed King.

When that is granted, what next? The search for the city of God within the cities of men is first the result of the presence within those cities of pilgrims of faith who can find no abiding place within. "Ye are the salt of the earth; ye are the light of the world." Salt has no power to change corruption into incorruption. Salt has power to stay the spread of corruption. Salt is aseptic rather than antiseptic. In this great city of London we seek for the city of God as we are true to the life which our Lord has communicated to us, and as salt, purify, preserve, and give to goodness its opportunity. I am particularly anxious that this principle should be recognized by young men and women who name the name of Christ, and have seen the vision of the city, and desire to help in the search for it. You are salt of the earth, your life absolutely yielded to Jesus Christ, in the office, in the warehouse, in the college, wherever you may be, is a life that makes difficult the spread of impurity, that gives a chance to the aspiration after God that is born in the heart of the young man at your side.

Light; I do not think our Lord used His figures carelessly when, illustrating His own word, He said, "A city set on a hill cannot be hid. Neither do men light a lamp, and put it under the bushel, but on the stand; and it shineth unto all that are in the house." The city on the hill is for the illumination of vast expanses. The lamp in the house is for the irradiation of private places. Wherever these pilgrims of faith live with their tent and altar; pilgrims, ever ready to be disturbed;

men of faith, never disturbed in the midst of disturbance; there is the light, revealing God to men, by revealing all that life means when men have found the Kingdom of God and have entered into it for themselves. By such living we make contribution to the coming of the Kingdom. By such living we seek for the Kingdom of God; and only by such living.

Why was it that Lot did not save Sodom? He could not help Sodom because Sodom knew that his motive for living there was selfish; that of gaining, getting. So also the Christian man, when London knows he is simply in the city for his own selfish gain, is unable to influence London for God. Unless London can discover beneath the legitimate exercises of life the passion for righteousness and truth; beneath all the activities of the passing days, the search for the Kingdom; that man has cut the nerve of his own endeavor. We seek for the city of God as we live the life of loyalty in the cities of men.

But further. There can be no such life that will not find opportunities for definite activity. The basis of all our activity must be love and light; not as though they were two things; they are but the two sides of the one great experience of fellowship in the life of the Son of God. God is love; it is an all-inclusive word. God is light; it is an all-inclusive word. They are not mutually destructive. They reveal the two qualities of the essential life of God. Love and light, passion and principle merging forever more in great and awful purity. In the proportion in which men are living that life of fellowship with God in the city, there will be activity, and it is only activity which proceeds from that inspiration and is governed forever more thereby that is powerful. The reason of all that we do if we would help must be love; and the method must be light. Our activity must be love inspired, but it must be light instructed. Love which is mere sickly, sentimental, humanitarianism, may destroy instead of building. Unless the love we feel for men is love illuminated by the awful purity of God that insists upon His holiness as well as His mercy, we cannot help men. Rose water is no medicine for the malady of sin. We never can understand love until we realize what it means, in the presence of the awful, brutal Cross of Christ which is His insistence upon holiness, and upon love. These are the things which are to master our activities if we are to seek the city of God. Alas, that we so often blunder into some selfish kind of desire to help men, forgetting these things! Take up the New Testament and see how these writers never forgot to relate the truths of everyday life with the fundamental truths of holy religion. "Husbands love your wives, even as Christ also loved the Church." Thus in one brief, burning sentence, home is saved and sanctified, and the flaming sword of the Divine anger is against all attempts to loosen the divorce laws of the country.

If we seek the city by the revelation of God and of man, and the interrelationship between them in our own lives, and thereby actual, positive endeavor inspired by love and light, which are of the essence of the life of God, we shall help toward the coming of the city.

Love will be angry in the presence of sin, in the presence of all oppression, in the presence of everything in our own city which is opposed to the city of God. Love is of the very essence of anger. Someone has said during recent years in writing of one of those old Hebrew prophets that the severity of the opening part of the book makes it impossible to imagine that the tenderness of the latter part was written by the same pen; that the man whose attitude was characterized by awful thunder could ever have merged into the infinite love song that describes Jehovah as singing over His people and resting in His love. That opinion is not true to the revelation of God. It is the severity of God which demonstrates His goodness. It is the goodness of God which creates His severity. It is the son of thunder who becomes the apostle of love. If we would help to build the city of God, we shall need the driving rage of a great anger. Do not forget that when Paul, the great embodiment of the Christian temper, came to Athens he was in a paroxysm, his spirit was provoked within him.

Our contribution toward the building of the city of God will be a great anger against sin and all that is opposed to the will of God; but it will become a great tenderness toward the sinner. These are the things of which a man cannot speak; he can feel them though he cannot say them. Anger with sin, but tenderness with the sinner; that is the Christian mystery. We caught her in the very act! What will you, pure Teacher, say to this woman taken in adultery? What did He say? He looked at them and said, "Let the man that is without sin, cast the first stone." And when they had filed out, single file, He said to her, "Where are thine accusers gone; did no man condemn thee?" "No man, Lord." "Neither do I condemn thee. Go, and sin no more."

Do you think by that word He condoned adultery? You know He did not. His fierce and awful word abides forevermore, the most fierce and flaming thing ever said against adultery; but for the woman taken in the very act, He had a great compassion and a great pity. O God, that I may be a man something like that, fiery, angry with sin; forever patient with the sinner. So the city will be built; so the Kingdom will be prepared for the coming of the King.

Where shall we begin? At home. We need that word in England today. At home. Oh the perils threatening us! The first of them is the break-up of home life, the failure of Christian men and women to maintain home life. Let us begin there. You can have a city of God where you live. Your house can be the city of God. The amount of the rent does not matter. The kind of furniture does not enter into the calculation. Your house can be the city of God. On thirty shillings a week, someone says? Yes, if that is your income. Your Father knows you have need of these things, and if you really needed more He would give you more. Remember, He has only promised you sustenance. Your bread and your water shall be sure. Home with Jesus King, and the law of His light forevermore recognized, and the law of His love forevermore yielded to is the city of God.

There is nothing this land of ours needs more than the multiplication of Christian homes; and the Christian home is not a home that bolts its door when all its own members are in, and excludes all others. The Christian home will leave its door upon the latch and welcome the homeless—and there are hundreds of them in London who for lack of a home which will give them, not charity and patronage, but home life, are drifting away. Let your home be God's city.

Then the Church, that must be God's city. The Church, a hospital for all spiritual malady and disease, a nursing home for all the weak ones; a barracks into which men shall be brought to be trained for fighting; a base of operations from which the army shall march, terrible with banners against the things that oppose. That also is the city of God.

If we begin at home, and continue in the Church, then where next? In your office tomorrow morning. If you are a member of Parliament, in the House, and God hasten the day when it may be true—I say it because it is on my heart—that not at the beck and call of any party whip, but under the control of the Lord Christ, men shall speak for Him and be true to Him in Parliament.

In other words, begin to build the city of God where you

are. Do not sit down and sigh, wishing that you might be somewhere else, in order that you might help. You can help where you are. George Herbert's philosophy is the philosophy we need to understand, that it is possible to sweep a room and make that and the action fine; and the maid in the house of her mistress tomorrow, who after this service will do that sweeping a little better for Christ's sake, is as surely helping to bring in the Kingdom of God as is the preacher in the pulpit here or anywhere.

This is Christian citizenship. This is seeking for God's city, and this outlook and conception will correct many popular fallacies such as that the Christian Church should catch the spirit of the age. A thousand times No! The business of the Christian Church is to correct the spirit of the age. Or that more manifest fallacy that when you are in Rome you should do as Rome does. Nothing of the kind. When you are in Rome do right though you violate all the conventionalities! Then there is that most devilish of all fallacies: It is no use, we must let things alone! That is what the devil wants us to do. That is what the devil said to Jesus; "Let us alone; what have we to do with Thee?" Our answer must be His answer, "Come out"; and in His name we are to be out upon the great campaign. Pilgrim of faith, soldier art thou, builder art thou!

> Thine to work as well as pray,
> Clearing thorny wrongs away;
> Plucking up the weeds of sin,
> Letting heaven's warm sunshine in.
>
> Watching on the hills of faith,
> Listening what the Spirit saith,
> Of the dim-seem light afar,
> Growing like a nearing star.

THE WESTMINSTER PULPIT

God's interpreter art thou,
To the waiting ones below;
'Twixt them and its light midway
Heralding the better day—

Catching gleams of temple spires,
Hearing notes of angel choirs,
Where, as yet unseen of them,
Comes the new Jerusalem!

Like the Seer of Patmos gazing,
On the glory downward blazing;
Till upon earth's grateful sod,
Rests the city of our God."

May we be builders with Him, as well as warriors and pilgrims.

CHAPTER XIII

CHRISTIAN CITIZENSHIP: THE BUILDING OF THE CITY

The city which hath the foundations, whose Builder and Maker is God.

HEBREWS 11:10.

THIS IS NOW THE THIRD SUNDAY EVENING THAT WE HAVE turned to the subject of Christian citizenship.

Speaking on the first evening from the words occurring in this same letter, "We have not here an abiding city," we considered the reason why men of faith have always had to make that affirmation; and have to make it still. The cities of men are cities in which the principle of selfishness is the master principle; and the law of life is that of the survival of the strongest; and the character of the citizens is to a large extent that of sordidness. The pilgrims of faith are those who have entered into life by self-death; who believe not only in the survival of the fittest—in that—but also in the possibility of the salvation of the most unfit; and whose law of life is that of sacrifice. Therefore, such can find no abiding city in the world.

We then considered the true attitude of the pilgrims of faith toward the cities of men. While it is true that "we have not here an abiding city," this also ought to be true concerning us, "We seek after the city which is to come"; not by gazing at the stars and waiting for the coming of a city; not by seclusion from the ordinary and everyday life of these cities of men; but by first seeing the vision of the ultimate purpose of God, and then by the response of life to all that vision means, the realization within the individual experience of the principles of the Divine Kingdom; and finally by earnest, actual, persistent effort in harmony with these things.

Now all this has seemed to be most excellent; but we are constrained to say: What of the chaos and misery in the midst of which we live? What of the sad habit of the Christian Church of withdrawing itself from the great centers of the life of the city? Or, what—and this is perhaps the question which overwhelms us most often—after all can be the value of our small contribution toward the building of the city of God and the bringing in of His Kingdom?

The answer to all these suggestions is contained within the compass of our text, "The city which hath the foundations, whose Builder and Maker is God." We shall surely be depressed and overwhelmed unless we learn the lesson which is crystallized into this declaration of the writer of this letter, that the Builder and Maker of the city is God. If that fact do but take possession of our hearts then we shall be content to live out our little day in the midst of the scaffolding, seeming to see very little of the beauty of the city, yet knowing that the plan is in His mind, He is the Architect; that the power is in Himself, He is the Framer; and that, therefore, at last the city must be built.

Let us remember as we come to this consideration, that the material city is but the shell containing the city itself. As today we speak of a school and think of the building, and yet know that the building is not the school; as today we speak of a club, and look upon the building, but know that the club is not the building; or finally as today we speak of a church and think of the building in which we gather, but know

CHRISTIAN CITIZENSHIP: THE BUILDING OF THE CITY

that the church is not the building; so let us remember when we speak of the city, we think, and properly think, of an actual material city, full of glory and beauty, built in the ultimate economy of God; but the glory and beauty of the material will be the outcome of that life which constitutes the city. The remembrance of that at the very beginning of our meditation will enable us to see that things which seem to us full of discouragement, may after all prove to be methods of God, and the very slowness over which we lament in our foolishness is assuredly part of the process necessary for the creation of a life so strong and true and abiding that at last the material city will result.

Let us glance at "The city which hath the foundations," as it was revealed to the Seer of the Galilean Lake in the Isle of Patmos. If you ask me if I really believe that some day, somehow, out of the mystic distance of heaven, there will descend to this earth an actual city, I reply that I am not Sadducean enough to think that only the things I can see and handle today are the real and final things. Whether that be so or not, for today, in the midst of the spiritual conflict, we are to take this vision and find in it spiritual elements which are of abiding value; and therefore, I shall for the sake of brevity pass by the descriptions of the city as to material construction, all of which are valuable and I think full of suggestion. I want first to set that vision in relation to the whole movement of the Book. The city according to the story of that Book is not heaven. Neither is the city to be built in the millennium, but beyond it. I am particularly anxious not to enter into controversy with your mental convictions. The writer may have been mistaken. I am only reminding you of what he wrote. There are no detailed pictures of the millennium in this Book. There are descriptions of events, full of awe and sublime majesty and terrible judgment, which usher in the millennial reign; but the millennium itself is dismissed in this Book in three or four verses in the chapter preceding that in which we have the story of the city. At the close of the millennium John says that the devil will be loosed again after having been chained for a thousand years. Another period of swift judgment will then fall upon the earth; after which, the great white throne and final assize, full of awful majesty.

Beyond all that, as to order, will come the city of God. This city will not be built immediately. The ultimate victory is postponed; not that God has abandoned His work, He is the Architect, the Framer, and He is building; but the victory is not yet. I shall be able to do my day's work better, however, if I can see something of the ultimate victory; and to John was given this wonderful vision of the city that hath the foundations, flashing with the splendor of the precious stones of earth, which in their preciousness are symbols of principle suffused with passion. A city in its form pyramidal, lying upon its base foursquare; a city with walls, and those of jasper, the stone symbolic of conflict, full of beauty.

The subject of supreme interest to us as we look on, out of the midst of the conflict, is that of the conditions of its life. The government of the city is that of the ever-present God, influencing all its inhabitants. All the life of that city is worship. No temple therein; because the Lord Almighty and the Lamb are the temple; and all life has become worship, because all life is communion.

Every city, according to these Eastern figures had a burgess roll, and this city has its burgess roll. A burgess is one who inhabits a walled town, having a tenement there which is his own property. The burgesses of this city are those whose names are written in the Lamb's book of life. The defiled of

CHRISTIAN CITIZENSHIP: THE BUILDING OF THE CITY

every class, such as work abominations and make a lie are excluded.

The vision of this city is that of the great Theocracy which is the true democracy. It is the vision of the true democracy which is the great Theocracy. All is of heaven; the ideal, the process, the realization. It is a city which comes out of heaven. The plan of it was not born in the brain of any man. It is a city entirely of the earth; the material is of the earth, gathered from the earth, returning to the earth. It is the city which Abraham saw but never reached. It is the city toward which all the pilgrims of faith have been looking, and in the building of which they have been co-operating with God by faith, but none of them have reached it. Abraham has not reached it yet. Moses has not entered into it yet. The great seers, and prophets, and psalmists of the past; statesmen, in the economy of God, who have seen it but have never found it. "These all, having had witness borne to them through their faith, received not the promise." They saw the city, but they have not yet entered it. The goal toward which they ran was not their crowning in heaven, but God's crowning on earth. The city which they saw was not in a land beyond, this to which they hoped to go; but this whole earth, governed by God, from a central city, the metropolis in which God is King, and which therefore is the Theocracy, the people constituting the instrument through which in every age He makes known His will. It is therefore the final and ultimate Theocracy. All attempts to realize the Democracy apart from God will issue in the most disastrous failure; and every attempt to preach the Theocracy which forgets the Democracy, will issue in failure equally disastrous.

Of this city the Architect and Framer is God. The whole plan is in the mind of God. What that is, no man can see finally, perfectly. Some vision has been revealed from time to time to men of vision, and in the vision they have seen something of the glory. Abraham saw it; Moses saw it. Isaiah saw it. Luther saw the city of God. Cromwell saw the city of God. Mazzini saw the city of God. William Booth has seen the city of God.

To take that latest illustration; what drove General Booth into that method which some people, who are nearsighted, criticize, the method connected with the social endeavor? What made him want to care for the flotsam and jetsam of this great city of London and all the cities? What put into his heart the passionate discontent with unholy conditions of life? His vision of the city of God. All the discontent that is constructive is born of a great content with the ultimate purpose of God. To have seen this vision of the city is to be forever restless in every other city, and so "We have not here an abiding city, but we seek after the city which is to come." The inspiring vision which has created the pilgrims and warriors and builders of faith has been the vision of the city which is in the plan of God. No man has seen it wholly. No man has been able, if he has seen it wholly, to communicate his vision to other men. The thing is too great to be finally stated. The vision is too great for two eyes to see and one mind, by symbols of pen or brush, to convey to the minds of other men. The city of God; not heaven, but the city according to the heavenly pattern; the heavenly city on earth.

Through all the processes of human history, God has been working toward this end. When Josiah Strong wrote that little book, *The New Era*, he used an illustration full of illumination as he reminded us of how, when Pilate wrote the superscription and had it nailed to the Cross of our Lord and Saviour Jesus Christ, he wrote other and better than he knew. That, which so far as Pilate was concerned, was only a method of annoying the priests, was the writing of God, and the method was of God. The superscription, "King of the Jews," was written in three languages, the Roman, the Hebrew, and the Greek. This, so far as Pilate intended, because Roman soldiers were there and he wanted them to read it, and Greek merchantment and travelers would be there and he wanted them also to read it, that they all might mock and laugh at the priests. There was a profound significance in the writing of that superscription in the three great languages of the hour, the languages of the three peoples most powerful in the affairs of men. Hebrew was the language of spiritual religion. Greek was the language of intellectual strength. Latin was the language of imperial empire.

God was building by all those great world powers. God was at work, in the midst of the Hebrew religion, in the midst of Greek culture, and at the heart of Roman power. Through all these, there were operative in the world forces making possible the mission and mastery of Christ. Not idly does Scripture declare that He came in the fulness of times. Let me say a thing that I hesitate to say in this way, lest there should seem to lurk in it something of irreverence, but yet let me say it: Had He come sooner He would have come too soon; had He come later He would have come too late. He came when the Hebrew nation had prepared in the history of the world the great spiritual atmosphere resulting from the monotheistic doctrine of God. The history of that people is a history of persistent sin against God. Oh the greyness of it all. But there is wonderful sunshine in it too. My spirit has been elated in many an hour of study as I have seen the overruling of God, the chaos coming to cosmos; God forevermore making the wrath of men to praise Him, and restraining the remainder. However much the Hebrew nation failed, after the captivity they never again set up an idol.

They went back to their land a broken, poor, miserable remnant only, under Zerubbabel, Ezra, and Nehemiah; with no king, no prophet, no priest; but a people who had learned the lesson with which they started, "Hear O Israel Jehovah thy God is one." When that master spiritual truth was embodied in the world's history, the Christ came. God was building.

Or, if we turn to the Greek outlook, and think of the wonderful history of Greek culture and refinement, that history of intellectual giants which made it possible to speak of Athens as the fairest shrine of pagan humanity; if there be no other thing to be said, let this at least be said, the Greek had provided, for that time, a language which was of universal use, in some dialect of which, the story of the Christ could be written, in some dialect of which, the messengers of the Cross could preach through all the known world and be understood. God was building. Rome was the center of imperial power, and if you want to know the value of it, read again the Acts of the Apostles and Paul's letters and keep your eye on Paul; the restlessness with which he wanted to get to Rome, the eagerness with which he looked toward it, the haste which made him unable to wait, and compelled him to sit down and write the Roman letter. What was it that made Paul want to reach Rome? It was not the restlessness of the tourist. It was the passion of the missionary. He knew that from Rome, the strategic center of the world, there were roads leading out to all the known world along which her legions traveled; and he saw that they ought to be captured for the traveling of the legions of the Cross. All the forces contributed to prepare the way for His coming in the fulness of the times. God was building.

But there was the preparation not only of what these forces contributed; there was the preparation of their failure. Hebraism, when He came, was degenerate; the home of

CHRISTIAN CITIZENSHIP: THE BUILDING OF THE CITY

ritualism and hypocrisy; and the spiritual ideal was not enough to create spiritual religion. By the failure of the past the way was prepared for His coming. The history of Greek intellectualism had become the history of Greek bestiality. When Paul came to Athens, he found Epicurean and Stoic philosophers who knew nothing of Epicurius or the original Stoics; men who had degraded their philosophies. Then He came, when the way was prepared for Him by this failure; and His evangel was presently published by the Hellenist-Hebrew Paul, and redeemed all that was best in Greek strength. Rome had failed; voluptuousness and brutality were the two facts of her government. By that failure the way was made for the building of the new empire, for the coming in of the Kingdom, for the proclamation of the new evangel. He came, and coming found the past had prepared for Him, the failure had created His opportunity; and in Him, all the essential forces of these three world powers were taken hold of, and their opportunity was created anew. The Spiritual religion; the opportunity for intellectualism; the method of true government, making for abiding strength, all came through Him. These things were the things after which men had groped, and by so doing had made way for His coming, and the imparting of His power. In that groping they had failed, and had made necessary the coming of Another; and He came, not only for the salvation of individual men; let us never make that mistake, for that He came, oh yes, but for more, to take hold of the essential world forces and to compel them to coöperate with the enterprises of God. So God was building, and has ever been building.

There is a great work waiting to be done among our young people. I want someone to write the history of England as Isaiah reveals the history of Judah. I do not think it would be popular in England, but it needs writing; the history of how God has been at work and is at work still, the history of the fact that amid all the chaos and break-up and disruption God is building; a history of the fact that through the centuries and today God is at work.

Ah, Habakkuk, thy trouble has been our trouble. What is God doing? I will get up to the watch tower and see. And he climbed, and God said to him, I am at work, but if I told you what I am doing you would not believe Me. I am bringing the Chaldeans to do My work. And Habakkuk was more amazed than ever; the Chaldeans are not in the covenant, the Chaldeans are people outside the privilege of the Divine government. How can God use the Chaldeans? Once again, I will away to the watch tower. What was the end of his watching? The great psalm, the psalm of a great triumph, a psalm in which a man could say amid the break-up and disruption:—

> For though the fig tree shall not blossom,
> Neither shall fruit be in the vines;
> The labour of the olive shall fail.
> And the fields shall yield no meat;
> The flock shall be cut off from the fold,
> And there shall be no herd in the stalls:
> Yet will I rejoice in the Lord,
> I will joy in the God of my salvation.

Whose Builder and Maker is God.

This is a dark day, you tell me. There are disappointing things abroad, heartbreaking things abroad; Missionary Societies languishing for lack of funds, indifference spreading over the Christian Church. Away with you; God is building! That is the highest of vision, and if you deny it me, then I will bow my head and die for very heartbreak. But if you will grant it me, I will build, and fight, and sing, because the city will be built, and God's victory will be won.

CHRISTIAN CITIZENSHIP: THE BUILDING OF THE CITY

There are abundant proofs of the tending of humanity toward that ultimate city of God. Do not be at all alarmed at that statement. Some people are very much alarmed. Do you not think the world is getting worse? I am asked. Certainly! But do you not think it is getting better? I know it is! I mean that in all seriousness. Wheat and darnel, "Let both grow together until the harvest." Some men are always looking at the darnel and they say the world is getting worse. Some men see only the wheat and they say the world is getting better. The man who sees the whole field of the world, sees the darnel and the wheat, he sees that evil is becoming more evil and growing into clearer manifestation in all its dastardly devilishness; but he sees that the world is being prepared for the coming of the King. I affirm that there are abundant proofs of the tending of humanity toward the city of God. Compare the world when Christ came with the world today. Then the nations were in thraldom, class in bondage to class. Have you ever thought of this very remarkable statement in the gospel story. "There went out a decree from Caesar Augustus that all the world should be numbered, and it is declared that every man went up to Jerusalem." I do not know whether that impresses you, but to me it is an amazing thing. If they want to number us in this country, they have to come to us; we would not think of going up to report ourselves to be numbered. It is a very slight thing, but it is a revelation of the despotism that existed in those days, but which is gone in the countries of the world influenced by Christianity, and gone forever. Spiritual freedom is becoming civic liberty. Divine Fatherhood is whispering the story of human brotherhood. Laws are being made, or men are attempting to discover laws, for the ennoblement of the people. Care for the helpless is a new element in human history.

If you point to the evil that abounds, and tell me of the

breakdown of these very principles to which I have been referring, then I tell you that as it was, so shall it be again. Not only the work of the great Hebrew, Roman and Greek people prepared for Christ; but their failure also prepared for Him. The very fact that failure is everywhere today is to me a revelation of the necessity for some new work of God in the world; and the corroboration of the great prophecies of Scripture, which declare that by another crisis, an advent in the history of humanity, He will at last establish His Kingdom.

Not consciously, any more than Greece or Rome of old did consciously prepare for His coming, but surely all the forces are preparing for that Advent.

"God's in His heaven," therefore ultimately, finally, "All's right with the world." Failure itself shall prepare the way for the coming triumph. He will again purge His floor and gather the wheat into His garner and burn the chaff. The city will be built, the victory won, God vindicated.

> I looked; aside the dust-cloud rolled—
>   The Waster seemed the Builder too;
> Upspringing from the ruined old I saw the new.
> Take heart! The Waster builds again—
>   A charmed life old goodness hath;
> The tares may perish—but the grain
>   Is not for death.
> God works in all things; all obey
> His first propulsion from the night
> Wake thou and watch!
>   The world is gray with morning light!

CHAPTER XIV

CHRISTIAN CITIZENSHIP: CO-OPERATION IN THE BUILDING

Let us therefore go forth unto Him without the camp, bearing His reproach.
                                    HEBREWS 13:13.

THIS IS THE FINAL INJUNCTION OF THE LETTER TO THE Hebrews, and the final application of our study during these four Sunday evenings.

In our previous studies, we have seen that the ultimate passion burning in the heart of the men and women of faith, inspiring their pilgrimage, creating their battle, enabling their building, was not a passion for their own personal salvation, but for the ultimate victory of God in the world, that which is figuratively described as the building of the city of God. All these men of vision, revealed to us in the Divine library, were men who looked through the mists and fogs to the dawn of a glorious day, to the establishment of the order of Heaven on earth, to the completion of the city of God, to the restoration of the sin-blighted world to the Kingdom of God.

Because we also are pilgrims, warriors, builders of faith, we have no abiding city here, for the city has never yet been built in which the principles of the Divine government obtain full and perfect mastery. Nevertheless, we, pilgrims, warriors, builders of faith, do not spend our time in useless lament—we seek after the city which is to come. By the clear vision of it, by acceptation of all the principles of the government of God and obedience to them within our own lives, and then by definite endeavor we prepare for the coming of the Kingdom —we become workers together with God both in His battle against evil and in His building of His city. "Let us therefore go forth unto Him without the camp, bearing His reproach."

The word is as startling and as revolutionary today as it was when the Lord first uttered the principle in the ears of Peter and the disciples at Caesarea Philippi. "From that time Jesus began to shew unto His disciples how that He must go unto Jerusalem, and suffer many things of the elders and chief priests and scribes, and be killed, and the third day be raised up."

Let us first reverently attempt to look upon the position of our Lord as indicated in these words, "without the camp." Quite simply they mean that our Lord was crucified outside the city of Jerusalem; that is the thought embodied in the hymn of our childhood, sacred to us all—"There is a green hill far away Without a city wall."

Now it is quite evident that He set His face from the beginning of His ministry toward death as the culmination of His mission. In His own heart, and according to His own conception, the ultimate warrant for all His teaching and all His doing was the Cross. When they challenged Him as to the right by which He cleansed the temple in Jerusalem, He answered them in figures of speech, which they could not then understand, but which were explained afterward by John: "Destroy this temple, and in three days I will raise it up"; thus claiming that His right to cleanse the temple of God was the right of His Cross and coming resurrection. Passing over all the intermediate spaces in His ministry, we come to the final movements, and we see how with calm, definite deliberation, born of a clearly defined purpose, He set

His face toward Jerusalem. The Cross lay before Him as part of the process leading on to resurrection, which was the culmination of His mission. Neither the ideals of His teaching, nor the splendor of His example, completed the meaning of His work; but always, in His thinking and deliberate intention, the Cross and resurrection. Apart from these, to use His own language, He was straitened, limited, and prevented from fulfilling His high and holy purpose. Therefore, as we see Him going out through the gate of the city, away from the center of the life of the people, outside the city over which He had wept, we are to remember He is going, out of His own deliberate choice and will, to the Cross arranged for and accomplished by the Lord Himself. That is the historic background of our text.

He thus left the city because of the sin within the city; because of its godlessness, its selfishness; because these things were not only manifest, but held mastery over every department of the city's life; the priests, the princes, the people, and the publicans, were against Him at the last. Against Him, not for personal reasons, but upon the ground of His presentation of the Kingdom of God, and His call to men to repent. Against Him, because His ideals were wholly spiritual. He touched life always at the spiritual center and from there moved out to all the suburbs of the mental and the physical. For that reason the city of Jerusalem, through its priests, its princes, its publicans, its people, was entirely opposed to Him. It was impossible for Him, in the city as she then was, to fulfil the Divine ideals. The whole movement of life was against Him. He gave Jerusalem His high ethic, and all His peerless example; but not by these things could He build the city of God or ransom the lost. It was necessary to move outside the gate, and beyond the camp, for the accomplishment of the work.

He went outside the gate, as the writer here says, "that He might sanctify the people." This was separation from the city in order to create an evangel for the city. It was the excommunication of a nation, in order to the making of a nation; the dooming of a city, in order to complete the building of a city; the passing out of chaos, in order to set at liberty forces which would restore the cosmos.

Then mark the nature of His activity; "He suffered without the gate." Look back upon the scene. If we could only see it in all simplicity as it actually happened; He was crucified as a malefactor between two thieves. To the ideal presented, to the ethic enunciated, that is man's answer; the answer not of those whom in our foolish pride we describe as the lower orders; but the answer of light and learning and intelligence; of the highest intellectual capacities in Jerusalem. "Outside the gate . . . without the camp."

There through suffering He created a new center. The old was to be destroyed because of its departure from the Divine. He returned to the Divine, and made possible the new. In Exodus we have the same principle illustrated. When the people had sinned, Moses came into the midst of the camp, and carried the tabernacle outside the camp and pitched it there. He said in effect: "By your sin you have exiled God, and by this act you are all excommunicated; there is but one way back, it is that you find your way to the new center created; for God Whom you have exiled can only return to you as you return to Him in obedience and repentance."

At the moment when our Lord turned his back upon Jerusalem and passing through its gate, suffered without the camp; He excommunicated the nation, put an end to the temple, abandoned the economy; but He did it in order that He might make a new tent of meeting, a new tent of testimony, a new point at which God and man should come together, a new center where God and man could be restored to fellowship with each other.

In the mystery of that hour, outside the city, outside the temple, in His suffering and His dying, He was standing, in the eternal economy of God, inside the veil as the great High Priest, accomplishing for humanity that infinite mystery of sacrifice whereby it should be possible for man to return to God, and God to return to man.

It may be that in the mind of someone listening to me the question may be arising, What have these things to do with our Christian citizenship in London? Everything. In the first sermon of the series, we saw that the city cannot be our abiding place because it is contrary to godliness; in the next we considered our responsibility of seeking the city of God, in preparation for the coming of the King; in the third we saw that God Himself amid all the chaos is working toward the cosmos and building His city. The present study shows that we can only be workers with God, and builders with Him, as we pass by the way of separation and sacrifice to the place outside the city gate; the place without the camp, where is to be the new center of the new city; because there new forces are operative by which individual men, and so the city, the nation, the race, can be made fit in the economy of heaven.

If we are to help God in the building of His city, we must be men and women outside the city, discontented with the city as it is; so living that the city becomes discontented with us.

Has the offence of the Cross ceased? It has not ceased. If we know nothing of the offence of the Cross, it is because we have not yet followed Him without the camp bearing His reproach. With absolute sincerity it may be, but with appalling ignorance let me also hasten to add, we may hope to reconstruct the cities of men apart from the Cross of our Lord. We shall never do it. The only way is that of resurrection and ascension; and that is the way of true fellowship with Him in separation to the offence of the Cross. The offence of the Cross abides. The Cross of Christ is as offensive today as it ever was. It is foolishness still to the Greek, a stumbling-block to the Jew. I spoke last Sunday evening of the great world powers represented by Pilate's superscription. What does the Cross mean to them? What was the Cross to the Roman? A gibbet, a gallows, a thing utterly offensive. What was it to the Greek? Foolishness. What was the Cross to the Hebrew? A stumbling-block, something devoid of power, over which men stumbled, and which they were determined to be rid of as offensive to fine religious instincts. The Cross has been the power of God unto salvation for nineteen centuries, and there is no other power of God unto salvation. Men today are as surely offended by the Cross as ever they were; offended by the idea that man can only be redeemed through suffering which has its symbol in blood; and offended by this deepest fact of Christianity, because acceptation of redemption that way, and fellowship in redeeming others that way, involve personal communion with and in the Cross. Yet this is the appeal of the text, "Let us therefore go forth unto Him without the camp." Let us become disinherited men and women, suffering the loss of all things, content even to suffer the loss of rights if by loss of them we can help other men; men and women abandoned of all the powers of the world. The power of the world said to our Lord, just ere He passed through the gate away to suffering, through the Roman Procurator, "Art Thou then a King?" "What is truth?" The culture of the world looked at the Cross and said it was foolishness. The religion of the world looked at the Cross and said the Cross was a stumbling-block. The reproach of the Cross, the offence of the Cross. Only as we get into fellowship with that reproach, that offence, only as we are willing to be at the end of that pride which affirms the possibility of reconstruction apart from that Cross, shall we ever be workers together with God for reconstruction.

Of course, I am dealing with reconstruction; with the necessity for it in human nature as I find it. If you have a nature that needs no redemption, if you were born of such as need no redemption, then do not be angry with the preacher, but listen; Christ said, "I came not to call the righteous, but sinners to repentance." If it may be granted that there are men and women who need no repentance, righteous men and women, then let them remember that they must not take the Christian name, for Christ said He did not come after them. His business in the world is with sinning men, with ruined men; with chaos, in order that He may restore it to cosmos; in order that He may save—gracious word, never to be dropped out of our vocabulary—that He may save the sinner; that He may remake the flotsam and jetsam, until it is beautiful for the palace and home of God; that He may build the city that never has been built by reason of human sin; and build it by so dealing with sin at its devilish heart as to cancel it and break its power forever. That is the mission of Christ.

The appeal of this series of sermons, and of this evening's sermon, is to souls that desire to be with Him in that work, the work that is necessary wherever you look. My comrades, you cannot get very near to this world's heart without getting very near to its agony; and you cannot get near to the world's agony without getting near to its sin; sin underneath all the veneer of the West as well as patent in the vice of the East.

Sin; how will you deal with sin? With the liar who tells you he is a liar, and hating it cannot end it; with the polluted man dripping with filth, who hates his filth but cannot break away from it? How are you going to deal with these men and women, for Christ's mission is with such; "I came not to call the righteous, but sinners to repentance."

When I look at the city of God—at the vision of which we glanced last Sunday evening in the Book of Revelation—there are two things that fill my soul with wonder. On the gates are the names of the twelve tribes of the Children of Israel, and on the foundations the names of the twelve apostles of the Lamb. We have missed the significance of the symbolism of that great vision if we have thought that these are the names of men of naturally fine and noble character upon the foundations. Nothing of the sort. Let the man whom some of us most admire tell us—for I verily believe that Paul's name is among the apostles of the Lamb,—he says of himself that he was "chief of sinners." On the gates of the city are the names of a failing, disobedient crowd of men who handed on the forces of failure to their sons. The names on the foundations are those of men who were sinning men, and who chant the anthem of redemption as they say, "Who loveth us, and loosed us from our sin by His blood; and He made us to be a Kingdom, to be priests unto His God and Father." The city of God is a city of ransomed, redeemed, regenerated humanity, the work of One Who came into human history and laid hands upon the chaos in order that He might restore cosmos. If we are going to help to build that city, we must go with Him by the way of His Cross.

To speak only of the Cross is not to deliver the whole of the Christian message. Said Paul, "It is Christ Jesus that died, yea rather, that was raised from the dead." It is that "was raised" which is the final word of the Christian evangel. If I leave the city and find my way to Him without the camp, I am coming to a new center of humanity. He looked on to the Cross, and in the midst of a great multitude of men, in answer to the inquiry of the intellectual Greeks as represented to Him by two of His own disciples, He said, "Now is the judgment of this world; now shall the prince of this world be cast out. And I, if I be lifted up from the earth, will draw all men unto Myself." What did He mean by "now"? To what was he referring? Read the context and it will be seen that He spoke in anticipation of His Cross. By the way of the Cross is the judgment of the world, is the casting out of the prince of the world, is the drawing of humanity back to Himself, and the consequent building of the city of God. If we go forth bearing His reproach, we come to this new center of discrimination, of judgment; this new center of repelling power over the forces of evil; the prince of this world cast out; this new center of attraction and healing. "I, if I be lifted up from the earth, will draw all men unto Myself."

Mark the sacred, holy paradox. To come with Him without the camp is to come with Him within the veil, to the very heart of the sanctuary, into true fellowship with God. To come with Him through the gate, to the camp, to the place of reproach; is to find our way into the place of peace, of communion; is to find our way to the dynamic center from which the forces flow, for the doing of that which cannot be done in other ways.

That is one reason why I read not merely that one passage in the thirteenth chapter but that which is a part of it in the twelfth chapter, "Ye are come," not merely you will come, not merely the ultimate and final victory, but "Ye are come unto mount Zion, and unto the city of the living God, the heavenly Jerusalem, and to the innumerable hosts of angels, to the general assembly and church of the firstborn who are enrolled in heaven, and to God the Judge of all, and to the spirits of just men made perfect."

To follow Him outside the gate, without the camp, to the place of reproach is to come to the center of actual present accomplishment of the purposes of God; and to assurance of their ultimate accomplishment, to the widest bound and reach of the universe of God. We come to a new center. We pass within the veil. We come to a place where the old ideals are reborn and the old forces are renewed and remade. We come to the place which in the history of the world will finally result in the acceptance by men of the truth that government cannot be by might, but that it must be by right; we come to the place where the culture of the world will be reborn; science, art, music, literature were through that Cross of our Lord and Saviour Jesus Christ born anew. Whatever there had been of these before the age in which He came was decadent and ruined. The great philosophy of Socrates had withered, and men were disobedient. The idea of Epicurus that men should get back to the simple life; or that of the Stoics, who aimed at high ideals of virtue; these things were perished, and even while the words of the ancient philosophies were upon the lips of the Greek teachers, the vital forces were at an end. But they were reborn in the Cross. With all its rugged severity it demanded forever more simplicity of life and strenuousness of life in order to bring about the fulfilment of being and to co-operation with the purposes of God. At that center, outside the city beyond the gate, spiritual religion was reborn, and by way of that Cross men have come to know that neither in Jerusalem or in any mountain set apart do men find God; but wherever they turn to Him and meet Him at the trysting-place of His love as revealed in His Cross, there do they find Him.

The urgency of the appeal is this, there can be no sanctification of the people or of the city save by co-operation with Christ in this method of self-sacrifice; this consent to fellowship with Him in His Cross. Here only is the place untouched of storms, for here was the center of the whirlwind. Here only is the place of action with God, in the building of the city.

If we are truly pilgrims of faith, warriors of faith, builders of faith, then let us remember we cannot dwell in Jerusalem sharing its life, and by talking of the Cross, redeem it. We cannot dwell in London and be of London, of its desire and of its amusement and of its philosophies, and save it. There must be utter separation, with a clear line of demarcation between those who have seen the vision and are walking the way of God toward the victory, and those who are content with godlessness. That is the first requirement for being able to help the city, or to prepare for the coming of the Kingdom or to co-operate in the building of the city of God.

Our only business as Christian men and women in London is that of missionaries. "What," someone says, "are you saying that all we have to do is to preach this gospel at the street corners, and preach this gospel by the distribution of literature?" No, nothing of the kind. Every relationship is our opportunity for proclaiming this evangel and bringing men into fellowship with this Christ of the Cross; our business by our strict integrity therein, and even by denying self therein for the sake of the man who is struggling by our side is our opportunity for building. That is Christianity. In social life and in municipal life, by standing for the crown rights of the Lord Christ, we build the City of God. We are to be separated to these things on six days of the week as well as on the seventh; by definite, honest, sacrificial toil, declaring the evangel; and by getting hold one by one of broken, bruised, battered men and women, and leading them to this Christ.

It is very little in the great whole that I can do, or that you can do, my brother. Thank God for the great whole; but do not let us forget that there is no great whole of God if we neglect our little. He has chosen, in an infinite mystery, which is also infinite wisdom, to limit Himself in His work for the restoration and salvation of men and of the race, to those who name His name and wear His sign, and share His life. Thus, the final appeal is the word of the text: "Let us therefore go forth unto Him without the camp, bearing His reproach."

CHAPTER XV

CHURCH IDEALS: THE CHURCH INSTITUTED

The Church of God.

ACTS 20:28.

IN THE COURSE OF HIS CHARGE TO THE ELDERS OF THE Ephesian Church, Paul made use of this particular phrase; and I propose to spend four Sunday mornings in considering certain matters which it suggests; speaking of the Church of God as revealed in the New Testament as to its constitution, its government, its discipline, and its work; our theme this morning being that of the first of these four considerations, the constitution of the Church.

We are arrested in the first place by the word itself, which is by no means common in earlier books of the New Testament; being found in the Gospel of Matthew only twice, in the other Gospels not at all, and for the first time in the Book of the Acts of the Apostles in its fifth chapter. (In the Authorized Version, the word is found in the second chapter, where it declares that, "The Lord added to the Church"; but the reading of the Revision is "The Lord added to them"; and as a matter of fact the actual statement is that "The Lord added"; meaning, as I believe, that these people were added, not to the Church, but to the Lord.) At this point in the twentieth chapter is the final occurrence of the word in this book.

Let me remind you that our word Church has no true connection with the word of which it is a translation, save in a secondary sense. Our word is a word full of beauty, coming to us through Old English from the Greek word which signifies the Lord; our word, therefore, simply meaning the Lord's house. It was first used of the place where Christian people assembled for worship, and presently, came to be used in a higher spiritual sense of the people who assembled for worship in such a place.

The word in which we are now interested, the true word of the passage, the word of which *Church* is a translation, is a word occurring often subsequently, especially in the writings of Paul. The word "ecclesia" literally means *called out*, and is used of some company of people separated from others. In this Book of the Acts, it is used once of the congregation of the Hebrew people in the wilderness; and once it is used, though not there translated church, in the sense in which the men who first head it would be most likely to understand it, of the governing body in one of the Greek cities. On the occasion of the uproar at Ephesus there was called together the Church at Ephesus, not the Christian Church, but the Church of Ephesus, that is, the assembly, the governing body, in which no slave could possibly hold office.

Such is the word itself. Suffice it to say it is one of those words which Christianity apprehended, and transfiguring, consecrated to its own purpose. As to its essential meaning, it signifies a people called out into separation; and as to its uses, it suggested to the men who first head it, two ideas; the Hebrew idea of the congregation, the nation itself, the Theocracy, the people God-governed; and the Greek idea of a company of free men, elected to the business of civic government. The two ideas, therefore, most probably suggested by

CHURCH IDEALS: THE CHURCH INSTITUTED

the word to the men who first head it from the lips of our Lord, were those of a people under the direct government of God, and a people exercising in the world an authority derived from their submission to the throne of God.

Now this word is used in our New Testament about thirteen times in its catholic sense, having reference to the whole Church of God; and about nine times in reference to the local assemblies of the people of God; the church in Thessalonica, the church in Corinth, the church in Ephesus, the church at Smyrna, and so on. Yet the words are used so interchangeably that it becomes evident that the New Testament writers always looked upon the local assembly as a microcosm of the catholic Church; and all the things declared concerning the catholic Church are true concerning the local assembly.

In approaching our study of the New Testament conception of the Church, we are compelled to take time with what is perhaps a somewhat old and often debated matter, that, namely, of the distinction that it is quite necessary to draw between the Kingdom of God and the Church of God.

There is a distinction, and before we can understand the nature or the function of the Church, it is necessary that we recognize that distinction quite clearly.

Let me begin with that very constantly recurring phrase of our Bibles, and that constantly recurring phrase of the present day, "the Kingdom of God," and inquire as to what it really means.

I personally am always a little afraid lest we read into it an altogether too narrow meaning. Consequently, let us first attempt to grasp something of the breadth and spaciousness of the suggestion of the phrase itself. So far as is possible, let us free our minds from all ordinary interpretation of the meaning of the phrase, from all application of the value of the phrase; and consider the phrase itself, in order that we may understand that to which it refers.

The Kingdom of God suggests first the actual rule and reign of God; secondly, the realm over which God rules and reigns; and finally—and it is within this final thought that we generally confine our thinking—the realization of this Kingdom in the history of men, and in this world in which we live. We pray "Thy Kingdom come," and our Master taught us so to pray; and when we pray, we are thinking of an actual and experimental and conscious establishment of His Kingdom in the world. It is right that we should so pray, we must continue so to pray, and we must work as we pray toward the establishment of the Kingdom. But there is a sense in which that Kingdom has already come, in which that Kingdom is already established. We come into the most true understanding of the teaching of our Bible when we remember that the phrase itself means the rule and reign of God. Included within the phrase is a theology, a science of God, a doctrine of God. It assumes the Divine transcendence, the fact that God is seated high above all the affairs of the universe. Included in it also is the fact of the Divine immanence, His nearness to and perpetual sustenance of every atom of the universe over which He sits enthroned. It involves also the doctrine of a personal God.

I know the difficulty of using the word *personal* in this relationship; a difficulty born of the fact that we are constantly postulating the Divine Personality upon the basis of our own personality, which I submit is a wrong process of reasoning. Personality is only perfect in God. It is never perfect in man. Man is but a shadow of the Divine, a likeness, an image, a representation; and so in the matter of personality there is imperfection in man, while there is perfection in God.

CHURCH IDEALS: THE CHURCH INSTITUTED

This phrase of the Kingdom of God involves the doctrine of the personality of God; intelligence, emotion, volition; all the essential things of our own personality, but in absolute and infinite perfection.

The phrase reminds us that of this universe, of which we know so little and can know so little, God is the Creator, the Sustainer; arranging beforehand, as Paul said in Athens, the bounds of human habitation; fashioning, as the writer of the letter to the Hebrews declared, all the ages as they come, giving them all their tones and qualities and quantities. The whole universe is the realm over which God reigns. The Kingdom of God is a fact established from which there can be no escape on the part of angels or men or demons. All are within the grasp of His government, all are compelled to yield themselves, whether willingly or unwillingly, to the sway of His power, and to the ultimate purposes of His wisdom.

These are the profoundest things, the most spacious things, suggested by a phrase which we too often use as though it only had reference to things of this earth.

And at last, the phrase does stand for the establishment in this world of the Kingdom, where today we are supremely impressed by sin, and sorrow, and sighing; there will be established the Kingdom of our God, a Kingdom of love and joy and peace, of perfect human well-being in individual and social, national and international relationships. The establishment of the Kingdom, or Kingship of God in the world, is the last idea suggested by the phrase itself.

Now this great thought is the fundamental truth of Biblical revelation. The first chapters of the first book in the Bible suggest these things pre-eminently. Whatever difficulties we may have concerning what we are pleased to speak of as the authenticity or the historicity of these chapters, at least we must be perfectly agreed that they teach that all things have had their origin in the will and by the power of this one God. That as I understand it, is the fundamental teaching of the earliest chapters of the Book of Genesis. "In the beginning God created the heavens and the earth." And in all that remains of the Old Testament, that is the perpetual chord of the dominant strain; and all the music, sometimes in major and sometimes in minor cadences, is true to that underlying chord; proclaiming the throne of God, and the government of God. The whole history of the Hebrew people is the history of the creation of a people recognizing that fact; and by obedience to it come to power and influence in the world; or by forgetting it, becoming a people scattered and peeled over the face of the whole earth. This throne and government of God, this sovereignty of God, is the great truth that runs through all the Old Testament.

When I turn to the New Testament, I find that this is still the theme. The first word falling from the lips of the forerunner of the Christ is, "Repent, for the Kingdom of heaven is at hand." The first words falling from the lips of the Christ Himself as He commenced His ministry of preaching is, "Repent, for the Kingdom of heaven is at hand." The whole of His administration—judged by His ethical standards, and His spiritual interpretations, by His works as well as His words—circles around this one word, "Seek ye first His Kingdom, do His righteousness; and all these things shall be added unto you." The supreme passion of His heart, as crystallized in the prayer which He taught His disciples, and which we constantly repeat, is the same. He did not teach us to pray first for the things we need individually, but for the coming of God's Kingdom in this world, and its establishment here.

If we watch the ministry of the Lord Jesus Christ, and

CHURCH IDEALS: THE CHURCH INSTITUTED

observe His dealing with His own nation after the flesh, we find that there came a solemn and awful moment, when with quiet dignity, in the metropolis of the nation, and in the Temple, the center of the metropolitan life, He said this most significant thing to the rulers of the people, "The Kingdom of God shall be taken away from you, and shall be given to a nation bringing forth the fruits thereof."

Or, if we remind ourselves of the first occasion upon which He used the word "Church," let us note very carefully, not all the values of His announcement, but one particular emphasis thereof. To the confessor Peter, He said, "I also say unto thee, that thou art Peter, and upon this rock I will build My Church; and the gates of Hades shall not prevail against it. I will give unto thee the keys of the Kingdom of heaven: and whatsoever thou shalt bind on earth shall be bound in heaven: and whatsoever thou shalt loose on earth shall be loosed in heaven." In other words, I will make My Church the standard of moral interpretation, binding or loosing the standards of conduct among the affairs of men; the keys of the Kingdom were thus committed to the men who for the moment stood as the sole representation of that Church which He was about to build.

Or, if we turn to those pages in the New Testament which deal with the sacred ministry of the Spirit, the fundamental fact is still that of the Kingdom of God; interpreted through the Christ as the Spirit unveils the Christ; realized within the Church as the Spirit creates a race of men who will say, in answer to all opposition and all persecution and all criticism, "We must obey God rather than men." That was Peter's answer on behalf of the apostles and the whole Christian community to the criticism and opposition and persecution of the Sadducean high priest and governing board. "How dare you," said the priest, "preach in the name of Jesus when we straitly charged you not to do so?" And the answer was, "We must obey God rather than men"; or, in other words, we are in the Kingdom of God, submissive to His throne, recognizing no other authority that we can allow to interfere as between us and Himself. We must obey God.

As we glance on at what the New Testament says concerning the future, we find that it declares that this Kingdom is to be preached and realized beyond the age of the Church; and eventually in one mystic passage the apostle declares that when He, the Lord Christ, has subdued all rule and authority and power to His own sway, having reigned until even death is put beneath His feet: then He shall deliver up the Kingdom to the Father, that God may be all and in all.

Now we come to the phrase, "The Church of God," which is not of the Old Testament, which no prophet ever understood; and to the fact, to which no prophecy of the Old Testament has any reference whatever; a fact hidden in the past, revealed in these times, the fact of the Church. The Church according to this New Testament teaching is an elect race, a company of people called out, and unified by a common life; to create which, Christ came, and the Spirit came to abide; an entity, which ultimately is to be complete within itself; an entity, the full and glorious vocation of which does not begin in this age, but in the ages to come; an entity, nevertheless, which has most intimate relationship with that Master principle of the Kingdom, to which we have been giving our thought; a company of those in the world today in whom that Kingdom principle is realized, through whom that Kingdom principle is manifested, through whom that Kingdom fact is to be propagated amongst men.

Let me again refer to words of our Lord already quoted: He said to the Hebrew people, "The Kingdom of God shall be taken away from you and given to a nation bringing forth the fruits thereof"; and when Peter wrote his letter, he described the Church among other phrases, by this suggestive one, "a holy nation." The Church of God then is that holy nation in the history of the world; realizing the Kingdom principle; manifesting the Kingdom value; proclaiming the Kingdom fact; propagating the Kingdom forces.

Then if that be so, let us now ask, What is the constitution of this Church?

The two references made to it by our Lord I have already referred to, and do not propose to deal with at any length, but I am compelled to commerce with them, because in them I find in germ, all truth concerning this elect company, the Church. He said, "Thou art Peter"—and I should much prefer to render with absolute literalness of translation, "Thou art rock, and upon this rock I will build My Church." Do not forget to link that word of Jesus at Caesarea Philippi with the first thing He ever said to this man. When He first met him, He said, "Thou art Simon the son of John: thou shalt be called rock." At Caesarea Philippi He said, "Thou art rock, and upon this rock I will build My Church." What rock? That master principle which, obtaining in the life of this man, had changed him from weakness to massive and perpetual strength. Not the man, not the man's humanity, not the apostle, blundering and failing; but that principle which had made him rock. And what was the principle that had made him rock? His discovery of God in Christ, and of the administration of the Kingship of God in Christ; Thou art the Christ, that is, the Messiah; the Son, that is, One showing the essential being of the living God. So that the ultimate word in the confession of Peter was the living God; and he recognized in Jesus the revelation of the living God; the Son; and he recognized in Him, the administration of the will of the living God, the Messiah. Upon that rock, that essential rock of Deity, of Deity revealed, of Deity administered, so as to change Simon from the weak changing man that he was into the man of rock, "upon that rock I will build My Church."

Or more briefly, to take the second reference to the Church on the part of our Lord, when speaking of the Church's discipline and power in prayer, He declared, "Where two or three are gathered together in My name, there am I in the midst." That reveals the fact that the Church consists of all those who are gathered about the living Lord, and who by the administration of His Holy Spirit share His very life and nature, and are the instruments of His discipline, as He is the medium of their prevailing prayer.

The next historic reference to the Church is found in the fifth chapter of the Acts. What has happened? Our Lord foretold the Church, and now I find the Church referred to as an existing entity; great fear came upon the whole Church when the fiery discipline that purged the fellowship of the presence of Ananias and Sapphira was manifested. Then suddenly, without introduction, the Church is referred to as existing. Whence came it? The answer is to be found in the second chapter of the book. By the coming of the Spirit upon a company of waiting disciples, that company was baptized into a living unity. They became one; they were joined to the Lord; and became one Spirit with the Lord; and being one Spirit with the Lord, they were also so with one another. It was a baptism into life, the dawn of a new light, the power of a new love taking possession of them; and the life was the life of the Christ; and the light was the light of the Christ; and the love was the love of the Christ. Not that they loved Him, but that He loved them, and that love took possession of them, and became the impulse of all their doing and serving and suffering. Behold in the upper room on the day of Pentecost, after the coming of the Spirit, a company of men and women, no longer geographically near to the Lord, for He was absent as to all human appearance and presence; no longer one sentimentally with the Lord; but one with Him by the mystic tie of spiritual life. His life and their life made one by the baptism of the Spirit. So the Church came to be.

In view of that, the apostle wrote that which we read as lesson in the Corinthian letter, "In one Spirit were we all baptized into one body, whether Jews or Greeks, whether bond or free; and were all made to drink of one Spirit. For the body is not one member, but many." That is the Church; the Christ Himself the Head; and all individual believing men and women, baptized by the Spirit into relationship with Him, the members; quite independent of nationality, Jews or Greeks; quite independent of social position, bond-slaves or free men. The great baptism of the Spirit destroys the differences, and creates the unity; the great baptism of the Spirit whelms human life, and brings it to the realization of its own powers, by linking it to the Master life, the life of the Lord and Master Himself. So was the Church originally constituted. And so the Church has grown through all the ages.

Paul, when in the Ephesian letter, dealing with the great theme of unity, which is the theme of our morning meditation, said, "Giving diligence to keep the unity of the Spirit in the bond of peace. There is one body, and one Spirit," and the great vision of the catholic Church filled his mind as he wrote that. Then he suddenly breaks it up, that we may see and understand it, showing us the way of entrance into this new and holy relationship; "one Lord," that is the Lord Jesus Christ presented to the vision of the individual man; "one faith," that is the faith of the man who sees the Lord, ventures everything upon Him, trusts in Him; "one baptism," that is the baptism of the Holy Spirit whereby that believing soul is made a member of that one Lord. So the Church has grown through all the ages. No man has ever been made a member of the Church by the vote of a Church meeting, or having his name written upon a Society Class book. All these things may be valuable in their place; but they are external and accidental. Men become members of this great Church of God when the Lord is presented, and they call Him Lord by Faith, and as a result of the Spirit's interpretation; and then by the Spirit's baptism are made sharers of His very life, sharers of His very nature.

And what is the purpose of this Church? Let Paul finish that which I have partially quoted in the Ephesian paragraph, and we shall know. "One God and Father of all, Who is over all, and through all, and in all." The Church is the one Body, the members and the Christ; the way into the Church, one Lord presented, one faith exercised, one baptism received; the issue of the Church, the Kingdom of God, "one God and Father, over all and through all and in all." The Kingdom of God realized, manifested, proclaimed.

Therefore, I am a member of this catholic Church, if I have believed on this one Lord, and have received the baptism of the Spirit whereby I am made a member of this Lord. The baptism of the Spirit is not a second blessing; the filling may be; the enduement for power certainly is; but we cannot interpret our doctrine of the Spirit, in the light of the New Testament, without recognizing that the baptism, the whelming into life, is in answer to that faith, whereby a man becomes a member of the Lord.

The first practical value of this teaching is that of a recognition on our part of the unity of the Church. Brethren, are we praying as we ought, for that recognition? Are we living as we ought in order to the realization of it? To the

CHURCH IDEALS: THE CHURCH INSTITUTED

passage already twice quoted, let me refer again. "I therefore, the prisoner in the Lord, beseech you to walk worthily of the calling wherewith ye were called." And how shall we do it? First "giving diligence to keep the unity of the Spirit in the bond of peace"; and I always feel that I want to change that translation a little. Not that it is inaccurate, but that we have such strange ideas of what keeping may mean. "Giving diligence to keep" does not mean to guard as with a garrison. That is the thought when Paul says, "I know Him Whom I have believed, and I am persuaded that He is able to keep," the word there means to guard as with a garrison. But that is not the word here; and I do no violence, nay, I illuminate the passage by translating thus, "Giving diligence to keep in view the unity of the Spirit," not to create it. We cannot create unity; we can keep it in view, never forget it, and live in the power of the fact of it. Then remember, it is the unity of the Spirit, not the unanimity of the mind. There may be many mental moods and methods of approach to the great fact of the Lord Himself and His Church. Not the uniformity of the body. I care very little, less and less for that; but the unity, the oneness of the Spirit. In proportion as the Church of God comes to that recognition, that keeping in view, with the corresponding answer of life to the fact of the unity of the Spirit, in that proportion we shall be content to sympathize with the differing mental convictions and bodily manifestations that the Church may take. These are the great lessons of study; the unity of the Church, and the continuity of the Church, and the certainty that the Church will at last be completed, and be presented to the Father for all that high and awe-inspiring vocation that lies beyond the present age.

Another practical lesson that we need to remember is that membership of the Church consists in fellowship with the life of the Lord of the Church. That life is light, and all the outlook is changed wherever it comes. That life is love, and the central passion and impulse of life is changed wherever it comes.

We have no right to hold any lower conception of the Church than this; and no lower conception of the nature of Church membership than this; and if that with which I commenced be true, that the local church is, or ever should be a microcosm of the Church catholic, the realization within a limited area of all the great truth which applies to the whole fellowship; then the local church should be one consisting of all those who have seen this Lord, and yielded to Him; and who have received by the Spirit's baptism the gift of His life; and whose central, burning, consuming passion therefore is the Kingdom of God established in the individual life, revealed to the world, proclaimed to men; and toward the ultimate victory of which all endeavor is consecrated.

May we be, so much as is possible to us, such a church; and to this end, may we who form the fellowship, be such men and women as sharing His life, yield to it, for the glory of His name. Amen.

CHAPTER XVI

CHURCH IDEALS:
THE CHURCH GOVERNED

He is the Head of the Body, the Church: Who is the beginning, the Firstborn from the dead; that in all things He might have the pre-eminence.
COLOSSIANS 1:18.

IT WILL AT ONCE BE CONCEDED THAT THERE ARE VERY many matters full of interest and full of value suggested within the compass of this sublime declaration of the apostle. Let me say at once that I am now proposing to deal only with one aspect of the truth included in this statement, that, namely, of the Headship of the Lord in the Church.

Having considered the subject of the constitution of the Church, we have now to deal with the Church as a separate entity, unified by a common life, while yet made up of distinct individualities. Our present theme is that of authority within the Church, the nature of the government of the Church of God which has thus been constituted, and which is thus growing into a holy temple in the Lord.

The question of government is one of difficulty, because of the fact already referred to, that the Church is made up of separate individualities; that men and women, believing in the Lord Christ, and being by the Holy Spirit baptized into living union with Him, do not in the hour of that baptism and reception lose their personality, their individuality, their separateness, in some sense of the words. There would be no difficulty in this matter of government apart from this fact.

If the figure of the apostle incidentally referred to in our text, and wrought out into fuller detail in his Corinthian letter, the figure of the Church as the Body of Christ be borne in mind, then at once the whole question of authority within the Church, of the government of the Church, is revealed so patently that there can be no misunderstanding of the ideal. As is the head to all the members of the body, so is the Christ to the whole of His Church.

But the difficulty referred to remains, and experience shows it to be a very serious difficulty; and therefore, we need carefully to consider what the New Testament teaches on this matter. And let me again say, as I said in connection with our previous study, not merely that we may know, but that by the grace of God we may be conformed to His Will in this matter as members of His Church, and so fulfil His purpose according to the measure possible to us.

The first affirmation of the New Testament to which I would draw your attention is that contained within this text. It is the declaration of the absolute Headship of Christ, that He is Himself, in some special and wonderful way, the Head of the Church—special, that is—in distinction from the fact of His Headship over the whole creation. And yet, the fact of that Headship over creation must be borne in mind in this connection, for to take this particular verse from its context will be to rob it of much of its virtue and many of its values.

Let us take time to remind ourselves that this declaration occurs in the passage which we read as our lesson, a passage in which we have perhaps the most full and wonderful statement in the whole system of Paul's doctrine of the Person of Christ. It is indeed a great passage, and it was written in order to set forth clearly—as clearly as such infinite mysteries may ever be set forth—the truth concerning the personality of the Lord Jesus Christ.

The apostle first shows the relation of Christ to God in one sublime and swiftly ending sentence, "Who is the Image of the invisible God?" In greater detail he then sets forth the relation of Christ to the whole creation; and that relation may be summarized in this brief word taken from the fuller description, He is "the first-born of all creation, and He is before all things, and in Him all things consist"—that is, hold together. Thus the apostle affirms the pre-existence of this mystic Person, and His activity in that glorious hour when the sons of God sang together in the presence of the dawning wonders of a new creation, declaring that He was Himself the Creator. The apostle speaks of Him further as Sustainer of the Creation, as he describes Him as holding all these together by His own power, so that in Him they consist.

He then passes to the subject of the relation between Christ and His Church, declaring that He is Head over all things to the Church; and here again he uses the phrase already employed in connection with creation, but with a modification that demands our attention, "The Firstborn from the dead."

Let us now pause to make the distinction to which we have already drawn attention incidentally. This Person is described as "Firstborn of creation," and it is at once recognized that the word is figurative, and suggestive of abounding life, and used in reference to that primal origin, the mystery of which is always beyond us, but the solution of which is always ready to our hands when we open our Bible and read, "In the beginning God created."

But in the midst of this creation is the fact of death, and we are everywhere conscious of the dark pall of it, the tremendous mystery of it, the alarming pain of it! Then the apostle draws attention to One emerging from it, Who is the selfsame Christ, Firstborn from the dead! By virtue of all that strange and mystic phrase connotes, He is Head of His Church, Head of that gathered-out company of men and women, who, having had a vision of the one Lord, have exercised in Him the one faith, and have received the one baptism of the Spirit, and thus have been created His ecclesia, His called-out people, under His authority, exercising His authority in the world.

Now from these spacious outlooks and these magnificent heights of the apostolic vision and teaching, we may safely and reverently turn, in order to declare that the one only and absolute authority within the Christian Church is that of the Lord Himself. He is the Founder and Builder of His Church. His work made it possible for the Spirit of God to come in that new method discovered to us in the story of Pentecost. Belief in Him precedes that baptism of the Spirit whereby we are quickened into a new life of fellowship with God. He abides forevermore, the sole Possessor of His people, and His will must be the final authority within His Church concerning every individual member, and concerning every detail of the manifold and complex life of every individual member, and consequently, concerning the whole Church, as to the methods of its service, as to the meaning of its service, and as to the processes by which it fulfils that service. We inquire, then, what is the government of the Church? To that inquiry we reply inclusively and exhaustively when we say, "He is the Head over all things to the Church."

So far all Christians are in perfect agreement. Our disagreement or our difference—or shall I rather say our difficulty?—begins when we inquire how the will of that one Lord and Master is to be made known to His Church.

Let us for a few moments turn from the fundamental

consideration in order that we may inquire whether, in the days of His flesh, He said anything that will help us. And immediately our thoughts revert to His Paschal discourses, to those final words spoken, not to the promiscuous multitude, but to the inner circle of disciples in the upper room, to those wonderful words recorded only by John. To those words, therefore, let me take you back for brief quotations only.

In the fourteenth chapter of the Gospel I find these words: I pluck them out of the rest, I hardly like to do so, and yet, they are what we specially need for our present consideration—"I will inquire of the Father"—and that is not satisfactory, but a little more so than "I will pray the Father," for when we read "pray," we think of asking, as we present a petition; and Christ never so prayed. His word for His own prayer is always different from that used to describe our praying; He asked upon the level of perfect equality and fellowship: "I will inquire of the Father, and He shall give you another Comforter, that He may be with you forever, even the Spirit of truth, Whom the world cannot receive." Or, turning to a declaration a little later in the sixteenth chapter of John, I find these words: "When He, the Spirit of truth, is come, He shall guide you into all the truth: for He shall not speak from Himself: but what things soever He shall hear, these shall He speak; and He shall declare unto you the things that are to come: He shall glorify Me: for He shall take of Mine, and shall declare it unto you. All things whatsoever the Father hath are Mine: therefore, said I, that He taketh of Mine, and shall declare it unto you. A little while, and ye behold Me no more; and again a little while, and ye shall see Me."

Now in the last declaration of that passage there is no reference to a second advent, its reference being rather to the new and spiritual vision that should be granted to these men by the coming of the Spirit; to that fact to which Paul referred when he said, "We henceforth know no man after the flesh, even though we have known Christ after the flesh, yet now we known Him so no more."

Christ said to that little band of His own disciples, whose hearts were breaking because He was going away, and who were strangely perplexed as to the mystery of the things He was saying to them, who did not, even after He had finished His speech, understand Him, but were compelled to wait for this selfsame enlightenment of the Spirit: "A little while, and ye behold Me no more." John will no longer be able to lay his hand on Mine as we sit at the board, or lean his head upon My bosom as I tell him secrets of love. "And again a little while, and ye shall see Me." You will see Me as you have never seen Me before, and John will be able to write: "That which was from the beginning, that which we have heard, that which we have seen with our eyes, that which we beheld, and our hands handled, concerning the Word of life." And this change would all be wrought, he declared, by the coming of the Holy Spirit. The Spirit came, in the first place, to reveal to the inner circle of His own disciples the Person of the Lord perpetually, persistently, perfectly. The Spirit came to reveal to them the meaning of things which Jesus had said, and which they did not yet understand. The Spirit came to abide with loyal men and women and children, and to reveal to them the will of the Lord about all the details of their lives.

And consider, brethren—thinking only for the moment individually, for presently, the corporate question will become more difficult, thinking only individually—how wondrously the living authority of the Lord has been established in the lives of men by the Holy Spirit. He came to reveal the

CHURCH IDEALS: THE CHURCH GOVERNED

Person of Christ. One of the central and perpetual wonders of Christian experience is that of the individual acquaintance of individual men and women with the Lord Christ, an individual acquaintance of individual men and women with a Person Who is to them in their thinking as human and as real as the Man of Nazareth was to Peter, James and John. I feel the difficulty of the thing I am trying to say. I know this Christ—suffer the word of experience—I know what it is to live with Him, and walk with Him, and talk with Him, and travel with Him, and have Him rebuke me; ah, and have Him whisper to me, "Well done!" And I have in my heart the picture of Him. He is as real to me, more real than any other earthly friend, and that, too, in human seeming and semblance; and that is why I very much dislike pictures of Him. Oh, there are a few I tolerate, and yet I seldom look at them without becoming critical, and without having to say, "No, that is not the picture of my Lord." It was a portrait of Him, the Lord, to the man who painted it! If by some sacred magic at this moment this whole audience could become artists, and each person could rapidly sketch the portrait of the Lord as he or she knows Him, what infinite variety, and yet what underlying unity, we should have. If we could merge the myriad photographs of Him into one picture, what glory, what beauty! Four men did that long ago. Matthew said, "This is how I saw Him"; and Luke said, "Theophilus, I want to draw Him for you as I have found him"; and Mark said, "This is how Peter saw Him, and how I saw Him"; and John said, "Wait, just a few touches more, there are many things not yet described!" And they are all different; but we bring them together and merge them, and, lo, this is He! How did Matthew write his gospel? On the human standpoint he wrote it with perfect naturalness, and with no conception that he was inspired; but the Spirit had come, and He was revealing his Master to him, calling back to his memory things he saw Him do, and heard Him say; and so he wrote. And that inspiration did not cease when the gospel stories were written. It lives until this moment. I ventured a moment ago to say experimentally to you, I know this Christ, and, as I said so, I saw a light on many faces which meant, We also know Him, we walk with Him and talk with Him; He is as real to us, more real than any other earthly friend.

The Master said, "Yet a little while I am with you, and yet a little while and I will come again"; and He came, and He has since been the perpetual presence. I know Him personally, individually, and that by the ministry of the Spirit of God, taking hold of what I am in myself, finding the recesses of my need, and filling them with the revelation of my Lord's sufficiency, indicating to me the dynamic force of His energy for the overcoming of the weakness of my frailty; and not of me only, who am less than the least of all the saints is this true; it is equally true of the whole company of the saints for nineteen centuries. And when at last we reach His heaven, the picture we have seen of Christ will have become our own portrait, for we shall be like Him. Then, when God has gathered the varied and matchless splendors of the whole host of the ransomed into one effulgent glory, behold the Firstborn from the dead! Thus He is making known to us His authoritative will by individual interpretation.

Brethren, the Church of God is not a company of people gathered around the memory of a dead and lost leader; it is constituted, not by the acceptance of a final ethic uttered nineteen centuries ago, not by the adoration of a great ideal that passed across the vision of humanity in Judaea long ago, but by the Abiding presence—where two or three are gathered in His name—of the Lord Himself. By the living pres-

CHURCH IDEALS: THE CHURCH GOVERNED

ence of that living Lord, and by the interpretation of the abiding Spirit, we know Him; and His will is made known to His own who desire to know it, amid the hurry and the hubbub of London; in the Houses of Parliament; as that Christian man sweeps the streets; upon the professional round; in the midst of a thousand and one domestic duties. He is with us by the Spirit, to say what is now to be done, to all such as are yielded to Him, and desire to know.

What, then, should be the Church's attitude toward these facts? The acknowledgment of His Headship; submission to the indwelling Spirit Whose office it is to interpret His will to all His people, and therefore initially—cessation from self, consenting to that separating redemption that brings us away from the world, abandonment to those cleansing fires that purify us from iniquity, a yielding of ourselves to that impulsing love, that makes us forevermore a people zealous of good works.

Now to turn from these things which are the true things and the deep things, and yet which are in a measure mystic. We inquire, how is this authority of our Lord to be applied in the actual corporate life of the Christian Church? I would remind you of what we considered in our previous meditation, that this word "Church" occurs about thirteen times in our New Testament in reference to the whole catholic Church of God; that it occurs over ninety times in reference to local assemblies, such as the church at Thessalonica, the church at Corinth, the church at Colosse; and that as we watch these occasions, and observe what doctrines gather about them, we discover that most evidently in the mind of these new Testament writers the local church in a microcosm of the catholic Church.

What, then, we ask, are we to learn from a study of these Scriptures concerning the authority of Christ, and its application as within the Church of God? First of all, I think they teach us that the authority of Christ by the Spirit in the Church is apostolic in principle, but not in detail. Apostolic in principle, that is as to these very things which we have been considering; the apostolic teaching concerning the Headship of Christ Himself; the apostolic teaching concerning the priesthood of all believers, and their right of access within the Holy of all for thanksgiving, as the eucharistic priesthood; and for intercession, the priesthood of prayer; the apostolic teaching concerning the guidance of the Spirit and the laws of spiritual life; and I venture to add personally, of conviction, the apostolic teaching concerning the ordinances of our Christian faith, the ordinance of baptism, and the ordinance of the observance of the Lord's Supper. These are great principles laid down by the holy apostles for our perpetual instruction, and to all these we are to be in obedience, and know that as we are living in obedience to them we are acting according to the will of the indwelling Christ, Who is our Lord and Master.

But we are not to be obedient to apostolic example in detail. I do not want to stay with this subject very long, but must touch upon it. The questions of music and of buildings, of times and seasons, of feasts and fasts, as we may find them in the New Testament, are questions of detail rather than of principle. We are not to be bound by the details of apostolic habit, but we are to be governed by the principles of apostolic teaching.

The reason for this is that this ministry of the Spirit for the interpretation of the will of our Lord is immediate and direct. The Spirit will, within the assembly of His people today, indicate His will if His people are waiting to know that will; and the Spirit will perfectly equip His people for the doing of His work in the world by the bestowment of gifts necessary for that work. Let us ponder these simple things carefully; first, that we cannot find a complete list in the New Testament of the gifts of the Spirit; that this great apostle of the Church, Paul, gave one list when he wrote to the Corinthians, and another when he wrote to the Ephesians. Some included in the first list are found also in the second; some are omitted; but in the second there will be those not in the first. We cannot find at any one place a list of the gifts of the Spirit, and therefore, let us never make the mistake of gathering out from all the different passages the gifts, and writing them in order, and saying, "These are the gifts of the Spirit." No, the Spirit giveth to everyone severally as He will, which means that, according to the necessity, so is the gift bestowed. There were gifts named by the apostle in the early Church that we cannot find in the Church today. If you tell me that that is a sign that the Church is degenerate, I answer, by no means, for there are gifts in the Church today not found in the Church in apostolic times; and that is not a proof that the Church in apostolic times was degenerate. The Holy Spirit is always changing the gifts according to the changing needs of changing times, and one of the gravest perils threatening the Church is that it does not discover the gift when bestowed, and make way for its use. "He gave some apostles, and some prophets, and some evangelists, and some pastors and teachers," abiding gifts for the ministry of the Word; but many others, helps, governments, healings in the past, and in the present new gifts bestowed constantly; so that if there be a piece of work to be done peculiar to London, the Spirit of God will give a man the gift he needs, which would be of no use in New York; so that if there is to be a peculiar work done in New York, the Spirit will bestow the gift upon some man for that work. The trouble is we send men out to India that God wants for London, and keep men in London that God wants for India.

Wherein, then, lies the failure in the Church in the matter of government? We have been trying to govern the Church otherwise, and by our own wit and our own wisdom to find out the way to do God's work, instead of remembering that the living Lord, and not a dead Leader is at the center of the Christian Church, and that the living Spirit, and not past interpretations, constitutes the method of guidance and direction in all our work. The Spirit calls whomsoever He will. He qualifies whomsoever He calls. He sends whomsoever He qualifies. The trouble is that the Church of God so often is not prepared to do what the church at Antioch did, and to say, "It seems good to the Holy Ghost and to us to send forth Saul and Barnabas."

The Church should be in direct contact with this supreme Will, apostolic in her attitude, but direct in her obedience. Our Lord is not divided from us by the distance even of the holy apostles. They did their work; they formulated the doctrines; they pioneered the way along which others have followed in the proclamation of the evangel; and, so far as their writings have been preserved for us, they become the basis of authority; but so far as their own example was concerned, it is not binding upon us. I do not ask what the Church in Jerusalem did in the matter of its worship, or in the matter of its work. I ask what will the living Lord have us to do in London? Let Him tell us by His Holy Spirit Who is with us now.

All attempts, beloved, to substitute an authority within the Church for that of the living Christ are wrong. Nay, I will go further. All attempts to create mediation between the authority of Christ and His Church, save the meditation of

CHURCH IDEALS: THE CHURCH GOVERNED

the Spirit, are wrong; and whether it be the substitution of an authority, or whether it be the attempt to discover His authority through other meditation than that of the Spirit, these are the lines, following which we wander from the way of His will, and make ourselves weak in our testimony to the world.

We require no pope who is God's vicar, because the Lord is not absent. We require no king to ratify our appointments, because the King Himself appoints and ratifies. We require no bishops to prescribe for us the order of our service, for the Lord Himself will arrange. We decline to allow any Conference, or Union, or Synod to interfere with the freedom of our work, for we are in glad bondage to the Living Lord. We deny that the Church meeting is authoritative by reason of the fact that a majority is in favor of this or of that. That is not Church authority; and where the Church—if my brethren of other ecclesiastical convictions will be patient with me for a moment—where the Church is Congregational, and gathers together in its Church meeting, and proceeds always upon the basis of the vote of a majority, it is surely going astray. In the life of the spiritual church there will come mystic hours in which a majority will say, "This is our thought and will, but we will not do it. We will wait and consult and pray with the minority, and wait upon the Lord, until the unanimity of the Spirit possesses us all." It is the authority of the present, living, reigning Lord in the assembly of His people, which is the true Church authority. The Lord has never delegated His authority. We believe in the real presence of the living Lord, and the result of that is unity, not uniformity, the unity of His Kingly Headship, differing in detail at different times and under differing circumstances, caring little and less for ritual, for uniformity of dress, or even of creed. Not mental unanimity, not bodily uniformity, but spiritual unity, is the great result of the recognition of the presence and Headship of the Lord, and the submission of His people to His rule.

But the final and the personal word under such consideration is that this government of the Lord Christ within His own Church is principally interfered with when we are not in right relationship with the Paraclete, the Advocate, the Comforter, the Spirit Himself.

Let me but recall to your memory three little words of the New Testament which seem to me to exhaust the perils confronting us concerning the Spirit: "Resist not the Spirit," "Quench not the Spirit," "Cause not sorrow to the Spirit." To resist Him in the working of His mighty energy for the accomplishment of Divine purpose, to quench Him in the bestowment of His fire-gifts whereby we co-operate with God; to cause sorrow to Him by our disobedience and our disloyalty; these are the ways in which we prevent His fulfilling His ministry within us, and among us, and through us; these are the ways in which we lose the vision of our Lord and our sense of His nearness, and wander away from the pathway of His will, and fail in our attempts to realize His purposes.

May these be granted to us, first of all a new and abounding consciousness of the supremacy of Christ, and then a new and more complete yielding of ourselves to the Spirit of interpretation; that so there may come to us a larger, fuller, richer sense of the unity of the Church; that so, finally, God through us may be able to move forward toward the goal of the establishment of His Kingdom, through Christ our Lord.

CHAPTER XVII

CHURCH IDEALS:
THE CHURCH DISCIPLINED

And if thy brother sin against thee, go, show him his fault between thee and him alone: if he hear thee, thou hast gained thy brother. But if he hear thee not, take with thee one or two more, that at the mouth of two witnesses or three every word may be established. And if he refuse to hear them, tell it unto the church: and if he refuse to hear the church also, let him be unto thee as the Gentile and the publican. Verily I say unto you, What things soever ye shall bind on earth shall be bound in heaven: and what things soever ye shall loose on earth shall be loosed in heaven. Again I say unto you, that if two of you shall agree on earth as touching anything that they shall ask, it shall be done for them of My Father which is in heaven. For where two or three are gathered together in My name, there am I in the midst of them.

MATTHEW 18:15-20.

It is actually reported that there is fornication among you, and such fornication as is not even among the Gentiles, that one of you hath his father's wife. And ye are puffed up, and did not rather mourn, that he that had done this deed might be taken away from among you. For I verily, being absent in body but present in spirit, have already, as though I were present, judged him that hath so wrought this thing, in the name of our Lord Jesus, ye being gathered together, and my spirit, with the power of our Lord Jesus, to deliver such a one unto

Satan for the destruction of the flesh, that the spirit may be saved in the day of the Lord Jesus. Your glorying is not good. Know ye not that a little leaven leaveneth the whole lump? Purge out the old leaven, that ye may be a new lump, even as ye are unleavened. For our passover also hath been sacrificed, even Christ. Wherefore let us keep the feast, not with old leaven, neither with the leaven of malice and wickedness, but with the unleavened bread of sincerity and truth.

I wrote unto you in my epistle to have no company with fornicators; not at all meaning with the fornicators of this world, or with the covetous and extortioners, or with idolaters; for then must ye needs go out of the world: but as it is I wrote unto you not to keep company, if any man that is named a brother be a fornicator, or covetous, or an idolater, or a reviler, or a drunkard, or an extortioner; with such a one no, not to eat. For what have I to do with judging them that are without? Do not ye judge them that are within? But them that are without God judgeth? Put away the wicked man from among yourselves.

I CORINTHIANS 5.

I HAVE READ THE WHOLE OF THESE PASSAGES BECAUSE, IF I may be permitted the phrase, they constitute the classic passages of the New Testament concerning the theme of our morning meditation, that of the discipline of the Christian Church.

We have on previous occasions considered the teaching of the New Testament concerning the constitution of the Church and the government of the Church, and we come this morning to this—shall I say—most difficult and yet most necessary and important subject, of the discipline of the Christian Church.

CHURCH IDEALS: THE CHURCH DISCIPLINED

The discipline of the whole Church, of the catholic Church is necessarily part of the government of the Church, and is therefore the prerogative of the Head of the Church. That in itself is a theme full, not only of interest, but of importance, and I think of great encouragement. It is not, however, the phase of the subject to which I am now proposing to give anything like special consideration. But that we may be reminded of the fact that the discipline of the whole Church is within the government of the Head of the Church, and that He perpetually exercises that government, and maintains that discipline; we have read together the wonderful passage from the book of the Revelation, in which the seer describes the vision of the Lord which was granted to him before the letters for the seven Asian Churches were given to him.

That is the vision of the Head of the Church in the midst of the churches, exercising government and maintaining discipline. There are seven lampstands, representing the individual churches. Christ in the midst of them, by His presence and oversight, makes them the One Church. He holds in His right hand the stars of the churches, and deals in discipline with the churches individually; and so with the catholic Church, through His dealing with the angels, or the messengers, or the stars of the churches.

There in figurative language, full of exquisite beauty, every point of which is suggestive, the Head of the Church is seen maintaining His discipline. That is a vision full of encouragement; If, perchance, some one of us had found ourselves in the midst of one of these Asian churches, say that of Laodicea, we might have been tempted to write an article —if there had been a religious newspaper to receive it—lamenting the fact of the lost discipline of the church, and there would have been an element of truth in the complaint.

But the true vision is the vision of John, who saw that if this be so, the Lord is still in the midst, and is dealing with Laodicea. Not by resolution of all the churches in solemn assembly can you deal with Laodicea, but by leaving Laodicea to the government of the living Lord.

Our attention, however, is fixed upon the symbolic and mystical vision of the Master Himself.

It is a night scene, the world's night. The Church is seen in its capacity of witness bearing. The light is shining in a dark place; lampstands and stars are things of the night. But it is a day scene; Christ is the unifying center amid the churches. He is the directing authority, and His face shineth as the sun in its strength. The Church's light in the night is derived from the fact that Christ has made day for her, and her members are children of the day, and walk in the light of His countenance; they are light-bearers for the sake of the night round about them.

But behold the Central Person. He was like, not "the Son of man," as though John here were borrowing the phrase so often upon the lips of our Lord as descriptive of Himself, but something bringing the vision a little nearer to our actual and essential humanity. Not that the earlier phrase removes Christ from our humanity, but that every title that describes Him has for us become associated with unspeakable dignity. And so John says: "I turned to see the voice which spake with me. And having turned, I saw seven golden candlesticks; and in the midst of the candlesticks One like unto a son of man," of our very humanity, but so entirely and utterly and absolutely different that all the description which follows is needed. I do not pretend to have the right finally to interpret the mystic symbolism of this vision; yet there are patent suggestions.

There is, first of all, the symbolism of function. He was

"clothed with a garment down to the foot, and girt about at the breasts with a golden girdle"; and immediately we are reminded of that passage in the prophecy of Isaiah: "And it shall come to pass in that day that I will call My servant Eliakim, the son of Hilkiah: and I will clothe him with thy robe, and strengthen him with thy girdle, and I will commit thy government into his hand: and he shall be a father to the inhabitants of Jerusalem, and to the house of Judah." He Who walks amid the golden candlesticks is clothed to the foot with a garment, and girt about at the breast with a golden girdle—the garment symbolic of His activity in judgment, and the girdle of His absolute fidelity or faithfulness to God.

Then there is the symbolism of character. "His head and His hair were white as white wool," suggestive of His purity and His eternity; "His eyes were as a flame of fire," suggestive of His intimate knowledge, perceiving, penetrating, so that nothing escapes His observation; "His feet like unto burnished brass, as if it had been refined in a furnace," suggestive of His procedure, brass forevermore being the symbol of strength, and the furnace that of purification; "His voice as the voice of many waters." I do not know a single statement in the Bible that more overawes my soul than that, "His voice as the voice of many waters," and I never came near an understanding of it until I first saw Niagara. I had been told that I should be overwhelmed with the thunder of Niagara. I was not so overwhelmed. I was overwhelmed with the majestic music which never ceased, and yet never interrupted peace, but created the sense of it through all the district around. Many waters—waters that had run from the hills and through the valleys; the running rivers and the singing waters from far and wide, sweeping at last through the peaceful stillness of great lakes, and then finding final utterance in a perfect harmony as they swept over the height. His voice:

"God, having of old time spoken unto the fathers in the prophets by divers portions and in divers manners, hath at the end of these days spoken unto us in His Son." The rivulets and the rivers and the streams of the past merge to the one music, and become the final speech of the Son; and His voice is as the voice of many waters, the perfect concord of infinite diversity, in the harmony of final speech. "He had in His right hand seven stars," suggesting administration, power, and protection: "Out of His mouth proceeded a sharp two-edged sword," finding verdicts, passing sentences, and uttering beatitudes; "His countenance was as the sun shineth in his strength."

Thus the Lord is seen in all the fulness of His glory; presiding over the witness bearing of the Church in the midst of the darkness; perfectly acquainted with all its folly and its failure, with the peculiar sin of this church and the peculiar difficulty of that; knowing the subtle peril which confronts the near, acquainted with the faithfulness of the far, and disciplining the whole. That vision, I repeat, is full of comfort.

Yet beyond that—or shall I say rather, as I would prefer to say—as part of it, there is the responsibility of individual churches concerning the maintenance of discipline within the borders of their own fellowship. As I have tried to think of this subject—and that, let me say, under the personal conviction that one of the weaknesses of Church life today is its lack of discipline—I have been driven to the two passages chosen, because in them I find the suggestion of two lines of discipline for which the local church of Jesus Christ must be responsible. The teaching of these passages is solemn, gracious, and clearly defined. In the first we have the words of our Lord Himself, words in which discipline, in order to the maintenance of perfect fellowship within the church, is dealt with; and then we have words of the apostle—stern words and severe words as they certainly were—in which the church's duty toward individual members in the matter of conduct is brought clearly before us. While I read the whole passage, all that is possible this morning is that we should attempt to see the general line of teaching suggested by each.

Let us, then, first consider our Lord's words. They are so old, so familiar, that this whole congregation could recite them; and yet I was almost startled at a question John Wesley asked after reading them. He said: "If this be the true order of dealing with men who sin against us, where do the Christian people live?" That question is as pertinent this morning as when it was first asked; and it is because I think that inquiry is pertinent that I propose that we should listen to these words of Christ as though we had never heard them.

"If thy brother sin against thee." The true emphasis there is not on the word "against thee," but on the word "sin." The reason for action is not that I have been wronged, but that my brother is harmed, and the fellowship of the Church is injured by his sin. Notice the final words, "thou hast gained thy brother." That is the heart of the whole matter. The purpose of our going to our brother is not that we compel him to confess the fault! No, a thousand times no. That will be the process, the method. The purpose is the gaining of our brother. "If he hear thee, thou hast gained thy brother." I am to go to my brother, not because my brother's sin has made me suffer, but because my brother's sin is harming my brother. Thou dost not go to thy brother to establish thine own right, to break his will, and bend his neck to own he was in the wrong, but to gain him.

Thus, we become conscious of the supreme matter, which is not on the surface. Supreme matters are never on the surface. The supreme matter is that the discipline of the Church is to be exercised in that which is the essence of the Church's life—love.

But if he will not hear thee, what then? "Take with thee one or two more." The "more" does not refer to the number, but to the persistent action. Do not give him up because he will not hear you. Yet, further, take one or two; and take trusted men, take men of the very spirit of the love which makes you go. And if he will not hear them, then tell it to the Church, the ecclesia—that called out, separated company of men bound together by the bond of the one life in Christ, impulsed by the one law of love, walking in the one illumination of light; tell it to them, that where you have failed they may gain this sinning man. And if he will not hear them, then "let him be unto thee as the Gentile and the publican." Then he must, if he will persist in sin, in spite of Thy attempt in love to win him, and in spite of Thy persistent attempt as Thou hast taken the one or two with Thee, and finally sought the persuasive power of the Church; if he will persist in sin, then he must be put outside the Church, he must be put outside its fellowship, he must not be suffered to continue to make his fellowship in the Christian Church a garment under which he hides sin. The Church is not to afford sanctuary to any man who persistently, and in spite of every attempt of love, continues in sin.

Now, my brethren, there must be no—forgive the ugliness of my word, I use it deliberately—there must be no shirking of this duty on the part of the wronged person. If your brother in this fellowship or in any fellowship has really sinned against you, because of his sin it is your duty to go and see him, and to deal with him. There is a false charity abroad within the fellowship of the Christian Church, which makes men say: "Oh, yes, this man wronged me, this man sinned against me; the thing he said was a sinful thing, the thing he did was a sinful thing; but I would rather not take any action." We have no right to say that, because there is no purely personal matter among Church members. The whole assembly is affected by the sin of one. The tides of the Church's life are weaker because one in the fellowship continues in sin. The Church's testimony to the neighborhood, to the city, to the nation, to the world, is feebler by reason of that fact. Thus not in the interests of the man alone, although that is always first, but finally in the interests of the fellowship, we have no right to refuse to exercise the discipline of love in the case of anyone who has flagrantly sinned to our knowledge.

Take one brief glance at that more terrible passage in the writings of Paul. The inclusive law which the apostle enunciates is that the leaven is to be purged. Leaven communicates itself, spreads its own corrupting force wherever it comes. Leaven must be purged out of the fellowship. A little leaven—one man sinning, and permitted to remain within that vital fellowship and relationship of the Church—will spread, first unconsciously and insidiously, but most surely throughout the whole Church.

The individual case quoted by the apostle was flagrant illustration, such as in all probability we should rarely, if ever, have to deal with in these days; and I am not going to dwell upon it. But Paul gives us general illustrations. I read them again, not to consider them in detail, but to ask you to notice one or two simple matters. Notice, first, that if some of these forms are not present today, others are; and notice, in the second place, what strange and apparently unequal things, according to our moral sense, the apostle puts very near together. "Fornicators, covetous, idolaters, revilers, drunkards, extortioners."

A man said to me some months ago: "I am a church member, and if I were found drunk on the streets there would be a church meeting. But did you ever know a church meeting held to discipline a man for covetousness?" No, brethren, I am not going to deal any further with this list, but let it be very carefully considered.

Leaven is to be purged; the sinning man is to be put outside the fellowship of Christian men and women. The particular case, as we have said, was a most flagrant one, a terrible example of wrong-doing; and the most terrible fact was that the Church had tolerated this man, and allowed him to remain a member of the fellowship. I cannot tell what lies behind this picture in the Corinthian letter; I dare not dogmatically affirm; but because human nature abides so much the same through all the passing centuries, I wonder whether this man was a wealthy man! I wonder whether he was, in that false sense in which we use the word, an influential man! I do not know; perhaps I have no right to libel the Church in Corinth by the habits of the Church today; but this is the truth we have to learn: That for a Church to allow any man who is living in sin, and is known to be living in sin, to retain his fellowship, is to permit leaven to remain, which is corrupting the life of the whole Church, and rendering it weak where it ought to be strong.

Now, how are these sinning men to be dealt with? That man to whom you go, and he will not hear you? He is to be accounted as a heathen man and a publican—that is, he is to be put outside the fellowship. By what authority? "Where two or three are gathered together in My name, there am I in the midst of them." The sinning man in Corinth is to be put outside the fellowship of the Church. By what authority? When you are gathered together in the name of the Lord Jesus. The whole matter resolves itself into this: that it is in the living presence of the living Christ that discipline is to be exercised.

In the case of the sinning man in Corinth, Paul said he was to be handed over to Satan. He had already given himself over to Satan by his sin. Then the Church must deny him the shelter of her fellowship, that he may work out to finality his own wilful sin and his own chosen relation to Satan. The Church—I reverently say in this connection—is to act in harmony with the abiding method of God in dealing with persistent sin. It is to give sin its opportunity to work itself out to finality. It is to create circumstances for the man who persistently sins, which will compel him to make his sin visible; or else to turn back again from the sin, that he may be delivered, as this Corinthian man undoubtedly did. I hasten to add that, for when you read the second letter you have full instructions for receiving him back, for he was filled with sorrow.

It is a solemn method, but I pray you ponder it—it is God's method. Is there lust in your heart? God will put you into circumstances where that thing will be manifested sooner or later. Is Judas a thief? Give him the bag, and he will either demonstrate himself a thief, or be driven back to Him Who can make him honest. The Church of God is not only disloyal to her Lord, and paralyzing herself; she is violating the eternal order of the universe if she permit men to retain their fellowship with her, who are wilfully and deliberately continuing in sin.

One other glance at the two stories, taking now the Corinthian one first, and repeating that which for other purposes I have already said. When Paul wrote again to these Corinthians in his second letter, he said: "For out of much affliction and anguish of heart I wrote unto you with many tears; not that ye should be made sorry, but that ye might know the love which I have more abundantly unto you. But if any hath caused sorrow, he hath caused sorrow, not to me, but in part (that I press not too heavily) to you all. Sufficient to such a one is this punishment which was inflicted by the many, so that contrariwise ye should rather forgive him and comfort him, lest by any means such a one should be swallowed up with his overmuch sorrow. Wherefore I beseech you to confirm your love toward him" (2 Cor. 2:4-8). There is no doubt that the same person guilty of incestuous sin is here referred to, and that the discipline exercised had wrought within him repentance of soul. The attitude of the Church toward the one who repents is to be that of readiness to restore, comfort, and love. That we are never to forget.

This becomes far more powerful and forceful when we turn to the words of Christ Himself. If he will not hear the Church, what then? Now we need to be most careful! What then? "Let him be unto thee"—what? "A heathen man and a publican"? No! What then? "A heathen man and a publican"! You certainly cannot print that. The different tone is the evidence of different temper. We can say an orthodox thing in such a way as to make it the most damnable heresy. The supreme business in all this discipline is not that of mechanical activity, but that of spiritual tone and temper. If this man will not hear the Church, what then? Let him be a heathen man, excommunicate him, banish him, damn him? No. That is Rome, and that is hell; and let us be done with it! What then? Let him be the man for whom I came to die; let him be the heathen man, the Gentile, the publican whom the Son of man came to seek and save. That is what he is to become to you. He is to be the man that you will pray for, as you never did before; for whom you will watch, and whom you will follow to the ends of the earth, in order to bring him back, won by the compassion of your love.

CHURCH IDEALS: THE CHURCH DISCIPLINED

That is Christian discipline. Not the anathema that rejoices in its curse, but the wail and the agony and the patience and the sacrifice which never lets this man alone until he is home again.

"Let him be unto thee as the Gentile and the publican." We must put him outside; we must not allow him to have the shelter of the Church; but the moment he is over the borderline, after him, after him, though the way be rough and long, and it means wounding and suffering; never give up hope—let him be the heathen man and the publican.

When the Church exercises its discipline in that tone, and in that temper, discipline becomes beneficent, gracious, producing purity, not only within her own borders, but in the very lives of those whom it becomes necessary for her to discipline.

The theme is difficult. I can talk freely here. I am under my own vine and fig tree. I hate discipline! I would rather do anything than go and tell a man about his fault. I would rather do anything than have to tell a man he has done something wrong. I always feel I am the culprit. But evil must not be tolerated within the fellowship of the Christian Church. You have no business, if there is someone over there with whom you are not on speaking terms, to remain inside the Church. Out with you, and get it settled! You are paralyzing the fellowship. Evil must not be tolerated; wrong conduct must be judged; the tolerated evil is leavening the whole camp and corrupting the Church of God.

To allow a wrong-doer to continue in Church membership is to inflict wrong on him by giving him a false sense of security. Put him out, in order that he may see the darkness, and that the lurid light of judgment may arrest him. Let him know there is no shelter for a man who persistently sins. Do not lull him into false security by allowing him to stay in the fellowship, and imagine that he may continue in sin that grace may abound. The Church must be pure. No consideration of delicacy, of sensitiveness, of peace, must prevent our loyalty to Christ.

But if, indeed, we thus act in obedience to the pure and holy impulses of the Christ life, that same Christ life is full of tenderness, full of compassion; and, as I have tried to say, will drive us out after those who must be dealt with in discipline.

And let it never be forgotten that repentance is always a door to reinstatement. Let us have no lengthy probation for a sinning brother. Get him in. The Church is not the abode of absolutely perfect men and women—at least, this is not! The Church is a nursery; the Church is a home. Home! That is the most sacred room in your home where the little child is sick, where the aged pilgrim lingers on. The most beautiful thing about home is that it is the place of refuge for the weak. Yes, for those full of trembling, and full of sighing and of sobbing; this is the place. Lest they be swallowed up of overmuch sorrow, lest repentance should become hopelessness, they are to be received.

And the last thing of all, what is it? "I turned to see the voice which spake with me. And having turned I saw . . . One like unto a son of man . . . And when I saw Him, I fell at His feet as one dead. And He laid His right hand upon me, saying, Fear not."

There is no more difficult or delicate thing awaiting us in our Church fellowship than this of discipline, but amid the golden candlesticks walks the Son of man.

"In His feet and hands are wound-prints, and His side." May He give us of His Spirit that we may dare to deal with sin, and refuse to find it harbor or refuge within our fellowship; and then that we may dare to suffer and die to save the sinning man, that he may find his place again in the fellowship of the redeemed.

CHAPTER XVIII

CHURCH IDEALS: THE CHURCH AT WORK

From you hath sounded forth the Word of the Lord.
I THESSALONIANS 1:8.

THIS IS THE CONTINUATION AND COMPLETION OF THE BRIEF series of meditations on the subject of the Church of God according to the New Testament. We have considered the constitution of the Church, its government, its discipline, and now our final theme is that of its work. This is the necessary sequel to all that has gone before.

Given a Church, constituted by the life of Christ communicated in answer to faith by the baptism of the Holy Spirit, governed by the one supreme, final, lonely authority of the ever-present Lord Himself, and disciplined with all tenderness, and yet with all earnestness, the leaven put away, and we have found that which is at once a propagative society, an equipped army, and an instrument of Divine activity.

When we approach the subject of the work of the Church, we are not considering a privilege granted to the Church. We are hardly considering a responsibility devolving upon the Church. We are considering, rather, the necessary and inevitable activity of the Church. If there be failure in those matters which we are about to consider, the reason of such failure will be discovered in failure in some of those things which we have already considered. Either discipline is lax and loose, and the Church tolerates within her borders impure men or women, or continues to manifest the spirit of antichrist in bitterness; or we have sought mediation as between the government of our Lord and ourselves, and so have not perfectly understood His way or His will; or it may be that the Church is a mixed multitude, rather than an assembly of the saints, because, through some loose method of admitting to membership, we have included men and women who do not share the life Divine, even though they sing the songs of the sanctuary. If the Church is failing in her activity, it is in all probability due to some of these causes.

The declaration of my text, this word that Paul wrote to the Thessalonian Christians, "from you hath sounded forth the Word of the Lord," constitutes a revelation, and the Church referred to by the apostle an illustration of these great matters. In that word and in that particular Church great principles are focused as in camera obscura, or, perhaps, I should say in camera lucida. We see, as in a picture, the great mission of the Church.

Let us first, then, concentrate our attention for a few moments on the picture presented, and then, passing outside, attempt to see in broad outline the more spacious meaning of the service of the Christian Church. This letter was written to the Thessalonian Christians. Writing to this Church, which he describes not as the Church in Thessalonica—that was a later method of address when he wrote to Corinth—but to the Church of the Thessalonians, he deals with fundamental things, both concerning life and service. Service is not dealt with at all fully, but in this passage service is very clearly seen in its relation to life. We read as our lesson the first chapter. Let that suffice for contextual interpretation. At the beginning he addresses these people, and he thanks God for three things, the "work of faith," the "labour of love," the "patience of hope"; and, when at the close of this particular chapter, he is at the end of the introductory portion of his letter, he says that they "turned unto God from idols, to serve a living and true God, and to wait for His Son from heaven." These two descriptions are identical; that at the close of the introduction standing over against that at its commencement, and we have only just to look at them for a moment that we may see the Church, for in the opening and closing words we have the whole fact of Church life revealed to us. Between these opening and closing words is my text.

Take the opening words, "Your work of faith," which does not at all mean the work they were doing in Thessalonica as the result of faith, but that very work of faith whereby they became Christian men, "the work of faith." When men asked our Lord upon one occasion, "What must we do that we may work the works of God?" His answer was, "This is the work of God, that ye believe on Him Whom He hath sent"; and that is the thought embodied here, "the work of faith." That is the first fact. What is the work of faith? Turn to the concluding description of the introduction, "Ye turned unto God from idols." That is the work of faith.

And, secondly, the "labour of love"; that is the outcome of the work of faith, that which necessarily, inevitably follows it, for the work of faith on the part of man is answered by the gift of life on the part of God; and that life is His life, and that life is love; and therefore, immediately the life of love becomes the inspiration of labour. What is that labour of love? I go to the final description again, "to serve a living and true God"; that is the labour of love.

I turn back again to that first and introductory word, and the final phrase is the "patience of hope"; and that is explained by the final word, "to wait for His Son from heaven."

Thus, in the opening description, I see the inspirational

things of the Christian life—faith, love, hope; and the expression of each; of faith, the work; of love, the labour; of hope, the patience. And then, in the final description, that is all stated again in another form.

Now, of course, that might be the whole theme of the morning, but it is not. Between these two descriptions comes my text, "from you"—that is, from the people of faith, and love, and hope, the people who have turned to God from idols, and serve the living and true God, and who are waiting for His Son from heaven, "from you hath sounded forth the Word of the Lord"; and that is inevitable, and that is the whole theme of the morning. Given a church according to the pattern, then there is found the fulfilment of function according to the purpose.

"From you hath sounded forth the Word of the Lord." "Sounded forth"; that is, quite literally, echoed forth. Chrysostom said, "sounded as a clear trumpet note." "Sounded forth." It is not that these people went everywhere preaching; but it is that these people, in their unity of life as a church, became an instrument through which the Word of the Lord was sounding forth. I would like to use another word than "sounded forth," another word than echoed forth. I would like to use this word: "from you the Word of the Lord reverberated"; through the valleys and over the mountains, and away through Macedonia and Achaia, the Word of the Lord reverberated. I learned the value of that word reverberated in this sense from my beloved friend, Dr. Pentecost. When speaking of Moody's missions in this country, he described them as missions which reverberated. When Moody was preaching in Newcastle, the thrill was felt to the southern coast. From you reverberated the Word of the Lord.

Dr. Findlay says that the expression "the Word of the Lord" is the "designation for God's revealed will" in the history of the Old Testament, a fine and perfect definition of the meaning of the phrase there. In the New Testament the phrase means Christ Himself inclusively. Particularly it means, first, always an argument for the Lordship of Christ. The Word of the Lord is the argument for His Lordship, and that is supremely the Word of the resurrection of Christ; and then it is the fact itself of His Lordship; and then the Word of the Lord is the whole system of His ethical instruction, the laws of the Kingdom. The Word of the Lord is the argument that proves Him Lord, that resurrection wherein He was horizoned as the Son of God, and by the vision of which the disciples were born again unto a living hope; the fact that He is Lord of all, and all the laws which govern those who are underneath His Lordship, all that is within the Word of the Lord. That Word of the Lord sounded forth, reverberated through Macedonia and Achaia; and the instrument was that fellowship of man and woman who had turned to serve, to wait—in faith, in love, and in hope.

This, I repeat, is a picture in camera of the Church at work. Let us leave the passage, and take the wider outlook on New Testament teaching; first, concerning the place of the Church in the scheme and the work of God; secondly, the work of the Church in fulfilment of that intention; finally, the power of the Church in the doing of that work.

First, then, the place of the Church in the Divine scheme. Let us attempt to see that scheme by quotation of three well known but apparently separated passages. You will immediately detect the connection, and the purpose for which I bring them together.

"God is love."

"The Word became flesh, and tabernacled among us (and we beheld His glory, glory as of the only begotten from the Father) full of grace and truth."

"The Church, which is His body, the fulness of Him that filleth all in all."

I now look back again at this particular passage in the Thessalonian letter, and I observe that in its very first verse the apostle writes: "Paul, and Silvanus, and Timothy, unto the Church of the Thessalonians in God the Father and the Lord Jesus Christ: Grace to you and peace." We begin in that salutation with the final result, "the Church of the Thessalonians," "the Church which is His body, the fulness of Him that filleth all in all"; and then we see the sphere, "in God the Father and the Lord Jesus," the Church in Him Who is love, but in Him Who is love because in Him Who is the unveiling of the love, the revealing of the love.

"God is love." That is a fact altogether too great for human speech or understanding, out of which all the movements for man's uplifting have sprung. I quarrel entirely with the theologian who talks of love as an attribute. Love is essence; and if you would understand it, you must take all the attributes, and see them in their interdependence and mutual inter-relationships. It is the final word. If you at all object to it, it is because you do not understand love. If you are a little afraid that in the saying of a thing like that we are robbing God of the awful fact of His holiness and righteousness, it is because you do not understand love. Yes, but love is love; and "Love is not love that alters when it alteration finds." Love is strong as death, mightier than the grave; love will pause at nothing to make possible the recovery and restoration of the sinner. That is a height I cannot climb; it is a depth I cannot fathom; it is a spaciousness that defies me; but you know it, and I know it. The supreme, the ultimate fact is that God is love, and out of the being, God is love, proceeds the doing, "God commendeth His own love toward us, in that while we were yet sinners, Christ died for us."

And so naturally, we pass to the next of these three declarations: "The Word became flesh, and dwelt among us (and we beheld His glory, glory as of the only begotten from the Father) full of grace and truth." Christ was first the Revealer of the love in its attitude toward man in his need; but he was more, and we fail sadly if we use only the word Revealer about our Lord.

Christ was the instrument of that love, the One through Whom it operated in the activity of redemption. He was the Revealer of an attitude, and the instrument of an activity. The Word was made flesh, pitching His tent among us, by the side of the place where our tents are pitched, in the same campus. May God the Holy Spirit make these things real to us. He pitched His tent among us, by the side of man as Man, not by the side of a Jew as a Jew, or of an Anglo-Saxon as an Anglo-Saxon. By the side of a Jew, yes, thank God; by the side of an Anglo-Saxon, yes, thank God; and in each case because by the side of man as Man. What for? To unveil an attitude and to accomplish an activity.

Thus, finally, we have the last of the three declarations: "The Church, which is His Body"—His instrument, as He is the Instrument of God—"the fulness of Him that filleth all in all," as it pleased the Father "that in Him should all the fulness dwell." The Church is the Body of the Christ, that through which Christ is still active, that through which God is in Christ, reconciling the world unto Himself.

The Church, being the Body, at the disposal of the Lord, the Word of the Lord will reverberate in the thunders of an infinite music over all nations and continents and peoples.

What, then, is the inclusive and complete work of the Church? It is that of the proclamation of the Word of the Lord. From you hath sounded forth the proclamation of the Word, the fact of the Lordship of Christ. Is not this the need, the supreme need, the differentiating need, that which distinguishes itself from all others? Yes, it is perfectly true, thank God, and we are coming to see it more clearly; that He has left no nation or kindred or class absolutely without light; that there are gleams of light wherever man is found, and we are coming to understand that the message of the missionary is fulfilment of the gleam by correction of the surrounding darkness, and by presentation of the final Light. All that is true. Yet there is a distinction, a separating quality, that makes our evangel the one and only evangel; it is that of the Lordship of Christ. Christ is Lord by virtue of His absolute supremacy in human life; but Christ is Lord by a victory won in the tragedy of His overwhelming passion, and Christ is Lord supremely by the triumph of His resurrection from among the dead. Is not that what the Church is in the world to proclaim? When the Lord Christ is thus known and proclaimed, the laws of His Kingship and the value of His supremacy are revealed. Our minds are dwelling upon all the ends of the earth; but let us come back for a moment to a narrower outlook. Mr. Gladstone once said that the severest malady threatening England was its loss of the sense of sin; and every preacher knows that to be true, if he be a preacher of the Word. Is not the reason partly to be found in the fact that we have not with sufficient emphasis and intelligence preached Jesus as Lord? We have assumed His Lordship, but have we preached His Lordship? I do not know that I am making clear the thing in my mind. I will try again. I believe there are thousands of young people in our land today who will never tremble when you preach the Ten Commandments. The reason is not now to be discussed; I state the fact. I do not think you can find man or woman of intelligence, if you can but bring them into the actual presence of this Lord Christ, but that they will say, "If that be

CHURCH IDEALS: THE CHURCH AT WORK

the meaning of human life, then, oh God, how have I failed!" I am talking out of my own experience. I have to repeat some things; I will repeat this. I never trembled under Mount Sinai in my life; but oh, when I measure my life by His life, and listen to the words that pass His lips, and see the central inspiration of the life of my Lord and Christ, then I put my hand upon my lips and cry, I am unclean. The proclamation of His Lordship is needed in England, where the Gospel is stultified, because men think they know it, and where preachers are afraid to preach it in its simplicity, because they imagine congregations know it; it is needed also for the ends of the earth. He is Master of all the forces destroying, He Who death by dying slew, He Who hell in hell laid low is the great Victor over all the forces that destroy. That is the Word of the Lord.

But the Word of the Lord is not only to be proclaimed as a theory by the Church; and it will never reverberate in thunder by such proclamation as a theory. It must be vindicated within the Church. The life of the Church must witness to the truth of the Gospel the Church preaches, in service definitely and positively rendered, and finally in sacrifice.

"In His feet and hands are wound-prints, and His side"; and, my brethren and sisters in Christ, whether it be here or there, we only begin to preach the Word of the Lord, to proclaim it with power, as there enter into our work the elements of travail and sacrifice.

Finally, a word concerning the power of the Church for her work. What is the Church's power for service? I want to begin and state it thus, passing, presently, perhaps to a deeper note. I do not know that it is deeper, but I will put first something which is not always put first. What is the power of the Christian Church? The spirituality of her own life. Not the power of the Spirit bestowed, but the Spirit, the power, working through. I make the distinction carefully. I might, if I were sitting down quietly with some of you, admit that there is actually very little distinction; but I think we make a great distinction, because we put it in the wrong way. Not the power of the Spirit bestowed, but the Spirit, the one Power, working through the Church; the Church thus becoming, not the Medium only, but in her very life the operative power, and in that sense the Medium of His work. Not the power of the Spirit bestowed, as though the Spirit bestowed some power apart from Himself, and gave it to us, a stored dynamic force that we take and use until it runs out; but the Spirit Himself, resident within, molding, fashioning, shining out, moving through; that is the power of the Church.

Yes, but how shall we know whether we have that power or not? The Church is constituted by the Spirit. It is by the Spirit's baptism into life that men come into the Church. The Church is governed by Christ, Who interprets His will through the ministry of the Spirit. The Church can only be disciplined when the Church is living in that Spirit, Who is at once the Spirit of love and of light.

So I go back to my position, and abide by it. The power in itself is the true spiritual life of the Church. Give me a church anywhere, two or three, units, tens, hundreds, thousands—which matters nothing, for in the mathematics of heaven one shall chase a thousand, and two shall put ten thousand to flight—but give me a little company of men and women, who have seen the one Lord, and have exercised in Him the one faith, and have received the one baptism of the Spirit, and are now living in answer to the inspiration of that life, and obeying its impulse. There is God's instrument, and from that Church will sound forth the Word of God. The power in itself is that of the spiritual life of the Church, and the Church is only spiritual as the Holy Spirit unresisted, unquenched, ungrieved, has His own highway through all its membership.

And yet again, if that be the power in itself, observe the power in its working. I have nothing other to do than to go back to those descriptive phrases that we dwelt upon by way of introduction.

How does this power of the Spirit operate for the sounding forth of the Word of the Lord? In obedience, in service, and in perfect confidence. Obedience—the work of faith, ye turned to God. Service—the labor of love, ye serve the living God. Confidence—the patience of hope, ye wait for the Son from heaven. There is the threefold inspiration of faith and love and hope; and waiting for the Son. Where the expression is lacking, it is because the inspiration is absent; and where the inspiration is absent, the expression is lacking.

What, then, is the law of power in the Church for the accomplishment of her work? First, that of passivity, the cessation of all self-controlled effort; secondly, an entire yielding to the interpretations and energies of the Spirit of God; finally, activity going, speaking, doing.

First, passivity, the cessation of all self-centered effort. A man may deal with theory, and miss the whole impact of the truth. I am convinced, brethren, that during the past five and twenty years one of the greatest hindrances to the Church's progress has been her ceaseless fussiness in attempting to devise new methods for doing God's work. We are always trying by our own wit and wisdom to find some new method. Let us be done with it. What shall we do? Yield ourselves to the interpretation of the Spirit of God and to the energies of the Spirit. Let the Spirit of God have His way. That is where we fail. The Spirit is the Spirit of light; He flings a light upon our pathway, and indicates that which is God's will for us in service; and we are afraid, the Cross lies there; we draw back. The Spirit is the Spirit of love. He touches us with a sacred impulse to help that degraded man or woman whom we see on the highway, an impulse to give up the quietness and the comfort of the home life, and the home worship for the dark and desolate places of the earth; and we shrink back—the Cross is there. And because we have not yielded to the Spirit in passivity, we fail; and we attempt to make up for our failure in devotion, by finding out new methods of helping God. If we will only let the Spirit have His way with us, if we will walk where He indicates, and do what He says, counting no cost, holding back no alabaster box of ointment for ourselves, then, in the rush of the fire and the sweeping of the new force, far more than half of our mechanical activities will be burned up; but we shall be out upon the highway of God's great enterprises in the world, going because we are driven by this great Spirit indwelling, speaking, perchance, not with the education and the elegance and eloquence of old, but in power, which matters far more, doing—yes, I am bound to say it, though it hits my heart—not half so many things, but a few things better. And then—ah, then—the Word of God will reverberate, will sound forth.

My brethren, the Church of God thus at work is safeguarded against heresy. I am not going to describe any particular heresy; but the Church, obedient to the Spirit, answering the Spirit's interpretation of the Christ, cannot go far astray; and a Church thus at work is safeguarded against false motive in service, false initiations, false methods, false aims; safeguarded against all fear and panic, against all weakness. The Church thus constituted, thus governed, thus disciplined,

CHURCH IDEALS: THE CHURCH AT WORK

and thus at work, is a Church to which three great things are forever guaranteed: first, vision, and then virtue, and finally victory. She will see; she will have strength to move on to the doing of the thing seen, and victory will follow wherever she goes.

I close this brief series of four meditations on the Church with this word. After all is said and done, the individual responsibility is the only one for each individual man or woman; and, therefore, why should I say any more to you? Nay, rather let me get away somewhere from human eyes, and have this out with my Lord.

Am I of this Church? Have I been born anew from above? Do I know the life of God in my own soul by the touch of the Holy Spirit? If not, however much I admire the ethic, however readily I agree to the beauty of the example, I am not of this Church. I may be on the borders, but I am not in; though I may have had clean water sprinkled upon my brow, or been plunged beneath the water, though I may have had hands placed upon my head, or my name passed by solemn church meeting, I am not of the Church, I am not of the Christ.

And as to government, am I under the Lordship of Christ? No, I am not going to make confession here; but I must ask the question. I must ask it anew. A man is bound to go back at times to searching, to wonderment as to why there has been failure, and why not greater success.

Discipline, have I been eager to discipline the man with a mote in his eye, while there is a beam in mine? God help me.

Am I an instrument so ready to the Lord, that from me the Word of God is not simply heard—sounding brass, tinkling cymbal, a clang, and a clash, and a clatter, God deliver us—but as reverberating music is sounding, bidding lonely watchers look up and hope, and wounded souls listen, and stricken men crowd up and hope, and wounded souls listen, and stricken men crowd to my Lord? So may we investigate along, somewhere ere the sun set, as to whether we are fulfilling our responsibility in the Church of God.

CHAPTER XIX

THE KINGDOM: THE KING

He hath on His garment and on His thigh a name written,
KING OF KINGS, AND LORD OF LORDS.
                                    REVELATION 19:16.

THIS IS A VIEW OF CHRIST IN HIS GLORY, A POETIC AND PROphetic description of a glory upon which the eye of man has not yet rested in actual history.

John, as he wrote an account of the vision granted to him, was careful in the center of the descriptive paragraph to name the glorious One the Word, in the mystic language which he had used in writing the story of His mission in the world. In the loneliness of Patmos there were granted to the Seer such visions of his Lord as he had never seen before. In the presence of the unveiling of the glory of this Person, John became as one dead; and yet, he was conscious of the touch of a gentle, tender hand, thrilling with all human affection, and of the sound of a voice full of sweet tenderness, and ringing with all authority, saying: "Fear not, I am the first and the last, and the Living One; and I was dead, and, behold, I am alive for evermore, and I have the keys of death and of Hades." The One Who passes before our vision in this paragraph is the self-same One upon Whose bosom John had laid his head in the years that now seemed so far away, the one of Whom he declared: "We beheld Him and we handled Him." Now he sees Him, in the figurative language of this paragraph, riding from the opened heavens, a King, followed by armies; and on His vesture and on His thigh a name was written, "King of kings, and Lord of lords." I repeat that the eyes of the men of the world have never yet so seen Him; nevertheless, Jesus is today God's anointed and appointed King.

One of the great themes of the Bible is that of the Kingship of God. I am sometimes inclined to think, as I study and attempt to teach it, that whatever word, descriptive of Deity, one may be thinking of at a given moment, that word contains within itself the suggestiveness of every other word. A little while ago, in a careful and devout treatise on the Atonement, the author declared that in the word *Father* all essential truth concerning God is contained; for the Father is a King having authority, and the Father is a Saviour, forever seeking the realization of the highest life of His children. Would it not be equally true to say that when one speaks of Kingship all other thoughts are included therein? Would it not be equally true to affirm that if one speaks of God as Saviour, authority and tenderness and tears are all suggested by the word? From the beginning to the end of the Bible, the revelation of God is that of His Kingship, not declared in so many words in the stories with which the record opens, but as clearly revealed there as anywhere else. Take the ancient story, and see the placing of man in the garden; mark the spacious liberty, the glorious opportunity in the midst of which he found himself, in order that he might have dominion; but, as you gaze upon that spacious liberty and that wonderful opportunity, mark well the tree that indicated the limit of liberty and the condition for the fulfilment of opportunity: "Of the tree of the knowledge of good and evil, thou shalt not eat of it." That tree was the sacramental symbol of the limit of liberty, and therefore a revelation to man of the throne higher than the one upon which man himself sat, and to which he must bow in allegiance if he would reign in power over everything that lies beneath him. As I pass on and on through the library I find the same story of God as King, God governing, God lifted up and enthroned, and when the seers of the ancient economy came to the highest visions of God they were always visions of God enthroned. With the coming of the New Testament, there came the fulfilment of the things suggested in the Old concerning this very fact of the Divine Kingship and government. In the language of the far distance there had been indications of the fact that at last into human history there should come a manifestation of the Kingship of God—the seed of the woman should bruise the serpent's head. It was a prophecy of the authority which should overcome the forces that were against humanity. The great promises made to the father of the race all indicated the coming of manifest Kingship, and to the great tribe of Judah the promise was definitely made that out of it should come a governor. The psalms are full of a King yet to come. The prophets during the delivery of their messages among the failing thrones of time, and in the presence of all the breakdown of earthly royalty, looked on and on, and waited and hoped that this essential fact of government and authority would come into clear manifestation.

In the New Testament there is the fulfilment of the hope, the answer to the expectation, the aspiration, the desire, the longing, the passionate waiting of the long centuries. From the beginning to the end of the story of Jesus' public ministry, there is the note of Kingship and unquestioned authority in His teaching. When he ascended the Mount, and delivered to His disciples His ethic, there was no note of apology, no question of counsel taken with any other. Nay, rather, there was the note that set aside the old economy, because it was now superseded by the new ethic, "Ye have heard that it was said to them of old time . . . but I say unto you!" I listen to Him in all His teaching, and I watch Him in all His ways; and I see ever One Who is sole and absolute Monarch, calling no man into His counsels. I trace Him through all His life, and I see Kingliness manifest not only in His teaching and in His general attitude toward men, but also, and perhaps supremely, in His attitude toward God. Christ never used the same word to describe His own praying which He used to describe the praying of other men. The word He used when describing the praying of the disciples, and when He charged them to pray, was a word which indicates coming into the presence of God with empty hands, as a pauper asking for the bestowment of a gift, of a bounty. Jesus never used that word about His own praying. Martha once used that word of His praying, but that was her mistake. The word Christ used of His own praying was a word which indicated partnership, fellowship with the God to Whom He spoke, "I will inquire of the Father." It is equally significant that you never find Him praying with His disciples. He prayed alone. They watched their Lord at His prayer, and as they watched Him and listened to Him, they came to Him upon one occasion and said, "Lord, teach us to pray." The very petition they presented to Him, asking that they might be taught to pray, is demonstration of the loneliness of His praying. Jesus prayed on another level, on another plane. His fellowship with God was other than the fellowship of the men by whom He was surrounded. Whether I watch His attitude toward men, or His attitude toward God, this perpetual note of authority is to be discovered.

As the shadows of the Cross were falling upon His spirit, the shadows of the dark hours to which Jesus was coming, and to which He had so often made reference in the company of the disciples, and as they trembled in the presence of the Cross out of their very love for Him, it is perfectly evident that the effect it produced upon Him was not that of trembling. There was no tremor in the presence of men and what they could do; the trembling was reserved for the loneliness of Gethsemane, when He faced the infinite mystery of the passion, and men were excluded. In the presence of the Cross itself Christ said: "Now is the judgment of this world: now shall the prince of this world be cast out. And I, if I be lifted up from the earth, will draw all men unto Myself."

That authority was manifested with equal clearness in the hour of the Cross. If we watch Him carefully we cannot fail to see that Jesus compelled the hour of His own death. In the earlier days of His ministry He said: "I lay down my life that I may take it again. No one taketh it away from me, but I lay it down of myself." Watch Him at the last. Read carefully Matthew's story, and you will find two statements close together, though we have sometimes read them and never recognized their relationship. The high priests, plotting for His arrest, warned Judas that it was not to be effected at the Feast. Directly after, I see Him with His disciples, and Judas sat at the board; and Christ said to him, "What thou doest, do quickly." And He was arrested at the Feast, in spite of the priests. This was not a man driven by circumstances; He was a Man compelling circumstances. This was not a prisoner arrested at last, having been hunted to death by His enemies, who had now overcome Him. He held in His hand every foe that was against Him, and compelled the whole of them to co-operate in the fulfilment of His own purpose. He stood in the presence of the representative of Roman power, Pilate; and when he asked Him, "Whence art Thou?" Jesus gave him no answer. When Pilate said, "Knowest Thou not that I have power to release Thee, and have power to crucify Thee?" Christ replied, "Thou wouldst have no power against Me, except it were given thee from above."

Man of Nazareth, did you call Him? Verily yes, man of my manhood, bone of my bone, flesh of my flesh, humanity of my human nature, but a King. This is He of Whom all the prophets spoke, and Whose coming they anticipated. This is He of Whom all the psalmists sang, their expectation becoming the inspiration of their psalmody. This is He for Whom long ages have been waiting. This is the King, God's one and only King. In the great Kingdom of God Christ is King, an expression to men of the meaning of God's Kingship, and for the accomplishment in the midst of human history of all the purposes of God.

Now for one moment look beyond this hour in which we are assembled. Lift your eyes! It is not easy to look on into the mystic future; but look, I pray you, look on to the Advent. Place it where you will; I care nothing for the sake of the present argument and illustration as to your view concerning the relation to each other of the various aspects of that Advent; I am desirous only of drawing attention to this tremendous declaration:—

> Then cometh the end, when He shall deliver up the Kingdom to God, even the Father; when He shall have abolished all rule and all authority and power. For He must reign till He hath put all His enemies under His feet. The last enemy that shall be abolished is death. For He put all things in subjection under His feet. But when He saith, All things are put in subjection, it is evident that He is excepted Who did subject all things unto Him. And when all things have been subjected unto Him, then shall the Son also Himself be subjected unto Him that did subject all things unto Him, that God may be all in all.

The underlying truth of that declaration is that of the Kingship of God. Jesus is seen as the manifestation in human history of that Kingship. Jesus came for the demonstration thereof in the midst of the long failure. He came into human sight, into human consciousness, to destroy the works of the devil, to restore again that part of the Kingdom which was lost and in rebellion. The fisherman of Galilee who leaned upon the human bosom of Christ—and I sometimes think felt the very beating of His dear heart—John, in the isle of Patmos, with the waters washing inshores, and desolation in his heart because of absent friends, looked, and the heaven was opened, and that Man of Nazareth was seen, and "upon His vesture and on His thigh a name written, KING OF KINGS, AND LORD OF LORDS."

Let us, therefore, consider this Kingliness of Jesus, for it is a manifestation in time, and for us, of the real meaning of the Kingship of God. I shall ask you to consider three things: first, the Kingly character as revealed in Jesus; secondly, the Kingly qualifications as manifested in Him; and, finally, the Kingly position which He occupies even now, and which will be manifested before the eyes of men in the accomplishment of the purpose of God.

The Kingly character. Upon this depends the Kingly position. That is a revolutionary thing to say, by which I mean that it is saying something that the world has never yet come to understand. True kingliness must be based upon character. A sentence like that is quite naturally applied to kinghood among men; but, in order that the truth in that application should be emphasized more powerfully, I affirm that the Kingship of God is founded upon the character of God. That is a tremendous truth, and if we can but grasp it, what will be the confidence, the assurance it will bring to us in the midst of battle and strife? That truth had its unveiling in Jesus

Christ. Kings have become kings in human history by force of arms. Said this King, "Put up again thy sword into its place: for all they that take the sword shall perish with the sword." Nationality that begins with military power, that is built upon military power, ends by military power. Not by force of arms, not by policy and intrigue, not by succession does this King reign.

Let me but remind you of that great passage in the Philippian letter, in which Paul described the humiliation and consequent exaltation of Christ. Let us begin in the middle: "Wherefore also God highly exalted Him, and gave unto Him the name which is above every name; that in the name of Jesus every knee should bow, of things in heaven and things on earth and things under the earth, and that every tongue should confess that Jesus Christ is Lord, to the glory of God the Father." How that thrills with the music of the march to imperial power—every knee to bow and every tongue to confess! This paragraph commences with the word "Wherefore," and now I take that word and use it interrogatively. Wherefore? Why has God lifted Him high, and put Him on the throne? I go back to that which precedes: "Who, being in the form of God, counted it not a prize to be on an equality with God, but emptied Himself, taking the form of a servant, being made in the likeness of men; and being found in fashion as a man, He humbled Himself, becoming obedient even unto death, yea, the death of the Cross." Can you explain to me that patient, persistent, awful descent to the uttermost depth of the Cross? There is only one answer. The answer is in the word which never occurs in the passage, but which bathes the passage with infinite light. The answer is given in the word Love. "God so loved the world."

> Love brought Him down, my poor soul to redeem;
> Yes, it was love made Him die on the tree.

That is the character upon which the Kingship of Jesus is based. That is the character upon which the government of God is based. The Kingly character is love. Love is not a weak, sickly, anemic sentiment, which has in it no discipline, no strength, no anger, no fierceness. Love has holiness at its heart. Wherever we find true love we find the capacity for anger. Love is always angry with anything and everything, and with anyone and everyone, that harms, hurts and spoils that which is loved. Jesus once brought the prince of darkness into the light, and described him as a murderer, a liar. Love will judge the murderer, and fling the liar out. If love permit the murderer house room, and forgive the liar in his lie, it ceases to be love. Love can be stern, severe and hard, but always in the interest of redemption and renewal, and remaking. "The King of love my Shepherd is." In that great word there is laid bare so much as man may see of the Kingly character of Jesus, and the character of God upon which His government is based.

Then consider the kingly qualifications. "The King of love my Shepherd is." All the great kingly characters in the Bible were shepherds. Moses, uncrowned, but a king, learned the art of kingship not at the court of Pharaoh, but in the desert. David, the king after God's own heart, served his apprenticeship to human kingship while he was a shepherd boy. Jesus said the sweetest and profoundest thing about Himself, in some senses, when He said "I am the good Shepherd," and other writers described Him as the great Shepherd and the chief Shepherd. The work of the shepherd is to watch over the flock, to feed the flock, to protect them, to heal their wounds, to lead them to pasture, to restore the wanderers, to fight the wolves even though he die in the conflict. That is kingship. The true king is always a shepherd, living not for himself but for his flock, thinking for the flock, caring for them, putting all the thought of his life and the service of his being into the interests of the flock. Such was this great Shepherd. Because of the perfection of the shepherd character of Jesus, there was perfect qualification for government. I know how difficult that is to understand, how revolutionary it seems, when thinking of the kings of earth even until this hour. God's king is a shepherd, because God is a Shepherd. I take you back to the ancient word, "Jehovah is my Shepherd, I shall not want." So sang David the king, who also was a shepherd. He saw on the throne of majesty and government the Shepherd who leads and loves and restores.

A further qualification is that He is a prophet also. When I use the word "prophet" thus, I do not use it in the imperfect sense of foreteller, but in the larger sense of forthteller, law giver, one who interprets the perfect will to people who need such interpretation, one who is able to enunciate an ethic, which if obeyed, life will be fulfilled at its highest and best. How is it that other kings have so constantly failed in human history? Because they have had to be dependent on others to make laws. I believe in absolute monarchy, provided we find the true monarch. He has never been seen in human history, except once; and this is the once. All other kings have either consulted their parliaments, or made laws despotic and devilish.

Here is a King Who went to the mountain and enunciated an ethic of which the whole can be written in two or three pages, and yet the proportion in which the world has found its way into light and liberty is the proportion in which it has obeyed that ethic. It is a perfect law, perfectly adjusted to human need. Who is there today who is not prepared to admit that if this nation could be remodeled and governed according to the ethic of the Sermon on the Mount, all our problems would be solved? Men outside the Church know that to be true. Men who charge us with being other-worldly learned the ethic which they admire from the lips of One Who was the supreme other-worldly Man. From His lips there fell the perfect and final law for the government of humanity.

This King has as qualification not merely the Shepherd character and the prophetic gift; He was also a Priest, and He is a Priest in very deed and truth. A priest is one who becomes a representative of others, one who stands for all the rest, one who takes the blame of failure, one who stands in the gap. "Who is this that cometh from Edom, with dyed garments from Bozrah?" What is the answer of the ancient prophet? "I that speak in righteousness, mighty to save . . . I have trodden the winepress alone." Figurative and wonderful language, foretelling the fact that finally the King takes into His own Person all the sins of the people. That is atonement. That is the mystery of the Cross. That is the infinite, incomprehensible, wonderful, eternal love that was manifested upon the green hill. This is my King, for He is my Shepherd. This is my King, for He is my Lawgiver. This is my King, for He is my Priest. The qualifications of His kingship are that He is Shepherd, Prophet, Priest.

One final word. I pray you mark the authority of Jesus, His Kingly position. He stood at the end of His days upon earth on the Mount of Olivet, with a little group of men surrounding Him, and He said, "All authority hath been given unto Me in heaven and on earth." That was human speech in order to reveal to men the fact, and to fix their attention upon it, that in that Manifestation of the eternal principle of Divine government, all authority is forevermore vested in the Man Jesus. He utters the final word of life or death concerning every individual soul. There can be no approach to God save through Him. "No man cometh unto the Father but by Me." Forevermore He pronounces the word "Blessed" or "Cursed" upon men, according to whether they bend the knee to Him, or reject Him. No man or woman can disobey His ethic without being lost. He is not a capricious King, commanding that men shall be destroyed, or that men shall be saved, to please His own fancy. He is the embodiment of eternal law. He brings men to the judgment bar of His high ideal; accept it, fall before it, worship it, and He will make you; reject it, and turn back to the base, the ignoble, the mean, the dastardly, the devilish and impure, and He will blast and blight you by the fires of infinite and eternal law.

We need have no anxiety about the Kingship of Jesus. We need not imagine for a single moment, in all the fussy feverishness of this neurotic age, that the Christian religion is going to fail. Christ cannot fail. All authority has been given unto Him. The thing He says is true. Nineteen centuries have passed away, and His word is living and abiding—searching, tender, gentle, healing even yet. He is God's King. All power is His as well as all authority. Read carefully the stupendous description of Christ in Paul's Colossian letter, and see how true it is. He can stay the progress of life, arrest the planet, and gather the souls of men about Him when and how He will. He is King.

He is King executing judgment in the world. What is judgment? Judgment is that which the world needs more than anything else. Judgment is absolute rectitude, the holding of the balances, the readjustment of things that are wrong. Judgment! Great word, gracious word, beautiful word, tender word! But you say, "I tremble when you say judgment." That is because there is sin in your life, permitted and retained. I am afraid of judgment, you say. That is because you are oppressing. The men who are oppressed thank God for judgment. Judgment is heaven's love at work, correcting all the things that are wrong. "He shall establish judgment in the earth."

Remember finally that His Kingly position is not merely that of authority, power and judgment; it is that of infinite patience. How often have we said—if you have not said it, be patient with those who have, and I stand with them—How slow are the goings of God. We stand in the presence of wrong and oppression, we look out over the city scarred and seared with wounds, we listen in moments of high spiritual inspiration, and we hear the sob and sigh of broken humanity, and we say, "How long, O Lord, how long?" Then the answer comes back, the longsuffering of God is His patience. Supposing we go back a little way. Had God moved to a swift issue twenty-five years ago, where would some of us have been who today, by His grace and patience, have seen the light and walk in it, and are hoping towards it, and looking for it? There is a process by which all evil might be crushed; but it could not be crushed without crushing all the possibilities of good. Let the wheat and the tares grow together until the harvest. When the wheat and the tares have grown to their final development and manifestation, then the thunderstorm.

Thank God for the patience of the King, and part of His patience is this service. Shall we not find our way to the King, and, submitting to Him, bring our lives into harmony with the eternal and abiding things? Thank God for Him, on Whose garment and on Whose thigh is "a name written, KING OF KINGS, AND LORD OF LORDS." Oh, soul of mine, bend to His sceptre, kiss His sceptre, put thy neck beneath His yoke, and find thy life and find thy liberty.

CHAPTER XX

THE KINGDOM: "THY KINGDOM"

Thy Kingdom. . . . MATTHEW 6:10.

OUR THEME THIS EVENING IS THAT OF THE KINGDOM OVER which the King reigns. The phrase I have read as text is taken, apparently, almost ruthlessly from its setting. These words are selected from the Lord's prayer. My theme this evening is not the prayer, but rather the Kingdom for the coming of which our Lord taught us to pray. In speaking of it let us remember that He Who taught the prayer was Himself the King; that the prayer itself is formulated with wonderful care, and is part of the King's Manifesto.

At the fifth chapter in the Gospel according to Matthew, we have the account of Jesus looking upon the multitude, and as a result going to the mountain, taking with Him His own disciples, and there upon the mountain height, enunciating in their hearing the ethic of His great Kingdom. At the heart of the ethic is this prayer, and at the center of the first part of the prayer is this phrase, "Thy Kingdom come."

Of that Kingdom Jesus is King by way of manifestation and for the purpose of demonstration. The one sovereign Lord is God. In order that men may know the King, He came into human form; and so coming, not nearer to man, but nearer to his consciousness by the way of incarnation. Therefore in Jesus of Nazareth, Man of our manhood, Bone of our bone, Flesh of our flesh, Life of our life, there has appeared

THE KINGDOM: "THY KINGDOM"

in human history all that it is necessary for us to know concerning the Kingship of God, for in the King, the Kingdom is revealed.

With that thought in mind, we turn to the consideration of the Kingdom for which He taught us to pray that it may come, not that it may be created, not that it may be established, but that it may come, that it may be realized, that it may appear, that it may reach its ultimate fulfilment. In human history kings have often been great only by reason of the greatness of the empire over which they have reigned. But the greatest kings, even in human history, are the kings who have created a great kingdom. The greatness of our King is created by the greatness of the Kingdom over which He reigns, and the greatness of the Kingdom over which He reigns is created by the greatness of the King. Yet, it seems to me sometimes that we can only come to any recognition of the greatness of the King as we attempt to see the Kingdom over which He reigns. We spoke of the abstract things of Christ's greatness in our previous study; of His character, of His qualifications, of His authority. Now let us try to see the Kingdom over which He reigns.

I shall ask you to follow me as I attempt to speak; first of the actual fact and extent of the Kingdom; and secondly of the present expression of the Kingdom in human history.

First, then, as to the fact and extent of the Kingdom. We are in danger of limiting our outlook when we speak of the Kingdom. I am not going to enter into any discussion of the interesting problem of the difference between the Kingdom of God and the Kingdom of heaven. Whatever difference there may be of application, there is no difference in the central thought. All the realms of which we are conscious are in the Kingdom of God. "King of kings" was the word of our last meditation. As we remember it we think of rulers and principalities; of dominions and powers; of kings over certain restricted areas. Over all these Christ is claimed by Scripture to be King. All realms are in His Kingdom. The material universe is in the Kingdom of God. The mental realm is under the government of Christ. Over the moral realm He is the one supreme ruler. So climbing up the ascending scale from the material through the mental and moral, we reach ultimately and finally to this: that the whole spiritual universe is within the Kingdom of God and is under the dominion of Christ.

Let us begin with the first of these thoughts; the material realm. To declare that this is in the Kingdom of God is to utter something old and commonplace, and therefore difficult of belief; that is of the belief which touches the heart and moves the emotion and fires the imagination. Yet, I believe that we are losing greatly in our Christian thinking and teaching by forgetfulness of this fact. No words of mine can set forth that truth with such lucidity, with such force, as the words which I read to you at the commencement of our service, selections from the writings of John and Paul. I halt you one moment to ask you to think of the difference between these two men, because as we recognize that difference we shall see how remarkable it is that they both came to identical conclusions concerning the Kingdom of the Lord Jesus Christ. John was the mystic, the dreamer; a man of intuition and insight. If I were asked to designate John, I should never speak of him as Saint John the Divine, but as John the Interpreter. I never read "Pilgrim's Progress" and the account of the visit to the house of the Interpreter without thinking of John, the man who saw things never seen, and was conscious of things that other men did not dream existed. The dreamer, the mystic, the poet, the visionary, the seer. Paul was a man of sincerity and honesty; a man of logical acumen; a man who would bring to bear upon the most trivial matters the profoundest powers of the mind; the man who wrote the great treatise on salvation which plumbs the depths, and scales the heights, and shows accurately the movements of God toward the accomplishment of His purpose. I am not saying there was nothing of the mystic in Paul, no vision of the gleam, no consciousness of the glory. In this very treatise he adds to all his statement and his logic, the wings of song, and having begun with the degradation of the Roman Empire, describing it until we shudder at this description, he at last says, "Let us rejoice in hope of the glory of God." He was pre-eminently a man of logic, a man of argument, a man of debate, a man of strange and strenuous reasoning power, a man who saw his way through all the processes. These two men, brought in different ways into comradeship with Christ, came to the same conclusion. The mystic words of John concerning the Christ are, "The same was in the beginning with God. All things were made by Him; and without Him was not anything made that hath been made." "In Him was life," and there is dramatic magnificence and inclusiveness in that use of the word "life." There follows a fine differentiation between the lower forms of life and the highest, as John continued "the life was the light of men." Such is the language of the mystic. I turn to Paul and I read in his Colossian letter, "Who is the image of the invisible God, the firstborn of all creation; for in Him were all things created, in the heavens and upon the earth, things visible and things invisible, whether thrones or dominions or principalities or powers; all things have been created through Him, and unto Him; and He is before all things, and in Him all things consist." Such is the language of the logician. The conclusion in each case is the same. Jesus of Nazareth, the Christ of God, the Man known of the Galilean fisherman as an intimate human friend; the Man arresting Saul of Tarsus, learned in the law of his people and enthusiastic in his opposition to Christianity; impressed Himself upon the mind of the mystic, and upon the mind of the thinker, and the result was the same. They both saw Him as the Creator and Sustainer of the material universe. That is the Kingdom of Christ. In imagination I stand upon the mountain side, and I see the touch of His beauty in everything. I watch the procession of the seasons as they come and go, and mark their wonderful regularity, notwithstanding the impatient blasphemy of people who are afraid that a week's rain will spoil their harvest, and I know that "In Whom all things consist." There is no flower outside His Kingdom. There is no ploughed field sweeping up the hillside in folds of russet velvet which is not His handiwork. He holds the world in His hand, and is Master and Lord of the material universe. The first fact then for us ever to remember, is that the Christ Whom we crown as King, is King in the material universe; present at creation, He is the Word of creation; He upholds it by the word of His power; and all things made through Him, move toward Him, and will find their final glory when they have attained that form which harmonizes with the infinite perfections, which had their unveiling for the eye of mortal men in the strange and wonderful Person of Jesus of Nazareth.

He is also King in the mental realm. All the powers of thought are under His control, and under His government. There is rebellion in the world, in the universe; but ultimately all is under His control, for no thinking being in the universe can finally escape the strength of the mind of God. He is absolute Sovereign. All beautiful thought owes its origin to this one King; and every expression of beauty is the outcome of His reign and His Kingship. Of music, art, poetry and philosophy, He is the Lord and Master. Test your music

THE KINGDOM: "THY KINGDOM"

by the harmonies of His perfections, and it sings its last unutterable note when it celebrates the Messiah. Art comes finally to Him, and that in art which is untrue and unclean is that in art which is unlike Christ and against the purposes of His Kingship. Poetry sings itself out in highest strains when it celebrates the name of this one great King. Philosophy is final when it is true to His wisdom. Thus through all the mental realm He is King.

The fact of His Kingship in the moral realm is beyond dispute. His law is the standard of morality. Gradually the word in its progressive civilization is coming to understand His ethic and obey it. Men outside the Church at this hour, sincere men, are telling us that we need to set up a new social order, and the proportion in which these men are uttering the truth about society, the relation of man to man in brotherhood, is the proportion in which they have heard the ethic of Jesus. In civic life, national life, here or anywhere else; the proportion of its purity is the proportion of its approximation to the ideals of Christ. In our moral ideals for the individual, the community, the nation, the world; the final standard is the ethic of Jesus. Thousands of men who have refused personally and individually to crown our Lord and Master, are crowning Him indirectly when they accept His ethic and bow before His standard of morality. From His Sermon on the Mount, light has flashed upon every age, rebuking it, shaming it, and gradually men are coming to honor the great ideal. I will put the whole case in other words. No ethic has ever yet been enunciated so severe, so searching, so high, so perfect as the ethic of Jesus. Twenty years ago a man who was filled with doubt and questioning concerning the Christian religion, said to me quite frankly, "My only complaint against the ideal of Jesus is that it is impracticable; no man can fulfil it." I only quote that, I need not argue it. I agree with it, No man can fulfil the ethic of Jesus save as He receives from Him the necessary dynamic force. I quote it in order to say that it was a recognition that Christ is King in the moral realm. To obey Him absolutely, completely, finally, is to come to the ultimate in morality.

Christ is King finally over the whole spiritual realm. The highest side of life develops under His rule. He has so spoken to men who have questioned and doubted and groped in the darkness after God, that they have found Him and come to know Him. By His interpretation of truth concerning God, men have come to such conception of God as has enabled them to worship and to serve. The whole spiritual world has been opened to the consciousness of man by the ministry of Jesus. He has given us back into a present fellowship, the faces "loved long since and lost awhile." "We sorrow not as those that have no hope." The simple phrases of our holy faith link us in that communion of saints which laughs at the terror of the tomb. They are not dead, but gone before. "Absent from the body, present with the Lord." We know that when Christ shall appear, they shall appear with Him in glory. He has not killed the capacity for sorrow; but He has gilded the teardrop with His smile and made the desert garden bloom awhile, by opening before us the gates, and giving us to see the infinite distances, and to enter even here amid the dust and turmoil of this present life into the communion with the saints who have gone before. If we follow Jesus we have no need to mutter in the dark in order to talk with spirits that have gone. We are their fellow citizens. If for a little while we wait amid the conflict, in this waiting we are not divided, but one with those who have gone. And presently, when the end comes, the followers of this Christ, this King, will look into the face of the rider upon

THE KINGDOM: "THY KINGDOM"

the pale horse, and hail him as friend rather than foe, recognizing, as Bishop Taylor once so exquisitely put it, that Christ has taken from him his sting, and made him forevermore a porter at the gate of life. The consciousness of the spiritual world is born of the touch and presence and victory of this Christ King. He reigns over all things material, over all things mental, over all things moral, over all things spiritual.

Let us consider secondly, the present expression of the Kingdom.

I am speaking out of the midst of a world, and out of the midst of a condition of affairs, which made it necessary for the King to teach men to pray "Thy Kingdom come." The Kingdom is not apparent, it is not perfectly patent, it is not seen of ordinary men save in partial degree. It is an actual essential fact. It is seen of such as have seen the face of Christ. We remember the word of the writer of the letter to the Hebrews, that old and familiar world, let us recite it now with this particular meaning in it: "We see not yet all things subjected to Him. But we behold Him Who has been made a little lower than the angels, even Jesus." The writer of those words recognizes the fact that within the Kingdom there is rebellion; but he affirmed that at last the victory would be won, and all things would be subjected unto the King. His words suggest the unfinished work of Jesus, "Not yet all things subjected unto Him"; and the assurance that it will be finished, "We see . . . Jesus."

Yet, while we recognize His actual sovereignty in all these realms, let us also remember that it is not only actual, it is active. Think of the rule of Christ today. We must remind our hearts of it or we shall lose courage in many a day of battle and darkness. He holds the reigns of government over all the forces in the midst of which we live. Think of the crowned heads of the world, kings as we name them;

think of the merchant princes of today; think of the rulers of the scientific world; or yet again, think of the great spiritual leaders of this and every age. Think of all these, and then hear again this word, He is "King of kings." Begin on that first and simplest level where it sometimes seems impossible to believe it; He is King of all the crowned heads. It is not manifest; but it is an actual and active fact. Go back to the Old Testament and catch one gleam of light. Speaking to Cyrus, Jehovah said, "I have surnamed thee, though thou hast not known Me." There was a man of faith in the olden days who was agnostic in the presence of what he saw about him, and Habakkuk said in his honest agnosticism, "Why is God doing nothing?" The divine reply was, "I work a work in your days, which ye will not believe though it be told you." Then said Habakkuk, "If that be true, I will up to the watchtower and watch and see." Then God told Him what He was doing. "I am taking people outside the covenant, cruel, brutal people, and making them the ministers of My sovereignty, for the chastisement of My people, that they may be ultimately saved." The man who began his prophecy by saying that God was doing nothing, ended by singing:

> Though the fig tree shall not blossom,
> Neither shall fruit be in the vines;
> The labour of the olive shall fail,
> And the fields shall yield no meat;
> The flock shall be cut off from the fold,
> And there shall be no herd in the stalls:
> Yet will I rejoice in the Lord,
> I will joy in the God of my salvation.

Do not forget the significance of these old-world pictures. Things are different today you say. Only with a superficial difference. At this moment God girds Cyrus though

THE KINGDOM: "THY KINGDOM"

Cyrus does not know Him. The whole philosophy of the government of Jesus over crowned heads, and parliaments of the world, is contained in this Old Testament declaration, "Surely the wrath of men shall praise Thee: The residue of wrath shalt Thou gird upon Thee."

If you take all that away from me, then I am a lost man indeed, without any hope. My hope is not in Parliaments. My hope is in the fact that God reigns, and that His King holds the reins of government. I do not always understand the process; I get so weary of waiting. Oh, feverish heart of mine, be still! One day with Jehovah is as a thousand years, and a thousand years is as a day. Mount up to the mountains, and see the going of God; live in the spaciousness of eternity, and know this, that all hell, and all the devilishness of men, cannot finally defeat the enthroned King. He holds in His own right hand the government of the world. Though the process may seem long, and the conflict may be severe, Christ is reigning and ruling, this anointed and appointed King.

He is King also of merchant princes. Have you ever heard a business man talk about creating wealth? You cannot create wealth; you can amass it. God must ever create wealth. What is the ultimate, final wealth? Money? Surely not! The thing that He creates is wealth. Only that which comes out of life is wealth. A man may reap his fields of golden grain, and garner all the wheat, but he has not made wealth; he has reaped in order to make himself rich, which is quite another matter. It is the King Who creates wealth. If Christ hold in check the resources of His universe for one year and there is no harvest, then what is the use of money? He is King over all merchant princes, and can beggar them if He will.

Christ is King of science. Let every young Christian hear

that word. Never be persuaded for one single moment either by the man who attacks Christianity, or by the man who defends it, into believing that science and religion are out of harmony with each other. Of course we need to be very careful to draw a distinction between scientific facts and scientific hypotheses; and to draw a distinction between Biblical declaration and human interpretation of its meaning. I stand for no man's interpretation of the Bible, not even my own, but I stand for the Bible. I am interested in every hypothesis of science, but I hold in reserve my judgment, and ask for the ascertained fact; and when I find the ascertained fact, and the simple statement of Scripture, I find that they are one. In all the scientific world Christ is King. All scientific discoveries and investigations in modern years have been made possible by the coming of Christ and the preaching of the gospel. Every discovery is a revelation. You speak to me of the discovery of some force. It was there before you discovered it. Why did we not discover it before? Because the hour had not arrived, and we were not ready for it. Take electricity for example; when the hour arrived the King discovered the secret to man, who forevermore says he discovered it. It was revealed to him rather than discovered by him, in answer to his endeavor. Ask, seek, knock, that is not merely for the Christian man when he is praying in his own inner chamber; it is the law of life. When a man asks, there is the answer; when he seeks, he finds; when he knocks at the door of entrance to hidden secrets, the King discovers them. In all the scientific realm it is by the coming of the Christ that men have been set free for investigation and equipped for investigation. Christ is King in that realm.

Once again, and I need not stay to enlarge upon this: He is today King over all spiritual leaders. Men who lead in spiritual matters, men who help other men to vision, are all

THE KINGDOM: "THY KINGDOM"

men who have kissed the sceptre of Christ, and bent themselves before His Cross.

What is the present expression of this great fact of Christ's Kingship? We thank God for the measure in which His Kingship is acknowledged directly or indirectly in this and every land. We cannot, however, say that the Kingdom has come in England. Where then is its expression to be found? It ought to be found in His Church, for there He is crowned King, there His laws govern, there His commands are obeyed, there His interests form the supreme interest. No man can say that without shame. There is a measure in which it is all true; and the measure in which it is true is the measure in which the world knows something of the Kingship of Christ; but in how much greater degree it ought to be true than it is. I find it almost impossible to rejoice in the expression of the Kingdom when I think of the corporate Church of Christ, for very shame of our failure. Therein is the secret of the unrest and indifference and rebellion of the outside world. The rebellion is against the Church that fails to manifest the Kingship of Jesus. There is no rebellion against the Kingship of Jesus when truly manifest in the Church. We have not realized His Kingship in our corporate capacity. The armies of the Captain of Salvation are engaged in internecine warfare when they ought to be confronting the foe. Yes, we must recognize that the measure in which the world knows anything of the glory of the Kingdom is the measure in which the Church has revealed it.

Whereas criticism of the Church's failure is of very little use save as it may inspire us to face individual realization; I turn to that matter in conclusion. The reign of Jesus can be expressed in individual life. If life is in His Kingdom, then it expresses His Kingliness. He desires that His Kingdom shall be manifest through His Church and through His people;

and He has indicated the line of present expression and the value thereof. Salt is pungent, aseptic; potent for the prevention of the spread of corruption; and it gives goodness its opportunity, wherever it exists. Not only salt, but light; "Ye are the light of the world," said the King to His own disciples in His manifesto; and He explained His own figure. "A city set on a hill cannot be hid. Neither do men light a lamp, and put it under a bushel, but on the stand; and it shineth unto all that are in the house." The lamp is individual, local, personal; the illumination of private places by His own children; the city is the Church in its corporate capacity, flashing its light upon the darkness, illuminating the far distant places. These are the ideals of Jesus. The world can only know the King as it sees the Kingdom; and it can only see the Kingdom through those who are in the Kingdom.

I discard all larger applications, and close upon this note.

How far are we exhibiting to the world the meaning of the Kingship of Christ, and so revealing the King Himself? When we pray for the Kingdom, do we mean it? When we say, "Thy Kingdom come," if we simply utter words, allow them to pass our lips, we take the name of God in vain; and our blasphemy is more terrible than the blasphemy of the man in the slum. We can only pray that prayer out of our inner life when the Kingdom has come there. If we say, "Thy Kingdom come," while still the idol holds sway in our lives, and unholy, filthy things, which are an abomination to the King, are retained in our lives, then are we taking His name in vain. God have mercy upon us and deliver us from such blasphemy. Let every man, and woman, at this hour, by solemn affirmation and solemn oath, surrender to the King, saying: "Here, O King, is my life, rule over it, be Master in it, realize Thy purpose therein; take the territory and subdue it to Thy perfect will; and through it show, my children, the

THE KINGDOM: "THY KINGDOM"

servant maids in my house, the men to whom I pay wages, all the people I meet, what is the meaning of Thy great Kingdom." We can be microcosms of the Kingdom, in which its laws, its purposes, and its beauties are seen. God help us so to be.

CHAPTER XXI

THE KINGDOM: "OF SUCH IS THE KINGDOM"

Except ye turn, and become as little children, ye shall in no wise enter into the Kingdom of heaven.
MATTHEW 18:3.

OUR THEME TONIGHT IS THAT OF THE CHARACTER NECESsary for entrance to the Kingdom. The words of my text were not addressed to the promiscuous multitude. I do not mean by that statement to infer that they have no application for such a multitude, but to insist upon it that their first application is to disciples. That fact makes them all the more significant, all the more remarkable and weighty.

> In that hour came the disciples unto Jesus, saying, Who then is greatest in the Kingdom of heaven? And He called to Him a little child, and set Him in the midst of them, and said: Verily, I say unto you, except ye turn, and become as little children, ye shall in no wise enter into the Kingdom of heaven.

When His disciples asked, "Who then is greatest in the Kingdom?" He forced them back to the wicket-gate, and said: "Except ye turn, and become as little children, ye shall in no wise enter into the Kingdom of heaven."

There has been no revolt in the great Kingdom of God save among angels and men—at least, so far as revelation has enlightened us on the subject. When Heber, in his great missionary hymn, looking out over all the world, said

THE KINGDOM: "OF SUCH IS THE KINGDOM"

". . . every prospect pleases, And only man is vile," he wrote something which has often been criticized and often objected to, but which is perfectly true. Apart from the fall of angels and the fall of man—resulting from the revolt of angels who kept not their first estate, but left their proper habitation—the whole creation is unfallen.

The words of Paul, in his letter to the Romans, involuntarily suggest themselves in this connection: "The whole creation groaneth and travaileth in pain together until now. . . . The earnest expectation of the creation waiteth for the revealing of the sons of God." When by reason of rebellion man lost his sceptre, and so lost the power to govern, all nature suffered. We are quite conscious that everywhere in nature there are things out of harmony with the will of God which has been revealed to us by Christ. Suffering, sorrow, limitation are everywhere; and all for the lack of the authority of a true King. In proportion as man, individually, socially and racially, is restored to true relationship with God, the whole creation will be lifted, remade, re-established, and so will be restored the whole great Kingdom of God. The redemption of creation waits for the redemption of man. That is a large subject with which we have not time to deal now. I mention it only that we may see its relation to the theme which is to demand our attention.

Man, living in the territory of God, is in revolt against Him. That sentence is very easily uttered. I would to God that conviction of its meaning might come to all of us. Man, living within the area of the Kingdom, and in the territory of God, is yet in revolt. The emphasis I now desire is not upon the last part of that statement, but upon the first part. Every man is living in the Kingdom of God in some sense. There is no power of my life that is not a God-created power. I said power; I did not say paralysis. There is paralysis in my life which is not of God; but the power which is paralyzed is of God. Whatever there is essential to my manhood is God's creation. This is God's world. I am weary of the men and women who speak of it as the devil's world. It is God's world. In God's great Kingdom men are dwelling, and yet are in revolt, breaking His law.

The inquiry of this meditation is as to how a man may get back into the Kingdom. Now this may seem to contradict my assertion that all men are in the Kingdom. Let us, therefore, be very careful. Every man is in the Kingdom; yet men are in rebellion against the King. No man can escape the government of God, but he may fight against it. Hell itself is not beyond the reach of God. No man can utterly, finally, absolutely escape from God. It is impossible! It is possible, though a dire thought, that a man may live and move and have his being in God, and yet be out of harmony with Him, in revolt against Him. That man must still feel the touch of His power, but it will blast instead of bless. My own experience of God is created by my attitude toward God. God is eternal, unchangeable love. If I yield to the wooing of His love, I know its sweet and tender embrace; but if I am rebellious and set myself against the purposes of that love, by that very attitude of mine I find that God is a consuming fire. These are not two things, but the two aspects of one fact; the difference is always the result of the difference in the attitudes of men toward God. That fact runs through the Bible from the story of Eden and the flaming sword, to the last chapter in the visions of the Seer of Patmos. Out of the stately, wonderful movement of revelation in this matter let me quote an illustration, not very familiar, yet known I have no doubt. Malachi spoke of the day toward which men were looking. Notice his description: "Behold, the day cometh, it burneth as a furnace; and all the proud and all that work wickedness shall be stubble"; and he continued: "But unto you that fear My name shall the Sun of righteousness arise with healing in his wings." These are not two days, but one. The sunrise burns as an oven things that lack root and life, and heals and helps the things that are planted by the rivers of water. God is unchangeable. Man's relation to Him determines man's experience of Him.

How, then, may a man enter His Kingdom? How can he get back to Him consciously, to find the Kingdom; not the Kingdom of scorching, burning, destroying fire, but the Kingdom of breadth, beauty, and beneficence—of light, and life, and love, and liberty?

Taking the affirmation of my text away from its context for a moment—returning to that by way of application—we hear the great King Himself answering our inquiry: "Except ye turn, and become as little children, ye shall in no wise enter the Kingdom of heaven."

Now our danger is that we seek to read into this story and into these words certain generally accepted theological ideas. Would to God we could get back to the simple naturalness of the thing that Jesus said and did. Let us endeavor so to do. The matter of first importance is that we keep before us the picture of Jesus with His disciples round Him. They had come with an inquiry. He took a boy—our translation says a child, but the pronoun is masculine—I do not know who the boy was; in all probability he was playing near at hand, or standing on the edge of the crowd which had gathered around the Lord. He laid His hand on the boy, and put him in the midst of His disciples. Do not be angry with me when I say I do not think he was a Sunday-school boy. By that I mean, he was not a boy prepared for the occasion. He had not passed through the class and learned his catechism in order to be put in the midst. He was a boy at play, a boy of the common crowd, a boy not specifically and purposely prepared and brought there. He took such a boy, and put him in the midst, and said, "You ask Me who is the greatest in the Kingdom. I want you to know and remember, that unless you become like that boy you cannot enter into the Kingdom." That is to say, Jesus declared that forevermore the child character is the character of such as enter into the Kingdom. I am not yet dealing with the question of how a man can be restored to childhood. I am simply insisting upon the teaching of Jesus Christ as to the necessity for such restoration. To enter the Kingdom a man must have the character of a little child.

I wish I could startle you with that. Notwithstanding the fact that centuries have gone, we have hardly begun to understand it. Gradually, slowly, very slowly, the Church of God is putting the child where it ought to be put—in the midst—and is making the child the type and pattern of character in the great Kingdom of God. If we wanted to show a man what he must be like to enter into the Kingdom of God, we should in all probability take down from our library shelves the life of some mystic saint, and say, "That is the type of character in the Kingdom of God." Christ did not say so. He said something much more revolutionary, much more startling. He took a child, and put him in the midst of the quarreling, wrangling, office-seeking disciples, and said, "You cannot enter into the Kingdom until you are like that child."

Now let us diligently endeavor to discover what this really means. What is this character that Jesus declared to be necessary in order to enter His Kingdom? To tell all the facts would be difficult, for simplicity is ever most sublime. The only people who can tell you all about children are the people who never had any. They deliver most of the lectures to mothers. Is there a child in your home? Put that child in your midst tonight; your boy—if he is mischievous, all the better—put him in your midst. That child, in his artlessness and simplicity, is the sublimest revelation possible of the character that Christ demands and that God asks.

Look at the simplest things about this little child. There is its perfect naturalness; secondly, its impressionableness; thirdly, its natural confidence; and, finally, its imperfection. Take all the life of a child, physical life, mental life, and spiritual life, and all these things are true of it. I have not exhausted the subject; these are only suggestive things that are true of the life and character of every child.

First its naturalness. The child answers the impulses of its own possibility. The child is curious, and it will ask questions. It is not until it gets older that it wears the veneer of a false restraint. The child will manifest, if you watch it, all the facts of its own being. If a child loves you, it will tell you so and fling its arms about you. It is only when you get older that your respectability cools off the ardour with which you dare to declare your love. In the child there is perfect naturalness. This is a very searching word, if we will let it search us. You say, "My boy is not natural." Then mourn over your sin, because you are that boy's father. The life of the child naturally is perfectly natural; it is life that does not dissemble, life devoid of hypocrisy. Hypocrisy is acting a part. There is no hypocrisy in a child.

The child is impressionable, amenable to training, plastic to moulding, and receptive. I remember the statement of a Roman Catholic bishop: "Give me your child until he is seven, and I care not who has him afterwards. I will have made an impression upon him that can never be effaced." I know something of the controversy as to whether heredity or environment be the stronger force in the life of a child. Personally, I have no hesitation in saying that I consider environment is far stronger than heredity. If you begin soon enough, you can mould any child. There are men here who are Christian, because the hand of godly father or mother was placed upon their character early enough, in order to mould it in that direction. If there be no other man, I am that man. I am a Christian tonight because from the earliest years of my recollection the hands of godly parents were placed upon me. The child is naturally plastic, impressionable, confident, trustful. I know about the boys in the slums of London who are cunning and artful; but what has made them so? The devilish system in the midst of which they were born. Think of that great institution, to which my mind always goes when I think of neglected children, the homes connected with the name of Dr. Barnardo; if they can get a boy early enough, though he has never had the influence of father and mother to help him, the child still has the capacity for faith and confidence.

The child is imperfect. That is not a sin. When I say imperfect, I will illustrate what I mean entirely in the physical realm. A child lying in its mother's arm is not perfect. Of course, you must not tell the mother so. That little aside helps me to draw the distinction between what I do mean and what I do not mean. It is absolutely perfect, but it is not perfected. If it be healthy, it is perfect; yet the perfection that you admire is the potentiality of a grander perfection that lies ahead. There is room for development, growth.

Now, said Jesus to His disciples, "Except ye turn, and become as little children." The character that He demands for entrance to His Kingdom is that of perfect naturalness, that which is impressionable, the character which has in it the elements of trust and confidence, the character which is not yet perfected. Thank God He does not demand absolute and final perfection; but He does demand the perfection of naturalness, impressionability, and confidence; all the things that make it possible for him to command and guide and develop, and ultimately to crown and glorify.

Now, in order that we may return to that with still greater force, let us go one step further. If that be the character demanded, looked at so far as we are able to do so in all simplicity, listen to the condition He imposes upon men: "Except ye turn, and become as little children." In that condition there are two things we need to notice. First, that it suggests the necessity for change; and, secondly, that the suggestion of turning reveals the fact that the nature of the change necessary is going back to first principles, to first ideals, to the simplicity of beginnings.

May I attempt to illustrate by passing over the notes, to which I asked your attention, when considering character? Turn to naturalness, from that which is its opposite, hypocrisy. Turn to absolute truth and simplicity, from the life that attempts to keep up appearances; turn to willingness to appear what you really are. Do you mean to suggest, someone inquires, that men are all hypocrites? I do; and I not only suggest it, but I affirm it. The one outstanding difficulty in the way of men coming into the Kingdom of God is that of hypocrisy. Take the story of the ministry of Jesus as you have it in the New Testament. What do you find? He never said a harsh word to a sinner—that is, such as we would call a sinner, the woman taken in adultery, for instance—but scorn, satire, anger, were always manifest when He dealt with hypocrites. Why? Because hypocrisy hinders a man more than anything else. This audience is in perfect agreement so far. You agree with this whole attitude of Jesus up to a certain point. You know the man who masquerades as religious and lacks religion—how you denounce him; the man who professes to be in the world what he is not—how you despise him. Hypocrisy has fine shades, and there are subtle degrees of it. Here is a man who makes no profession of goodness, yet all the while, in the deepest of him, his heart is crying out after God. That is hypocrisy. There are scores of people listening to preaching who are moved by the messages they hear, who, nevertheless, go back to a godless life. Why? Because for years they have taken up a certain position, and if they confessed that they needed a Saviour and yielded to Him, it would give the lie to the position they have occupied for so long. There are hundreds of church members who need to be born again. Their difficulty lies in the fact that they are church members, that they are hypocrites, that they are naming a name that they do not hallow, praying for the coming of a Kingdom whose coming they hinder, asking for the will of God to be done while they do not permit it to be done in their own lives. From all hypocrisy men must turn and become as children, in simple, artless naturalness, ere they can enter the Kingdom.

Not only from hypocrisy to naturalness, but from hardness to impressionableness. Hardness; the fear of tears; the foolhardy love of false consistency; the rendering of the heart adamant against all appeal and argument. There are those who have so steeled themselves against the message, have so hardened their hearts in the presence of the declarations of truth, that they have become hard. They must turn and become children again; must get back to softness, simplicity, willingness to learn.

Once more; back from rebellion to confidence, from cynicism to trust. With the passing of the years, many have lost faith in God and in man. They are guided in all the doing of their life by doubt. They do business upon the assumption that every man is a rogue until they have proved him honest. They doubt their neighbour, every man; they doubt God;

THE KINGDOM: "OF SUCH IS THE KINGDOM"

they have become cynical. Back, says Christ, to the capacity for belief in something, someone; back to childhood. You laugh at your childhood; you say you have escaped the softness of childhood, the dreamings of youth. That is the tragedy. You have shed no tears for years. There was a time in your childhood when you shed tears, when one morning you found your pet canary dead in its cage. You have not cried recently, though you have left a track of ruined men and women behind you. Back to childhood. In the name of God, this is not a soft word. It is a veritable fire. It scorches me now as I preach. I become tremendously conscious as I stand before you of how little I know of the child heart and spirit.

This King, so sweet, so gentle, so loving, stands at the wicket; and as I would argue about greatness and position and fame in the Kingdom, He says, "Back, you cannot enter until you get back into childhood."

This word of command is an awful word; a word that fills my soul with fear; a word that wrings from me this inquiry, "How can I ever find my way back to childhood?" To this inquiry let us hear the answer. On a housetop in Jerusalem this same King once sat with one man. The man had come to Him, a man of culture and refinement and influence, a man that Jesus could trust because of his honesty and lack of hypocrisy. Sitting together there, as Canon Liddon once suggested, perchance they heard the sighing and moaning of the wind in the streets of Jerusalem. To that inquiring, honest heart the Christ said this strange and mystic thing—He said it to no other man, it was too profound and too wonderful to be commonly spoken—but He said it to this man: "Except a man be born anew, he cannot see the Kingdom of God."

Let us put these two things together. "Except ye turn,

and become as little children, ye shall in no wise enter into the Kingdom of heaven"; "Except a man be born anew, he cannot see the Kingdom of God." The human responsibility is revealed in the word "turn." The Divine activity is indicated in the phrase "born anew," born from above. If the King stands at the wicket-gate with a flaming, fiery sword, keeping back the hypocrite, the hardened man, the cynic, in His hand is the gift of life for that very hardened man, that very cynic, that very unbeliever. Thou mayest be born again—that is, thou mayest become a child. This King will lead thee back to the beginning of things. If thou wilt but turn back toward His ideal, He will turn to thee with dynamic suddenness, and the thing thou desirest shall be thine.

"Except ye turn, and become as little children." I can turn back in strong desire; I can turn back in solemn dedication; I can turn back in obedience; but I shall never become a child again until He touch me Himself, touch me with new life; then, wonder of wonders, He takes away by His transforming touch the heart of stone, and gives me a heart of flesh. Tears spring again, and tenderness permeates all my astonished life. I am willing to be taught and willing to be led; I put the crown upon His brow, and the Kingdom is within me because I have become a child by my repentance, and by the renewing touch of His life upon mine.

When can that be? Now. That Kingdom cometh, in this sense also, not by observation. It will come into observation presently, but it cometh not by observation. That Kingdom comes to the man who comes to the Kingdom. In the moment in which I turn back, and yield myself to His great demand, in that moment by the touch of His life He gives me back my childhood.

There are very many songs sung today which are full of nonsense; but there are some wonderful songs. There is an

THE KINGDOM: "OF SUCH IS THE KINGDOM"

old one comes to my mind now; some of you have sung it, perhaps idly:

> Backward, turn backward, O time, in your flight;
> Make me a child again, just for tonight;
> Mother, come back from the echoless shore,
> Take me again to your heart as of yore;
> Kiss from my forehead the furrows of care,
> Smooth the silver threads out of my hair,
> Over my slumbers your loving watch keep,
> Rock me to sleep, mother, rock me to sleep.

This is not a cry for toys. It is the wail of a weary soul for home, for rest, for God. Is there anything more pathetic in literature and poetry than Tom Hood's song?

> I remember, I remember,
>   The house where I was born,
> The little window where the sun
>   Came peeping in at morn;
> He never came a wink too soon,
>   Nor brought too long a day,
> But now I often wish the night
>   Had borne my breath away.
>
> I remember, I remember,
>   The fir trees dark and high;
> I used to think their slender tops
>   Were close against the sky.
> It was a childish ignorance,
>   But now 'tis little joy
> To know I'm farther off from heaven
>   Than when I was a boy.

Is not that what you are saying in your heart tonight? If so, the King confronts you, and says to you, "Except you come back and become a child, you cannot enter into the Kingdom."

I will take for granted your interest, and that you are saying with Nicodemus, "How can these things be?" The answer of Christ to you is this: "The wind bloweth where it listeth, and thou hearest the voice thereof, but knowest not whence it cometh and whither it goeth; so is everyone that is born of the Spirit." At this moment we are in the midst of everything that is necessary for our remaking. Whether in the church or outside of it, this is the day of Pentecost. Do not talk of Pentecost as though it were a day nineteen centuries ago. Westminster Chapel is as full of the Spirit as was the upper room on that Day of Pentecost. We are in the midst of the river of life. What, then, shall we do? Turn back to the King, yielding to all that He desires and appoints; then He will give to us new hearts and new life—the child nature.

The King said another thing one day, which sounds contradictory, but is not so, "The Kingdom of heaven suffereth violence, and men of violence take it by force." That does not sound like getting back to childhood. Yet it is true that before some of us get back to childhood, we become violent men and women. In what sense? Another word of the King will help us: "If thy right hand offend thee, cut it off; if thy right eye makes thee to stumble, pluck it out." So get back to childhood. I dare not, will not be untrue to the word of the Master, and end as though this were a lullaby. There is a lullaby beyond it. There is the mother-heart, the father-heart beyond it. Infinite peace and spaciousness are beyond it. The moment a man enters into that life, he finds all renewal. All restoration is beyond. But if we would be in this Kingdom, we must get back to childhood, however fierce the struggle be. May God help us to make that struggle for His name's sake.

CHAPTER XXII

THE KINGDOM:
THE OATH OF ALLEGIANCE

Blessed is he that shall eat bread in the Kingdom of God. Whosoever doth not bear his own cross, and come after Me, cannot be My disciple.

LUKE 14:15, 27.

OUR THEME TONIGHT IS THAT OF THE DEMAND WHICH the King makes in respect of His own enterprises upon those who enter the Kingdom. That is the real signification of His words, spoken in answer to one of those who sat at meat with Him in the Pharisee's house.

By bringing these two verses together, I have desired to direct your attention for a moment, by way of introduction, to the matters which precede my text in this chapter. The complete story with which this chapter, and the following two, deal, is full of interest, and to read it quite simply and artlessly, as for the first time, is to discover the growth of the teaching. We, in company with His first disciples, are led on, and ever on, by our Lord in an ever growing understanding of His mission; and in the heart of this whole paragraph to which I have referred, the words occur, "Whosoever doth not bear his own cross, and come after Me, cannot be my disciple."

I am going to crave, and perhaps tax, your patience for a moment while we attempt to see all this narrative which surrounds the text, for by extensive examination we shall come to intensive application. In the fourteenth chapter, we have the story of how Jesus went into the house of one of the rulers of the Pharisees to eat bread, and in that connection the significant declaration is made, that, "they were watching Him." What immediately follows reveals the yet more interesting fact, that while they watched Him, He watched them. Somewhere on the outskirts of the crowd was a man afflicted with dropsy; and the Lord challenged them as to whether it was legal for Him to heal him on the Sabbath; and when they held their peace, He healed the man and let him go. Then He observed how they chose the chief seats, and in a parable rebuked them. According to the law of the Kingdom of God, if a man makes a feast, a dinner or a supper, he will not call his friends, nor his brethren, nor his kinsmen, nor his rich neighbor. Why not? Notice this very carefully, "Lest haply they bid thee again, and a recompense be made thee." I do not know a more caustic piece of satire than that upon the whole business of entertaining even as it obtains today. Do not ask your friends lest they ask you again! That is often the very reason why we do ask them. In that remarkable contrast between the ideal of Jesus, and the habit of our own age, there flashes into view the difference between the self-governed kingdom of the world, and the Kingdom of God. As one of the number listened to Him—and I am never quite sure and I quite frankly say so, whether he was impressed with the beauty of the ideal, or whether he was a cynic and laughed at its impossibility—but whether for that reason or the other, this man said to Him, "Blessed is he that shall eat bread in the Kingdom of God." In other words this man said, that is a counsel of perfection, surely it must be a vision of the Kingdom of God that a man shall be so forgetful of himself as not to invite friends lest they should

THE KINGDOM: THE OATH OF ALLEGIANCE

ask him again, but that instead he shall ask and entertain and show hospitality to men who cannot return it. "Blessed is he that shall eat bread in the Kingdom of God." Whether satirically, or in admiration, he meant to say, "That will be a wonderful social order, blessed is the man that is in that Kingdom, blessed is the man that lives there." Then, catching up his own figure, that of eating bread in the Kingdom, Jesus said to him, "A certain man made a great supper; and he bade many"; and went on to describe how all that were bidden made excuses; not one of them gave a reason, they made excuses. One said he had bought a piece of land and must needs go and see it—and either he was an extremely bad business man, or a very bad dissembler, for no sensible man will buy land until he has seen it. A second man had bought five yoke of oxen and must go and try them—and the same criticism applies to him as to the first. The third man said he had married a wife and therefore he could not come.

All these were excuses! "Blessed is he that shall eat bread in the Kingdom of God," said the man; and Christ replied in effect, Men do not believe that; the supper is made, the invitations have been sent out, but the men invited will not come into the Kingdom, "they all with one consent began to make excuse"; because the bidden guests have refused, the master of the feast is now calling the poor, the maimed, the halt, the blind; and because these do not fill the table, he is sending forth again to constrain all to come in. God is anxious for the coming of His Kingdom because of the blessing its coming brings to men. Man is not anxious for the coming of the Kingdom, he is not prepared to pay the price of the Kingdom.

Then multitudes followed Him, and He turned and said, "If any man cometh unto Me, and hateth not his own father, and mother, and wife, and children, and brethren, and sisters, yea and his own life also, he cannot be My disciple. Whosoever doth not bear his own cross, and come after Me, cannot be My disciple."

"Blessed is he that shall eat bread in the Kingdom of God." Do you really think so? said Christ. Listen, the man that is going to help Me to bring in that Kingdom will have to do so through the process of suffering. The man that follows Me in the building and in the battle which issue in the coming of the Kingdom must be prepared to take up his cross and follow Me. Thus He explained the reason of the severity of His terms, and at the close I read, "Now all the publicans and sinners were drawing near unto Him for to hear Him. And both the Pharisees and the Scribes murmured, saying, This Man receiveth sinners, and eateth with them." He then answered their criticism of His attitude by the threefold parable of the lost silver, the lost sheep, and the lost son.

This is the outline of the great paragraph. If we think of it in its entirety, if we take that extensive outlook, we see at once that the mind of Jesus, throughout the whole process, was occupied with the work He had to do in order to bring the Kingdom in. The man who sat at meat with Him had some gleam of the social order. There came to him some conception of the beneficence of that Kingdom of God in which men should cease to be selfish and should care for their fellow men, and he exclaimed, "Blessed is he that shall eat bread in the Kingdom of God." The mind of Christ was centered upon the ultimate, but it was conscious also of the process that leads to the ultimate; therefore, He sifted the crowds that followed Him in order to find amongst them men and women upon whom He could depend for co-operation in the work that lay before Him. My text, therefore, is Christ's enunciation of the oath of allegiance to be taken by all such as desire, not merely to be in His Kingdom and of

THE KINGDOM: THE OATH OF ALLEGIANCE

His Kingdom, but to be workers with Him for bringing it in, and establishing in the world the order which all men admire and which God desires; but to bring in which, all men are not prepared to suffer and toil.

I am profoundly anxious that before we give a little closer attention to the actual terms of this word of Jesus, we should definitely understand to whom it was spoken, and what it means in broad outline. Jesus Christ was not here laying down the terms upon which men may be saved. He was rather laying down the terms upon which men may become fellow-workers with Himself. We have on more than one occasion in dealing with this passage drawn attention to the fact that the figures which our Lord made use of, those of building a tower, and of conducting a war, are applicable not to the men to whom He spoke, but to Himself. I do not desire to stay with that at any length, only we must understand it. He said to them, "Which of you, desiring to build a tower, doth not first sit down and count the cost . . . or what king, as he goeth to encounter another king in war, will not first sit down and take counsel?" by which He did not mean, if you are coming after Me you had better count the cost, but rather, I am in the world to bring in that Kingdom which you admire; I am here for the building of that city. I must count the cost. I cannot associate with Myself in the work of building, or in the work of battle, any save those who take this oath of allegiance, those who are prepared to take up their cross and follow Me. Christ is the builder. He is the King, and He sifts the rank of the multitudes that admire Him, to find the souls that are willing to suffer with Him, and die with Him, in order to accomplish His purpose.

Accepting that interpretation of the meaning of our Lord, let us observe carefully how in this paragraph our Lord revealed His consciousness of what lay before Him ere that

Kingdom of God could come which the man, sitting at the table with Him, had admired. I think the subject is a very pertinent one and a very immediate one. There are multitudes of men who are still saying, "Blessed is he that shall eat bread in the Kingdom of God." There never were so many men in the world as now, who admire the ideals of Jesus, His ultimate purposes for men, His great teaching concerning the Fatherhood of God and the brotherhood of humanity, His great conceptions for human life manifested in such remarkable words as these, "One is your Master . . . and all ye are brethren." That is but a brief sentence but it is the unveiling of the perfect ideal; one master, and all others brethren. I say men by the thousand today are admiring those ideals. If not in the words of the man who sat at meat with Him, still in spirit with Him, they are saying the social ideal of Jesus is perfect. "Blessed is he that shall eat bread in the Kingdom of God."

"Very well," says Christ, "if you mean it, are you prepared to go with Me along the road that I must travel in order to bring that Kingdom in? Between chaos and cosmos lies the Cross. Between the disorder that you lament, and the order that you admire, there is travail and bloodshedding and suffering. If you are coming with Me the way I am going, to the goal which you admire, you must take up your cross and follow Me."

Thus our contextual examination enables us to see what was Christ's consciousness of all that lay before Him. I turn again to words already referred to in order to discover that consciousness. He said, "Which of you, desiring to build a tower . . . what king, as he goeth to encounter another king in war . . ." "To build a tower"; "to make war upon another king"; these are significant words as revealing Christ's consciousness of what it was necessary for Him to do in order to bring in the Kingdom. All of you who are students of the Bible—not merely of small portions of it, restricted parts, but in the majesty of its sweep and the growth of its revelation—will at once recognize that when Jesus speaks of building a tower there is a remarkable suggestiveness in the illustration. The first occasion upon which we read anything of the building of a tower is in Genesis, in the account of the attempt at Babel. Why did men suggest the building of a tower, according to the Genesis story? I remember a Sunday-school teacher telling me years ago that they attempted to build a tower so high that if another flood came they could climb to the top and be safe! If you go back to the ancient story, you read "Let us make us a name." They said in effect, let us become confederate without God. There existed in their mind the passion of humanity for the solidarity of humanity, and they were trying to realize it, without God. They said, "Let us build a tower which shall be the symbol of our independence and our federation." Exactly the same thing men are still attempting, to confederate, and disarm the nations without putting God in the forefront; and they will never succeed. The passion is a Divine one. It is the method that is wrong. Go on through the Old Testament, and we read of building over and over again; sometimes it is a city, but constantly the passion for building, for construction is manifest; it is all material, and therefore doomed to ultimate failure. I track the movement from the Babel of Genesis to Babylon of Revelation, where I hear the strange and wonderful music, "Fallen, fallen, is Babylon the great." When? When the kingdom of this world has become the Kingdom of our Lord and of His Christ.

Christ came to build, to construct; to create the federation of men. He did not come into this world merely to save individual souls out of it; He did come to do that; but He came also to reconstruct human life, and the human order; and the mission of the King will never be complete, until the city is built, and the anthem rings through heaven and earth, and all the universe, "Behold, the tabernacle of God is with men." Then there will be reconstructed human society, reconstructed national life; no longer kingdoms, but *the Kingdom;* no longer nations, but *the nation;* no longer peoples, but *the people.* Confederacy upon the basis of loyalty to God. Thus Christ took the old figure of the Old Testament, and said, "To build a tower; to realize the aspiration of humanity; to accomplish the purpose of God; to lead broken, battered, bruised peoples into unity about the throne of God and in relationship to the most high; that is My work."

Yes, but if the mission of Christ is building, and that is constructive, the mission of Jesus is therefore that of war, and that is destructive. "To make war against another king." He was in the world to make war against the king who offered Him, in sublime impertinence, all the kingdoms of the world if He would give him one moment's homage; against the one presiding over all the things that hurt and spoil humanity. Let us gain the light of another simple saying of Jesus upon this great subject. "He that is not with Me is against Me; and he that gathereth not with Me scattereth." There are only two forces at work in the moral realm; the force that gathers, and the force that scatters. The prince of the force that scatters is the devil, and the force that scatters is evil, sin. The Prince of the force that gathers is the King of kings; and the force that gathers is the force of love and light and life. Said Jesus, "I am in the world to gather, to build; but in the process, I am in the world to fight, to destroy the works of the devil, to enter into conflict even unto death with all the things that harm and spoil, to enter into the

THE KINGDOM: THE OATH OF ALLEGIANCE

'. . . one death-grapple in the darkness twixt old systems and the Word.' "

This is the mission of Jesus, to build and to fight. Which of you if you had a tower to build would not select with definiteness and precision those who would help you in your building? What king of whom you ever read in the pages of history, deserving that name, if he were about to make war against another king did not count the cost, whether he could meet him who came with twenty thousand, himself only having ten thousand? In other words, said Jesus, "I need men upon whom I can depend. I am not in the world to give the world a spectacle. I am in the world to reconstruct, and I can only reconstruct as I destroy. I am a Builder, but I am a Waster too. I am here to fight in order that I may put an end to war, and lead humanity to God and so to peace." To build, and to battle. The coming of His Kingdom, of which we have spoken, can only be accomplished in this twofold way.

Nineteen centuries have passed away since He uttered these words, and the work is not yet accomplished. Nineteen centuries ago someone wrote the letter to the Hebrews, and in it these words occur, "We see not yet all things subjected to Him." The centuries have run their course, yet here and now I repeat the words of the writer of the letter to the Hebrews: "We see not yet all things subjected to Him." The tower is not built; the city of God is not established. The commonwealth does not perfectly exist; the warfare is not ended. The foes of God are in every land, and every city, and every village. I need only state that, you know it; and if you know anything of the ideal, I think you can say as much as this Pharisee long ago said, "Blessed is he that shall eat bread in the Kingdom of God." Yet that Kingdom is not perfectly come. The war is on; so is the building. The scaffolding is about the building; we have never yet seen all the beauty even of the outline. The enemies are all about the wall; and he who would have any share in the building must work with the sword and the trowel.

If, therefore, we are going to help Him we must take the oath of allegiance, and this is it, "Whosoever would come after Me, must take up his own cross and follow Me." In the days of Rome's greatness the Roman soldier took what was called the Sacramentum, which was an oath of allegiance, and when he did that he promised to obey his commander and not desert his standard. Our King says, "Those who would come after Me along this pathway of building and battle, toward that ultimate Kingdom, must take the Sacramentum, the oath of allegiance." What is it? Not a formula to be repeated. There is not a word sufficiently strong to express it; no vow that man can make can be depended upon in the day of crisis. The oath of allegiance is not a ceremony. Ceremony in itself forever fails, and there is none imposing and solemn enough to carry the meaning of the building and the meaning of the battle. The oath is an act, of which the Cross is the symbol. If the Cross is the symbol, what is the act? The silent, and actual surrender of the whole being to Christ. I do not know how to say this as it ought to be said! The thing I have said is a spacious thing if I did but know how to say it! If I could only utter it in the true tone, and with the right emphasis; if it could only ring as it ought to ring like a clarion call through this assembly, arresting us, startling us, there might be some hope. If I am to help to bring in the Kingdom of God, I must go after Him to building and to battle; but in order to do it I must take up my cross.

By the shores of the Galilean lake after His resurrection, He talked to Peter, and the last thing He said to him in the

THE KINGDOM: THE OATH OF ALLEGIANCE

wonderful process of restoration from wandering to service, was this, "When thou wast young thou girdedst thyself, and walkedst whither thou wouldest; but when thou shalt be old, thou shalt stretch forth thy hands, and another shall gird thee, and carry thee whither thou wouldest not. . . . Follow Me." John adds in parenthesis, "This He spake, signifying by what manner of death he should glorify God." Yes, but He also spoke of the principle upon which Peter should live and serve. In that word of Jesus there is the most remarkable unveiling of the meaning of taking up the cross. "When thou wast young, thou girdedst thyself, and walkedst whither thou wouldest." So long as I am doing that, I cannot help Him to build and to fight. Soul of mine, art thou girding thyself and walking whither thou wouldest; is the underlying reason even of thy preaching the pleasing of thyself? Then thy preaching never helps Him to build or to fight. You may be very popular with your friends, but you cannot help Christ to build. But, when you stretch out your hands and let Him gird you, and let Him command you; when you will take that life of yours with all its powers and possibilities, and all its resources, and sincerely hand it over to Him; when you will take up your cross; then you will help Him to build, and you will help Him to fight; your blow will tell on the strongholds of evil, and the influence of your life will hasten the coming of the day of God.

"Blessed is he that shall eat bread in the Kingdom of God." We all come as far as that. I think the whole audience comes as far as that. I do not believe there is a man or woman or child in this house who has seen anything of the vision of the Kingdom of God as revealed in Jesus, but would say, blessed is the man who lives there. Jesus saw the great multitudes; He sees them now; He holds us for the moment; let Him speak. Oh, that I could be silent and be hidden, and

Christ only heard and seen! The pierced hands seem to me to be sifting amongst us tonight, beginning here in the pulpit. He is after men and women who will help Him to fight. Am I prepared? If any man will come after Me toward that Kingdom, he must come My way. If any man will help Me in the building and the battle, he must take up his own cross. That is the Sacramentum. Are we prepared to take the oath of allegiance? Presently, many of us will gather about the table which we call the sacrament; and in that sense it is well so named. Any man who sits at that table and takes that bread and fruit of the vine, who does not at the same time deny himself and realize his responsibility to the world and to Christ, is a traitor as he partakes. "This is My body broken, My blood shed, for you." Let a man examine himself, and eat. This is the sacramentum and the symbol of it. Not that the taking of the bread and wine is sufficient; but it is the outward and visible sign of the inward and invisible attitude. There may be men and women here who have never yet enlisted under the banner of Christ, who have never yet begun to follow Him even for their own soul's salvation; let such begin to follow Him tonight for His sake, for the sake of the world, for the sake of His battle and His building; and if you will do so, I invite you to this table. Tonight there is no after-meeting, no inquiry room where we can speak together; none is necessary. Sit at this table, as one who says, "Tonight I will take up my cross and follow Him." By such act you take the oath of allegiance. God grant that the King may tonight find some men and women for His building and His battle.

CHAPTER XXIII

THE KINGDOM: TRAITORS

Men shall be . . . traitors . . . from these also turn away.

2 TIMOTHY 3:2, 4, 5.

WE HAVE IN THIS LETTER IN ALL PROBABILITY, THE LAST words of the great apostle. It is very largely a personal letter. One illustration of that will be discovered in the fact that there are twenty-three proper names found in its four brief chapters. It is the letter of an old man to a young man. It is a letter of an old minister of Jesus Christ to a young man commencing his work in the ministry of the Word. It is the letter of one who has borne the burden and heat of the day to one who stands facing the battle. It is the letter of one who has been careful to lay the foundations, and who charges men to beware how they build thereupon, to a man who is to continue to build. It is impossible to read this letter naturally, as a letter—that is, at one sitting, forgetting those false divisions of chapters and verses—without becoming conscious that the heart of the writer is full of conflicting emotions; full of sorrow, and yet full of joy; full of anxiety, and yet full of courage. He is perfectly conscious, as the time of his departure approaches, of the dangers that lie ahead. The peculiar message committed to him has been the doctrine of the Church; but he has never forgotten the Kingdom. Whereas it has been his work in the course of his constructive and educative ministry among the churches, to declare the truth concerning the Church of God; the passion in his heart has ever burned with vehemence for the coming of the Kingdom of God.

All about him are evidences of the foes, the forces that are against Christ and the Gospel of Christ. In his own personal experience he is conscious of the forsaking of friends. He bears in his body the scars, the stigmata that tell of his own buffeting. He sees ahead of the Church and of the enterprises of the Kingdom of God in the world, great and grave perils; and all these things make him anxious about Timothy, this young man—so dear to his heart, his own child in the faith, the fruit of his own preaching—as he recognizes that the ministry which awaits him will in many particulars be a more difficult one than his own has been. His letter, therefore, is a letter of warning. He says that in the last days perilous times—or, as the Revised Version has it, "grievous times," or as I venture to suggest even more literally, "difficult times"—shall come. Then follows a dark catalogue of evil things. I think I may be allowed to say that a hush of awe, of fear, fell upon this congregation as I read them tonight; one was conscious of it in the very reading—"Men shall be lovers of self, lovers of money, boastful, haughty, railers, disobedient to parents, unthankful, unholy, without natural affection, implacable, slanderers, without self-control, fierce, no lovers of good, traitors, headstrong, puffed up, lovers of pleasure rather than lovers of God; holding a form of godliness, but having denied the power thereof."

The one word that I have chosen from the dark and awful list is the word "Traitors." I take it because it suggests peril to the Kingdom. I have already said that this man was specifically, as far as doctrine is concerned, the apostle of the Church. I have also said that there ever burned in his heart the passion for the Kingdom. This man, looking ahead, saw perilous days, days in which evil men would become increasingly evil; days in which evil men and impostors shall "wax worse and worse." This does not mean that the world is to wax worse and worse, but that evil in itself will be worse and worse, as good will be better and better. The two elements are noticeable in their development in all the centuries, and in the day in which we live. Good is better than it ever was. Evil is worse than it ever was. The wheat and tares will grow together until the harvest, the full development of both good and evil; and then will come God's crisis and God's settlement.

Paul saw the development of evil things, and as he described the conditions of evil, one word passed his lips which reveals the truth of the thing I have already affirmed, that the passion for the Kingdom was still burning in his heart, "traitors." This is peculiarly a word of Kingdom relationship, a word indicating a peril threatening the work of the Kingdom.

This is the last in our series of meditations on the Kingdom. We spoke first of the King, the One upon Whose vesture and upon Whose thigh the great name is written, "King of kings, and Lord of lords"; of the Kingly character, the Kingly qualifications, and the Kingly authority of God's anointed King. In our second study we spoke of the Kingdom over which He is assuredly King, even though at the moment there may be rebellion therein; He is King in the material, mental, moral realms; and all because fundamentally, essentially, He is King in the spiritual realm.

We spoke next of the character of all such as are in His Kingdom; we heard the King standing at the wicket gate, saying, "Except ye turn, and become as little children, ye shall in no wise enter into the Kingdom of heaven." And then we listened to the King, speaking to men in the Kingdom, indicating to them what must be their sacramentum, or oath of allegiance, if they would be His helpers in building and in battle, "Whosoever doth not bear his own cross, and come after Me, cannot be My disciple."

I ask you tonight to think with me of the peril to the Kingdom, indicated in the words, "men shall be . . . traitors." In advance of our consideration let me say what I shall repeat at the close; that this is the gravest peril that threatens the Kingdom of God. The word indicates an appalling kind of resistance; that which postpones the Kingdom most successfully. "Men shall be . . . traitors." These are not the men outside, arrayed in battle against the King; but the men and women inside, who are untrue to the King.

"Men shall be . . . traitors." First, let us solemnly ask ourselves what does this word suggest to us. What is treachery? Let us, secondly, notice the concomitants of treachery; the companionships of treachery, which the apostle describes in these very words that surround the one word of my text. Thirdly, let us attempt to see the root of treachery as the apostle here in passing, and yet, quite clearly, indicates it for us. Then let us consider the punishment of treachery. Finally, let us take our way into the secret place and ask the King to show us whether we are traitors.

What is treachery? The word here translated "traitors" occurs only three times in the New Testament; in this passage, once in the Gospel of Luke, where Luke, giving the list of the men who were about Jesus in the days of His public ministry, writes this very remarkable and appalling word, "Judas the traitor"; and once in the Acts of the Apostles in that magnificent address of Stephen, when charging the men to whom he spoke with sin, he described them as betrayers, using exactly the same word. These are the only occasions

THE KINGDOM: TRAITORS

where the awe-inspiring word is to be found in the pages of the New Testament. It is a somewhat interesting thing to discover the simple, root intention of the word. A traitor is one who goes before. That, of course, does not express its full significance. We must find, not only the root meaning, but the common use of the word if we are to understand it. There seems to be no suggestion of evil in the word if we simply take its root intention; but when we observe its use, we find that it was always used in this sense; a traitor is one who goes before the enemy, one who leads the enemy, one who surrenders a position before the enemy can capture it. The traitor is one who unlocks the gate of a city and lets the enemy in; one who gives away a secret of the State, and so leaves the State at the mercy of its foes. Thus the use of the word is always an evil use, or rather, a use that always suggests an evil attitude and action; a traitor is one who surrenders a position to the enemy.

In its bearing upon the Christian fact, and in its relation to the great business of Jesus, that of bringing in the Kingdom of God, which He made the very inspiration of prayer when He taught us to pray, "Thy Kingdom come," and which He indicated as the master passion of life when He said to men, "Seek ye first His Kingdom"; this word describes one who names the name of Christ, but does not share His nature; one who recites the creed of the Church, but does not manifest the conduct of saintship; one who may be, and in all probability is, absolutely orthodox in doctrine intellectually, and absolutely heterodox in attitude volitionally; one who wears the livery of the Kingdom, but is disobedient to its government; one who hiding among the soldiers of the King becomes the vantage ground for the enemy; and, therefore, one upon whom the enemy can most perfectly depend, because he has a false position within; one, therefore, upon whom the King can not only not depend, but one who postpones, hinders, paralyzes the effort of the King most successfully, that effort that moves toward the bringing in of the Kingdom. The traitor is one who breaks the oath of allegiance, who takes the sacramentum in words, but not in deeds.

Said Jesus at Caesarea Philippi, immediately after telling His disciples that He would build His Church, and that He would give to His Church the keys of the Kingdom—mark the intimate relation of Church and Kingdom—"If any man would come after Me, let him deny himself, and take up his cross, and follow Me." The traitor is one within the company of those who are supposed to be obedient; but who reverses the whole process; denies the Cross, asserts himself, and refuses to follow Christ.

You say to me, that that is what the man outside is doing. But mark well the difference. The man inside sings of the Cross and refuses to be crucified; professes to be abandoned to Jesus, and asserts his own will, and his own self-life; lives a life self-centered, and sings a song as though he were God-centered. Traitors are men and women who are in league with the enemy, while to all human appearances they are marching with the soldiers of the King. I need not tarry now to survey human history so far as it has been written, to show how humanity in its deepest instinct hates the traitor. I suppose I am correct in saying that there are names in the history of almost all nations, not very many, but some, that are held in everlasting contempt. We forevermore hold in respect—I am now speaking along the line of broad human illustration—the foes of our national life who have fought us fairly, and whether we won or they matters little as the years go on. On the other hand, we hold in everlasting contempt the men in our ranks who gave away some secret to the enemy. There is no graver, greater peril to the Kingdom of God than that created by traitors in the camp. What then is a traitor? One who tolerates the evil against which the King is making battle; one who hinders the King in His building, refuses to help Him in the building, or pulls down what Jesus builds. He said, I came to build. His mission is destructive. The men within the ranks, those supposed to follow Him who never help in the building, the men who tolerate in their own lives and hearts the evil against which the King is fighting, these are traitors. The men who never help in the building—and I do not propose to speak of the men who attempt to pull down that which Christ is building, I content myself with the other statement, the men who do not help.

There is the great ideal of the Kingdom flaming like a vision before us, the great Kingdom of God for which He taught us to pray, for which we do perpetually pray with more or less intelligence, the one great Kingdom in which one law shall govern all human life, the law of perfect love: "Thou shalt love the Lord thy God with all thy heart, and with all thy soul, and with all thy mind, and with all thy strength. . . . Thou shalt love thy neighbour as thyself." There is the ideal—call it what you will, call it Utopia, speak of it as though it were a dream that can never be translated into actuality, I care not. Christ came to realize that dream. He came to build. Here are men and women who name His name and make His sign, and sing His songs, but they are doing no building; men and women who have never lifted a hand to hasten the coming of the Kingdom in the world. Their very neutrality—I am not yet touching the deepest note of treachery—hinders and postpones the coming of the Kingdom. You remember that fine, majestic Hebrew song, the song of Deborah, in which she let loose the splendid scorn of her angry womanhood: "Curse ye Meroz, said the angel of the Lord, Curse ye bitterly the inhabitants thereof." Why? Because they fought against the Lord? No! But "because they came not to the help of the Lord against the mighty." Read the whole song at your leisure. It is a song of infinite sarcasm, of satire—hear me very carefully for there is a very pertinent application of all this to our own age—satire poured upon those sitting by the watercourses of Reuben discussing the situation with great searchings of heart! Conventions, conferences, discussions, resolutions, but no building, nothing done! That is treachery of the worst kind; and every sanctified Deborah will sing her song of satire in the presence of it.

Or, will you come from the stately and almost tragic splendour of the song of Deborah, and listen to the quieter, calmer, more intensive word of Jesus, "He that is not with Me is against Me, and he that gathereth not with Me scattereth"? Mark Christ's implied claim for Himself, He is a Gatherer; to gather in the children of God who were scattered abroad, to heal the breaches, to bring humanity back into a common brotherhood around the Fatherhood of God; to end the strife of nations and of men by restoring them to the beneficence of the Divine government; to gather together; that was His mission. In view of that He said, "He that is not with Me is against Me," and if we are not helping Him to gather we are scattering. If we wear His livery and do not help Him in the building, we are traitors.

There is another form of treachery. He came not merely for building—that ultimately, finally, for that is the purpose and passion of His mission—He came also for battle. No word of inspired Scripture tells the whole truth with more graphic phrasing than this, "He was manifested to destroy the works of the devil." Am I helping Him in that battle? There are things that no preacher can say. There are searchings of heart that cannot find expression in the voice of a man. Am I tolerating—let me speak of myself and of no other—in my inner heart and life, in my thinking, in my living, something against which the King's face is set, against which He makes war; something of impurity, of unloveliness, something of greed? Then am I a traitor! I may sing all the songs of the sanctuary and recite all its creeds, and believe all its doctrines; and yet, if in some chamber of Mansoul, whether it be the chamber of the imagination, or the hall of the affection, or the palace of the intellect, I find house-room and hiding for some evil thing; I am a traitor. Such evil work is always done for a price—for thirty pieces of silver; and often for far less!

Traitors; not the man outside, the roué on Piccadilly; not the poor, sinning thief that we ought to rescue; but the man inside, who listens to the word Sunday after Sunday, and nought that it says touches him or makes him disgorge his ill-gotten gain, or cleanses his heart of lust. That man is a traitor. That man postpones the coming of the Kingdom, as all the forces of hell massed outside the Church can never do.

Look for a moment, now, at the things which surround treachery, the awful companions of treachery. The first two phrases describe the character of such; self-lovers; money-lovers; and immediately following there is a three-fold description of the conduct that grows out of that character, "boastful, haughty, railers." Once more Paul describes character, "unfilial, unthankful, unholy," and immediately again the conduct that issues from that character, "unloving, implacable, slanderers." A third time he deals with character, "uncontrolled, fierce, no lovers of good," and a third time describes the conduct resulting, "traitors, headstrong, puffed up."

Or take the list in another way. First we have the personal manifestations of godlessness; "self-lovers, money-lovers, unfilial, unthankful, unholy, uncontrolled, fierce, no lovers of good"; and then the social manifestations of godlessness, "boastful, haughty, railers, unloving, implacable, slanderers, traitors, headstrong, puffed up."

Then at last he touches the deep, underlying root, the very wellspring out of which the streams flow, "Lovers of pleasure rather than lovers of God; holding a form of godliness, but having denied the power thereof." Personal character is ruined, the social virtues are destroyed, because religion is dead. The form of godliness is ritual without religion; and this results in all the things that are unlike the Kingdom.

Now let us inquire, what harm traitors can do to the great Kingdom of which we have been speaking. First of all let me say this; our treachery cannot dethrone the King. It is well that we be reminded of that. What visions of God we have in this great and wonderful literature! Among them all one now comes back to me, that in the Book of Isaiah. Isaiah had never known another king than Uzziah. There came a day when Uzziah died, and Isaiah saw the empty throne and felt the sense of desolation. Then he came to the realization of the one great Throne, "In the year that king Uzziah died I saw the Lord sitting upon a throne, high and lifted up, and His train filled the temple." The empty throne; and the Throne that is never empty! So let us remember, in the midst of this solemn evening consideration, that our treachery cannot dethrone the King; but our treachery can postpone the Kingdom. As God is my witness, I speak to my own heart as well as to yours. The Kingdom of God can be hindered by treachery. Here is the heinousness of treachery; here is the diabolical nature of wearing the livery of the King while playing false to His purpose; we postpone the Kingdom. The sob and cry of creation is a sob and cry for a King.

THE KINGDOM: TRAITORS

The measure in which I am playing traitor is the measure in which the agony of creation continues; or to put it from the positive side, the measure in which I am loyal to the King is the measure in which He is brought nigh to the suffering creation. I cannot dethrone the King, I cannot finally prevent the winning of His victory; but I can make the road longer and rougher for God and for humanity by my treachery.

Once again, what is the punishment of treachery? Suicide, spiritual suicide! Stephen charged the Hebrew people with treachery. He was speaking to the people of the covenant, to the children of promise, and in his great address, he revealed to them their privileges, tracked the way of God's dealings with them through the centuries, until he came to the Deliverer Whom he described as "My righteous One"; and he said, "You murdered Him." But that was not the first thing; the first charge was, "You betrayed Him," and the word is identical in meaning with the word "traitor." You are murderers: but before that, and this is the deeper matter, you are traitors. Though Roman hands drove the nails, Hebrew inspiration moved the Roman hands to the deed. Roman hands were the hands of lawless men, men who were without the law; but you were men who had the law, and had light, and had the covenant and the word of revelation. You were traitors. You named the name of Jehovah, and when the ultimate Messenger of Jehovah came, you were betrayers, murderers. With what result? By that act the Hebrew nation as a nation committed suicide. I find the selfsame fact of suicide in the case of Judas. How did it all end? You know the tragic story. Thirty pieces of silver! Have you ever noticed the solemn fact that he never spent one of them? He carried them back and flung them at the feet of the men from whom he had received them. There is no purchasing power in the price of disloyalty. What then? By his own act he ended his life. This is a principle of perpetual application. It is not merely the story of the Bible; you may read it in all history. I go back to the history of Rome. You have read "The Decline and Fall of the Roman Empire." Have you ever pondered the spiritual and moral teaching of it? Have you ever discovered the fact that the nation that disobeys law dies by its own hand? All the King's enemies are their own executioners. By the act of my treachery, I strangle my own life. I go down into the darkness which I myself have made. By the act of disloyalty to the King I erect the scaffold for my own destruction.

Our final word is, "Behold the King!" Here once again I see the great ideal. Lift your eyes and behold the city of God, not yet built, the work not yet completed. Then know this, that the men and women inside the Church who name His name and do not help Him build, who tolerate the things against which He is at war; these are the men who postpone the Kingdom. Consequently, my brethren, the thing I have to say to my heart and to yours is this, in the name of God and for the sake of the world; quit the form of religion, or cease to deny its power. Infinitely better to have done with the singing of the song, and the reciting of the creed, and the profession of faith if the life is not in harmony therewith.

My last word is to the man who says, "I have played the fool. I have been a traitor, is there hope for me?" Back to the Cross. The Cross was the outcome of treachery, and is the only remedy for you. Share its deep significance and abandon yourself to its death. If I will but go back to that Cross and take anew the oath of allegiance, by handing myself over entirely; then with infinite pity and in that meek mercy that lies at the heart of His majesty, the King will forgive me, and take me back again, and allow me to build with Him and battle with Him. Oh, Simon Peter, thou didst curse and swear that thou didst not know Him, by the flickering light of the fire His enemies had built; but by the Galilean lake in the dawn of the morning, with the flush of hope upon the sky, He will take thee back and give thee all thy work. Oh, the comfort of it!

> The King of love my Shepherd is
> Whose goodness faileth never.

Even though I have been a traitor He will take me back. Let us gather about His feet, and from this day be true to Him, and so hasten the Kingdom.

CHAPTER XXIV

"IN THE BEGINNING GOD"

In the beginning God . . . .

GENESIS 1:1.

I AM QUITE CONSCIOUS THAT THE TEXT IS NOT A COMPLETE statement. It does not give us the full affirmation of the writer, but it reveals his assumption; and the affirmation is valueless apart from this assumption. To the affirmation itself, I do not propose to give anything more than passing reference by way of illustration of the larger subject suggested by and included in the assumption, "In the beginning God."

That phrase takes us beyond the seen to the unseen, behind the sensual to the spiritual, beneath the passing to the permanent, before the temporal to the eternal.

If then, I am charged with mutilating a text, I shall reply that the murder of the letter is in this case deliberate in order to the liberation of the spirit.

Let us consider the general spirit or atmosphere into which we are brought by these words. They constitute, first, the recognition of a starting-point. The phrase may have reference to matters of time or of place, to the subject of order or of rank. If you think of time, "In the beginning." If you think of place, "In the beginning." If you think of order, consecutive and regular movement, and progress, "In the beginning." If you think of rank, dignity, position, precedence,

"IN THE BEGINNING GOD"

"In the beginning." This recognition of a starting-point is in perfect and absolute harmony with science.

The phrase is also the recognition of a cause; and the cause is written for us here in that old Teutonic form which defies the attempt of philologists to place it or explain it, "God." On the page of the Hebrew Bible the word is Elohim, the plural form of El. The word stands essentially and simply for might. There are three numbers in the Hebrew—singular, dual, and plural; and the plural is constantly made use of to indicate intensity. When some thought possessing the mind of a writer could not be expressed for very greatness by the singular number, he would employ the plural.

That in this connection is the suggestiveness of the word Elohim. It is used here not to define nature, or to unveil character; not even to solve the mystery of personality; it is used rather to indicate the recognition of a cause at the beginning of time, place, order, or rank. The phrase thus recognizes a Being separate from everything hereafter to be described, and yet sufficient for everything hereafter to be described.

If the recognition of a starting-point indicated by the words "In the beginning" is in perfect harmony with science, the recognition of a separate, sufficient cause transcends the demonstration of science. Science has never yet found its way to the honest possibility of making the declaration with which this Book of Genesis opens. Science has at times been compelled to say there must be a first cause: but there is a very distinct difference between that affirmation and this "In the beginning God created." The one is the admission of an apparent though not demonstrated necessity on the part of men of sincere investigation; but the other is the quiet, dignified affirmation of a Person and a fact. Thus the Divine Library in its present arrangement opens with a phrase which is a voice from without, speaking to the deeps within, and its message when perfectly and earnestly considered is found to be in harmony with everything around.

Here is no apology for God, no argument for God, no defence of God, but the opening affirmation, which for the moment may be received as an affirmation and not necessarily believed; then, as we take our way through page after page, and book after book, of the library, it will be for us to say, when that work is completed, whether the revelation of the library, the revelation of the facts and forces within and around us, harmonizes with the great opening assumption of the Book, "In the beginning God."

It is not my purpose this evening to defend the accuracy of this assumption. I accept it as true, and, proceeding from that standpoint, submit that it is axiomatic, that courses and consummations must be related to causes. If I can find a beginning, then that which begins must inevitably in all its course and in its consummation bear some relation to that which was its cause. The deduction in the present case is self-evident. If this opening affirmation of the Word of God be true concerning creation, concerning the Library itself, concerning man, that the first originating cause is God, then there surely can be no escape from the fact that all the course of creation, all the course of the Divine Library, all the course of man, that crowning fact and wonder of Creation, must inevitably be in some form or fashion, in some way or other related to the original cause; and that the consummation of creation, of the Divine Library, and of man must also be related to that originating cause, God.

Thus we are confronted in this first verse in the first book in the Divine Library with a fundamental truth that has its bearing on all life, "In the beginning God." At the back of all the forces in the midst of which we live, forces blossoming in beauty, moving in rhythmic order, even startling us by their differentiations and changes and new manifestations and developments; at the back of everything is God. Therefore, all these forces, in their movements and in their working, and in what they produce, are related to God, and are moving toward a consummation which must in some way be related to Him.

Let us then attempt to give ourselves first to some considerations, and finally to some applications.

Let us consider our phrase in its relation to the actual affirmation of the writer, "In the beginning God created the heaven and the earth." Let me quietly, earnestly, and solemnly warn my young friends especially that in the study of the Bible we need to disabuse our minds of all human interpretations, ever remembering that not what the Fathers thought, or the schoolmen taught, or the theologians held, is necessarily true; but what the Word itself declares. The first fact declared concerning the creation is that the potential stuff—call it matter, if you will—is God-created. For the moment we are not considering the process by which the work was done, nor the processes which followed that initial act of God, through which the thing first made has come to be the things we now know and touch. The fundamental declaration, that with which I am now dealing, is that "In the beginning God created."

What is your particular theory of the origin of the things in the midst of which you live? Do you believe still that this universe came into being suddenly; that God, by some sudden, immediate act, made everything as you find it? I dismiss that as being utterly out of harmony with the first chapter of Genesis. Or, do you say, I have been compelled to the acceptation of what is known as the evolutionary theory? Then remember that the evolutionary theory postulates perpetual beginnings. What is its last product? Its last product is something self-evident. Whence came it? It is the product of something lower. Whence came that? From something lower still. Whence came that? From something still lower. In each case there was a new beginning; call it differentiation if you will. It was a new start, a fresh development, a coming of the new out of the old. Trace this process back and back, and where will you end? Thirty years ago the scientist would have told you, in the primordial protoplasmic germ. The scientist now says nothing of the kind; he whispers electrons, and then speaks of a psychological fact beyond. The scientist, with honest integrity and splendid heroism tracking his way back, finds ever a beginning proceeding out of something which also has a beginning, until at last he arrives where there is no place on which to step off; his last word has been said, and, beyond, the scientist of today tells us he hears whispers, thunders of mind, and is conscious of psychological mysteries. In that strange, magnificent gap my text stands, and out of it comes the word "In the beginning God." Let that be granted, and that which I have already declared to be axiomatic follows. All the developments, all the processes are related to that first cause from which everything sprang. All that which science has discovered is the method of God. Between the first and second verses of this chapter there is a great gap, so great that we cannot bridge it, a mystery so dark that we cannot explain it. "The earth was waste and void, and darkness was upon the face of the deep." That is not how God made it. That is not the suggestion of the first verse. The suggestion of the first verse is that of perfection, harmony, a cosmic order. What happened between the first and second verses? I do not know. There is no solution anywhere in the Word of God; but God did not create a waste.

La Place's theory of nebulae is exploded. He declared

that everything might be explained as proceeding out of nebulae; but when Rosse turned his reflector upon those cloudy masses, which even Herschel had described as nebulae, and had scientifically declared as impossible of resolution into order, they were seen to be perfected systems of stars. The first verse of the Bible declares that God did originally create, and from the third verse to the end of the chapter we have the account, not of original creation, but of the restoration of a lost order, the bringing of cosmos out of chaos. How the chaos happened none can tell, for the Bible has no whisper of the secret, and science has as yet not attempted an explanation, perhaps because it has not recognized the fact. Yet the marvel of scientific investigation is that it is going behind that chaos of the second verse, and is discovering the footprints of God in that earliest method of creation, in fossil remains which must have been lying hidden for millenniums. The testimony which it bears is that all the way, through all evolutions or devolutions, through all developments or progress, God Who started has accompanied. Paul, speaking of the Son of God in that marvelous Colossian passage, says not only is it true that by Him were all things created, but also that in Him all things consist, are cohesive, hold together and march forward in rank and order and rhythm toward the ultimate consummation.

If this great assumption be accepted as to the cause of creation, then the consummation is assured as being a consummation related to the God of creation and according to the purpose of the God of creation. I am not now speaking of man, but of creation itself. This Bible is not the Bible of creation; it is the Bible of redemption, and the story that we often speak of as the story of creation is in reality the story of the starting of redemption—that is, of reconstruction. The gospel flames upon the first page of the Bible, not perhaps in the terms in which we know it, the terms of our human salvation, but in terms that reveal the heart of God. That is the thought of the second verse, "The Spirit of God moved upon the face of the waters" for reconstruction, not for first creation; for renewal, not for origination. This is the gospel fact revealed to those who have eyes to see. That which he created, being ruined in some dark mystery unrevealed, He will make again a second time. Even though in this process of second making there shall come a catastrophe somehow growing out of the first, yet He will move forward toward the establishment of a new order, "Behold, I make all things new. . . . I am the Alpha and the Omega, the beginning and the end." So that from the first page to the last the consummation is set in relation to the first cause; and if that first cause be God, the courses are under His command, and the consummation must harmonize with His will.

For second illustration, which of course must be dealt with in the briefest way, let us take the divine Library.

What is the story of the Bible? The cause is again the same: "In the beginning God"; holy men of old spoke, as they were moved by God.

The course of the Bible is that of the chronicling of actual events and spiritual interpretation of their meanings. As to the story of their writing I use three words—selection, advancement, incompleteness. That is true from Genesis to Revelation. The Bible is perfectly complete in its revelation of all that man needs to know; but there are things about which the Bible never says the final word; it never finally explains the mystery of the Divine Being, it never attempts the solution of the problem of evil in the universe, it never explains the part that pain is playing in the economy of God. Then it is the result of a method of selection. There has been a great dispute about the first chapter of Genesis, as to who

"IN THE BEGINNING GOD"

wrote it, and how he knew what he wrote. Hugh Miller suggested, as you remember, that visions were granted to Moses or some other, in the same way as the visions in the Book of Revelation were granted to John. I should describe that as a pious hypothesis having no foundation in fact. It has been said that it is now established beyond a doubt that the man who wrote this, whether Moses or not, owed very much to Chaldean inscriptions, and we are perfectly certain that there is an element of truth in that declaration. Today we are in possession of Chaldean inscriptions in the reading of which things stated in the Book of Genesis are to be found, but it is interesting to note in passing that in no inscription yet found has the first assumption of this Book been discovered, "In the beginning God." What shall I say, then, when I am told that some of these things are found in Chaldean inscriptions, believing as I do that Moses wrote this book? I remember Moses' relation to Abraham, and I remember that Abraham came from Chaldea, and I have no doubt that he brought with him legends, traditions from Chaldea, which legends and traditions contained elements of truth, and Moses' account is the result of selection from the mass of material. The process was that of God revealing to this man the element of truth in the midst of the darkness in which he found himself. The true missionary ever comes, not to destroy but to fulfill, to find the gleam of light without which God has never yet left a people, to destroy the accretions, the things of evil that contradict the essential light. The Bible is the result of that Divine presidency over human thought through which there has been the separation of the true from the false. In poetic statement we have the account of that process by which the chaos became the cosmos. There was reconstruction, and as I read that first page, and watch the process described, I see also the process by which man wrote the story; it was accomplished by the presidency of the Divine mind over his mind, leading him to the selection of the thing that is true from the mass of false; and the result was that he wrote in such a fashion that while millenniums have passed he who considers the story in the light of advanced science finds how absolutely accurate it is. This element of growth and development runs through the processes.

The consummation of the Bible is found in the One to Whom the Bible leads, in the central Person Who is not merely the One Who speaks the Word, but the Word of God, the expression of God, pronouncing in human history the final, inclusive truth. The Bible leads at last to the Spirit Who interprets that Word. Jesus Himself declared that the letter killeth, but the Spirit giveth life.

Our final illustration of the things suggested by this phrase is that of man; and now we may leave behind us those dim distances full of light and glory, and think within the sphere of our own personality. What is the truth about man. "In the beginning God." Every man is the creation of God. In that fact the race is unified, in spite of all its apparent division. There is nothing in all Scripture more remarkable than what may be termed an incidental word in the letter to the Hebrews, in which the writer says: "We had the fathers of our flesh to chasten us, and we gave them reverence: shall we not much rather be in subjection unto the Father of spirits, and live?" It is incidental, but it is a word flaming with light showing that every individual man is related to God in his first creation, that the spirit-life of a man, which is his essential life, is not the creation of his father after the flesh, but the creation of God, the Father of the Spirit. In that spiritual fact, I repeat, lies the unity of the race, not the uniformity of the body, for we are differently formed and fashioned, not in the unanimity of the mind, for our mental outlook and temperament varies infinitely and gloriously; but in the unity of the spirit the race is united. Black and white, high and low, these are the incidental differences of the physical, and sometimes of the mental, but beneath the whole of them, unifying into the magnificent solidarity of the human race, is the spiritual nature which every man receives individually as the creation and gift of God. So that the essential truth concerning every man is, "In the beginning God." In a great and wonderful mystery, with which I cannot attempt to deal in this presence or time, God has linked Himself to the human race, so that in the creation of individuals He is forevermore in fellowship with man, even though man may have fallen and have sinned. The essential, central fact in the life of every individual is this, "In the beginning God."

If that be the true cause of every individual life, I pray you remember the course of every individual life is held in relationship to that cause. All the course is under His government. How often shall that be stated? How often shall I declare that which has become a great conviction to my soul? No man ever escapes for any five minutes of his earthly career from the government of God. A man may be in rebellion against that government, but he lives in the grip of it. By the laws of God each man is made or marred; which, depends upon his attitude toward those laws. It is impossible for humanity to separate itself from God. Take the lowest method of illustration; I breathe His air; I trample upon His earth; I derive the sustenance of the physical from the forces which have emanated from Deity; I employ mental powers which are the reflex of His own infinite knowledge; all my aspirations spring out of my spiritual being. I may degrade them, prostitute them, but they are all things which I am, and have, from God, and I cannot ultimately escape the touch of the government and law of God, the rule of God in my life.

All the course of every human life is related to the originating cause of every human life.

The consummation of every human life must therefore inevitably be related to the originating cause. No man can escape God here or hereafter. I am not now dealing with the experience of the man. Let me only say the experience of relationship may be blessing or blasting, according to whether our yielding to Him is the yielding of sane, spiritual loyalty, or our rebellion against Him is that of insane, carnal disloyalty. But escape Him we cannot; not for this evening, not for the hour in which we sin, not for the time in which we have tried to forget Him that we may indulge the passions of the flesh; never! The touch of God is on our spirits, and the hand of God is holding us even at such times. Never can I escape the originating cause, present in the course, and there in the consummation.

Already I have merged from consideration to application. Let me close by the enforcement of one or two matters. What is our relation to God as Cause? That is a fact, and there is no escape. I am His stuff. I take the old Hebrew figure of the clay in the hand of the potter; I am the potter's clay. The Hebrew figure breaks down, for no potter manipulating clay originated the clay; but this great Potter originated this clay, this stuff of my substance. The figure is a very beautiful one. Remember, the potter can never make a vessel either for use or ornament out of steel filings; he must have clay. Man is the very stuff God wants in order to accomplish His work. God is the originating Cause; man is His stuff, His design, His workmanship. These are the things from which I cannot escape. I live and move and have my being in Him, whether I will or not; the beating of my heart, the throbbing of my nerves, all these things are of Him.

"IN THE BEGINNING GOD"

If the fact of the originating Cause is settled, what shall I say concerning the course? That is forevermore the opportunity for my choice, the point of my responsibility. Write it as a motto everywhere "In the beginning God." In veiled language let me utter it in this assembly. With regard to the birthright of the bairns, fathers and mothers, "In the beginning God"! Then when the children are coming to adolescence, boys and girls, write over that sweep period, "In the beginning God." Help them to make their choices in relation to Him. Instead of asking your boy whether he has made up his mind what he wants to be, ask him if he has found out what God made him to be. A little further on, the great moment of human life, that of love's dawning, comes. Alas and alas! that we have trifled so long with the sacred subject of the love of youth and maiden. There also let us say, "In the beginning God." If the writing over that dawning wonder of love reveals something that is unlike Him, contrary to Him, banish it, though it be as dear as the right hand or right eyes. In the beginning of vocation, when looking to the future, choosing a calling in life, deciding what you will be, "In the beginning God." Then when in marriage a new world opens, you are to live no longer in your heroic and pure loneliness, but now and for tomorrow in association; then inscribe over the portal of your new home "In the beginning God," erect a family altar, and observe the same, upright recognition of God as interested in and presiding over all the affairs of home life. In other words, set the course in right relation to the Cause.

If you will, what then? Then in the consummation the relation will be one that results in crowning, in the ultimate fulfilment of life, in all spaciousness of being and of doing.

My brother, "In the beginning God," you are God-created. Submit yourself to Him so that your whole life may be God-governed, and that at last you may come to the full infolding of your own life, and be God-crowned.

I dare not finish there. Someone is listening, and saying, "Yes, I think you are right, but it is all too late. 'In the beginning God,' but I broke His law and set Him at defiance, spoiled my chance; I am waste, void, a ruin and a wreck." Is that so? Thank God the chapter is not ended, "The Spirit of God moved upon the face of the waters. And God said, Let there be light." O'er the waste and ruin and wreckage is seen the brooding Spirit of God, bringing back order. So that if you say you have no chance in the first verse, you have in all the rest of the Bible that follows! He can come to you in healing restoration as surely as He came to the scarred earth in the dim and distant past, and make you fair and beautiful as His own heaven. Let him. May God help you.

CHAPTER XXV

WHAT IS MAN?

The Jehovah God took the man, and put him into the garden of Eden to dress it and to keep it. And the Jehovah God commanded the man, saying, Of every tree of the garden thou mayest freely eat: but of the tree of the knowledge of good and evil, thou shalt not eat of it: for in the day that thou eatest thereof thou shalt surely die.
GENESIS 2:15-17.

THIS PASSAGE OF SCRIPTURE INCLUDES TERMS WHICH DEmand the context if we are to understand them or gain the full value of the statements made. The terms "Jehovah God," "the man," "the garden," "every tree," all demand the context for interpretation.

I have selected this particular paragraph, because it presents before the mind a simple picture of primitive conditions; the picture of a virgin garden, and of a man, perfect in condition of body, mind, and spirit.

These first two chapters of Genesis deal with Divine activity. The first activity is that of primal creation. There is no description; no account of the method; and no portrayal of the final issue of that primal activity. In a brief and comprehensive declaration, the fact is broadly and inclusively stated, "In the beginning God created the heaven and the earth." What that earth was, what its form and fashion, what its peculiar characteristics, who were its inhabitants; these are things not revealed. We have no story beyond that declaration of a primal creation. Then, with startling suddenness, the whole scene suggested to the imagination is overclouded, and instead of a creation fresh and bright and beautiful, and full of splendour, we look upon the earth void and waste, desolate and dark.

Then that which is the particular story of this second chapter commences, the account of another Divine activity, the activity of God in the restoration of a lost order. We know nothing of what happened between the facts chronicled in the first verse, and those described in the second; but we have the story of reconstruction, of the renewal of a lost order. All the processes of this restoring activity of God culminated in man. Everything moved toward that consummation. Everything was in preparation for the advent of man. The coming of light, the redistribution of land and water, the restoration of the earth to its solar relationships, the creation of new forms of life, vegetable and animal; all these prepared for the coming of another; and all culminated in man.

In this paragraph which I have read, that man is seen in all the strength and beauty and simplicity of his manhood. He is seen in a garden, a garden not yet cultivated, but a garden potential, and presently, under the touch of his hand to be prolific. It is the simplest of all scenes; it is the most primitive of all pictures.

According to the teaching of these Scriptures, this man is the father of the race, the progenitor of that humanity which in the process of millenniums has multiplied and divided into the strange and bewildering complexities of races, temperaments, and accomplishments, in the midst of which we live today. We turn to the picture, that we may escape for a little from the bewilderment of the complex and find the illumination of the simple, in order that by the blessing of God we may presently return to the complexity and live therein the true life of simplicity, and make our contribution toward the working out of the Divine consummation for the human race. It is difficult to escape from the complexity of the life of today; how complex it is, yet in the complexity I see no reason for grief or complaint. Let me say at once, that we are not now dealing with the subject of sin. We are dealing with essential humanity, and in doing so, it is difficult to escape from the complexities of life, complexities which are the outworking of the marvelous potentialities of the simple as we see it in the garden; for every city is the result of a garden. London is a garden, or it is on a garden! It is a long time since we saw it, but right underneath this great city with its appalling multitudes there is old mother earth, and flowers once bloomed and blossomed, and the harvest was reaped. London is humanity's complexity. By the inspiration of the Spirit of God let us get behind these complexities; away from the multitudes to the individual; away from all the marvels of humanity in its toil, and suffering, endeavor, defeat, accomplishment, back to this simple picture and see man as he is there revealed to us.

There are four things for our consideration. They are recognized in the text and explained in the context. First, the being of man; secondly, his true circumstances, surroundings, environment; thirdly, his vocation in the economy of God; and finally, his limitation.

As to the being of man, the context teaches us three things. First, it reveals his origin; secondly, it declares his substance; and finally, it unveils his nature.

It first of all declares that this being is the creation of God. In the declaration it makes use of two different terms to describe the Creator. In the first picture one name alone is used; in the second two are employed in conjunction. In the first chapter the name used is God, or—and I am bound to use the Hebrew word because of its values—Elohim; the Hebrew word in the plural number, signifying not two or three, but intensity, a method adopted by Hebrew writers when some fact is to be expressed, and the singular form will not convey all the strength and glory of the thought. This name stands for might, essential, sufficient might.

The second chapter of Genesis gives an explanatory account, in order that we may more perfectly understand the nature of the man described as the culminating glory of the process of restoration. Now the same word, Elohim, is linked to and prefaced by that word which we have translated and which has become familiar to us as Jehovah; a word suggesting voluntary and sufficient resource at the disposal of man. We see then that man, according to Scripture, was created by the God of all-sufficient might; and by the God Who in the interests of that man He has created is Jehovah, the becoming One, the One Who voluntarily becomes everything that man needs, or ever can need, for all the processes of his being to consummation. Man is the definite, direct, immediate, voluntary, creation of that Being.

The second teaching concerns the substance of man. He is of the dust of the ground; but as dust he is not man; even as dust when formed and fashioned into some external shape or manifestation, he is not man; he becomes man only when enswathed, enwrapped, permeated by the breath of lives. Man then as to substance is a mingling of dust, and the essential spirit-life of God.

Finally then, emerging from that declaration concerning the substance of man, we have the revelation of the nature of man. Because he is of the dust and of the very essence of the Spirit of God, he is, in the whole creation, the only link between the material and the spiritual. He is not material alone, and not spiritual alone; no man is a man as a disembodied spirit; no man is a man as body minus spirit. Every man is at once of the dust, and of Deity; of the material, and of the spiritual.

The final fact as to the nature of man is that he is made in the image and likeness of God. That is not the same thing said twice over. By the words "image" and "likeness", two separate ideas are conveyed. "Image" suggests the fact that he is the one by whom God is represented. "Likeness" suggests the fact that he is in himself like God. There may be an image which is unlike. A man may set up as representative of himself a sign or symbol which may not be in the least like him. Only yesterday, moving along one of our streets, I saw upon a waggon a vast block of stone, and one sign upon it, the broad arrow. Whose image and superscription is that? The king's. The broad arrow is the image of the king, but not the likeness of the king. Man is placed in creation as the image of the King, the representative of the King to all creation beneath him. He stands in the midst of the earthly order as the representative of God to everything beneath him; to all beasts, and fowl, and fish; to all fruit, and flowers, and trees. But man is not merely a broad arrow, something unlike God, nevertheless representing Him; he is in the likeness of God, modeled upon the pattern of the infinite mystery of the personality of God. Personality is not perfect in man; but perfect in God. Personality is perfect in the infinite God, but man is in the likeness, though he is finite. In the great essentials of human nature, intellectual, emotional, volitional, man is not only in the image of God, he is in the likeness of God; only it is necessary to remember that I am speaking of man as I see him in this garden, and not of man as I meet him in London. The image has never been entirely defaced, but the likeness has been almost entirely lost.

Now let us consider the simple suggestion of this passage concerning man's surroundings, his circumstances, his environment. We see him in a garden with—what for lack of a better term I will describe as a double environment. As he is dual in his nature, material and spiritual, so also his environment is dual, material and spiritual. His material environment was that of the garden. We have all sorts of foolish notions about the garden of Eden, notions unwarranted by the actual facts of the story in Genesis. I have seen pictures of it, and they were mostly pictures of Italian gardens. Genesis gives the picture of a garden uncultivated, in which God had planted trees; none of which had yet appeared, because there was no man; but they were there, in the soil, scattered there by God—and I hope that term does not suggest anything capricious, "I report, as a man may of God's work —all's love, yet all's law!"

The garden was potential. There was potentiality resident within the garden, not merely of tree and flower and fruit, but of the city which has never yet been built; for not only is it true that London today stands upon a garden; it is equally true that everything in London has come out of a garden; all the stones, all the woodwork, all materials have come from a garden. The garden was imperfect; the flowers not yet blossoming, the final issues waiting for the touch of power, waiting for the guidance of the hand of the man God made. Into that, man was placed. Materially, that was his environment.

But that was not the closest fact of his environment. There was a spiritual environment. This man was living in the midst of the very spirit life of God. That spirit life which being inbreathed had made him a living soul was that in which he lived and moved and had his being. Man lived in the deepest fact of his nature in immediate touch, and connection

WHAT IS MAN?

with God. Man as I see him here in the earliest picture of the Divine library was not only in immediate contact with God, he was in conscious contact with God. There was speech between this man and his God. There was, to use our great evangelical word, communion between this man and his God. The agonized cry that perpetually breaks from the lips of sinning and fallen humanity, "Oh that I knew where I might find Him" is the natural, and necessary outcome of the very nature of man himself. Here in this garden was a man conscious that the nearest fact of his environment, from which he never could escape, and from which he did not in these early days desire to escape, was not that of the garden which in some senses was outside him, but that of the God of the garden in Whom he lived and moved and had his being, and with Whom he had communion.

Let us take the next step, and notice what this picture teaches us concerning primitive man, original man, as to his vocation. There are two little phrases, how easily we read them, how glibly we pass them over, how little we understand them. His vocation was to dress and to keep the garden. The whole vocation of man in this temporary and probationary life in the economy of God stands startlingly revealed in that sentence.

What is this word, to dress? Quite simply the Hebrew word is one which in a score of instances is translated to work. If you feel after the heart of the word for its true significance and original intention, when the verb is transitive or causative, it means to enslave. We must not abuse that word by thinking of slavery as something cruel; man was put into the garden to capture it, to discover its secrets, to lead them out to fulfilment, to lay his hand upon its potentialities and guide them into generous realization. To dress it, to work it, to capture it, to realize it. Ponder that conception long enough, and you will see that the ultimate completion of it will be the city of God. As I have already said, there is more in the garden than flowers and weeds, all the potentialities of material life lie slumbering in any garden covered with green grass. Charles Kingsley manifested a fine instinct when in effect he wrote to his friend, "Don't be anxious to entertain me. Put me down under any hedgerow and in two square yards of mother earth I can find mystery enough to keep me occupied for all the time I stay with you." In the garden were all the potentialities. The vocation of man was to discover what God had hidden there, and in co-operation with God to lead it toward its ultimate blossoming and fruitage; and to its final, glorious perfection.

Not only was he to dress it; he was to keep it. I confess that to me is a startling word. What does it mean? Literally to hedge it about, figuratively to guard it. In that little word there is the suggestion of the fact that whereas this is the picture of a restored order, and whereas man is seen in all the primitive strength and simplicity of his new-made manhood, he is in a universe in which there are forces that threaten. He is not merely to capture the garden, he is to guard it; and his very vocation, as here revealed, is suggestive of the fact that somewhere, not clearly defined, there are forces that threaten his garden; that there is possibility of blighting, possibility of these forces spoiling the best fruit. He is therefore to capture and develop the garden; and to guard it against attack.

Once again, what does this simple picture of man in a garden say to us concerning his limitation? You will notice that the symbols here are trees. What else would you have in a garden? If I am asked if these trees were real trees, I ask, "Was the man a real man, and was the garden a real garden?"

WHAT IS MAN?

The symbols of this man's limitation were in the realm of the sustenance of the physical; for the physical is always in the economy of God the symbol of the spiritual. The outward signs and tokens of limitation were in the realm of the material, but they were the signs and symbols of limitation in the spiritual. I pray you mark the first fact, it is not that of narrowness, but of breadth; not that of restriction, but of infinite possibility; the first fact is not that of bondage, but of liberty. The word limitation does not necessarily connote narrowness; it simply indicates a bound and a boundary. Where is the boundary? Of every tree he might freely eat, of all the trees, including the tree of life. Surely you say, that is a figure of speech. By no means. You have here the picture of primitive conditions, and there was one tree the fruit of which was peculiarly good for the maintenance of life, that is for its sustenance. Of all these trees he was allowed to eat, and he had to cultivate them and keep them and find his sustenance therein. The material fact was the symbol of the spiritual fact. This man in material surroundings was a spiritual being, and the nearest fact in his surrounding was spiritual, and so the spaciousness of spiritual possibility was revealed; of all the great spiritual sources of strength this man might partake. It is a picture of wide and glorious liberty.

Then we come to the word "but of the tree of the knowledge of good and evil, thou shalt not eat of it." What was this tree? I do not know. It might be quite helpful to us if we cease talking about an apple tree; there is no warrant for it in Scripture. The fact as declared is that there was one tree which was made the symbol of man's limitation in the economy of God. One tree was marked off, looking upon which, man must remember that his moral life could only be led to perfection, and his spiritual life to glory, as he lived in relationship to God. In the activities of his finite life in that garden, that tree was the sacramental symbol, for which he must care, and which he must tend and guard, but of which he must not eat.

Such was his limitation. First the spaciousness "Of every tree"; then the boundary which indicated that he was not supreme but a subject; just one tree that reminded him of his relation to God.

Let it be remembered that this is a picture of primitive man, potential, imperfect, but sinless; elemental man. The only adumbration or shadow of sin or evil that I find in all the story is in the revelation of vocation in which he is told to guard the garden, and in the indication of his limitation, the one tree of which he must not eat. This man is sinless in his nature, perfect in his being; not perfected, not completed, because his work is waiting for him, and the essential glory of man is not that of his being, but that of his vocation. Until he had fulfilled his vocation, until by dressing the garden and guarding it, he had produced results, until he had become a worker with God, producing results after which God was seeking, he was not perfected. No man is perfect because he is a perfect being. It is only by fulfilment of function that man can be absolutely perfected.

These then are the simple facts of every human life. I say simple facts; these are not, in some senses, the facts of your life and mine; but these are the facts of our life, fundamentally.

In its being, human life is of God and like God. That is the profoundest truth concerning every human being.

In its environment, human life is placed among the things of God; this world is God's world, the seas are His, the hills are His, the birds are His, the flowers are His; all the mys-

WHAT IS MAN?

teries and forces which men today are discovering and harnessing for the accomplishment of their purposes in the world, are God's forces. The environment of every human life is that it exists among the things of God.

As to vocation, every man is made to be a fellow-worker with God. By co-operation with God, man perfects Creation.

As to limitation, according to this picture, human life is absolutely free within the government of God.

All this is strange to us today and one of the reasons men are so anxious to get rid of these chapters of Genesis is that they do not suit the facts of human life as these men know it. This is not a picture of human life as we know it. This is not even a picture of human life as we have found it in our own experience. Superadded to these things are other things with which we shall have to deal presently; swelling rivers of poison that desolate the life, great forces and fires that burn the life; great foes of evil that are against the life. We have not reached that point in this evening's meditation. We are simply considering what the Bible says about our nature in the economy of God.

Men do not start today where this man started. This man was innocent knowing neither good nor evil. Today innocence is only true of infancy, and ah me, how soon it is gone! How soon? I do not know; but ah me, how soon! Neither is the man in Christ standing where this man stood in the garden. The man in Christ is not innocent. The man in Christ knows good and evil; but blessed be God, he is made able to choose the good and to refuse the evil.

We have been turning back to elemental things. I have been trying to bring this life of mine, so full of mystery, to the measurement of this picture; and in spite of all the changed conditions, in spite of all the forces of evil, the presence of which we shall attempt to understand in the progress of our studies, in spite of all, I find that my own life beats true to this revelation. The very mystery of my being makes me believe I am after all of God. Dust is not the final word concerning me. Yes, I believe I am in God's garden even yet. I wander a little away from the place where man has bunglingly attempted to realize the city, and has always realized sorrow, and I know it is God's garden. Yes, I am among the things of God. Somehow I am coming to be quite sure that I am intended for co-operation with Him, for my life rises to highest heights, and feels the largest ecstasy, and becomes conscious of the greatest things, in those moments when I know I am doing something with God. I am not speaking only of Christian service—that ultimately, that is the crowning glory—but of the smallest things. When you are really in your garden, doing the thing in the garden that presently will smile back at you in all the colors and beauties that come out of God's earth, those are the days and moments when you live. Ultimately, when we are dealing with the spirit of man or woman, helping to lead such into realization of relationship to God, these are the moments, of all moments, the greatest. There is nothing like it. I believe I am intended to co-operate with God. Then as to limitation, how spacious it is. Would you have the story in the terms of the New Testament? "All things are yours; whether Paul, or Apollos, or Cephas, or the world, or life, or death, or things present, or things to come; all are yours; and ye are Christ's; and Christ is God's." That is the spaciousness of life. Yet, how definite it is; not a tree always, but that which is of your position, of your calling. For a man in a garden, it is a tree. You know what it is for you; your ledger, something else! As you turn your way back to tomorrow, to the office, or shop, or store, you know it, there it is; not some mystic heavenly vision, but simple and natural, close at hand, something reminding you of your relationship to God. These elemental things are still with us; we are of the first man, and of the God of the first man; sons of Adam, "the son of God."

CHAPTER XXVI

THE BEGINNING OF SIN

I DO NOT PROPOSE TO TAKE ANY ONE VERSE IN THIS CHAPTER as text. It is complete in itself for all that it is intended to teach, and it is required as a whole if we are to understand that teaching. Of course it is impossible now to deal with all the details of this story, and for the purpose of this meditation it is not at all necessary that we should do so.

This chapter is supremely interesting because it is the first in the Divine library on the subject of sin. The fact of the existence of evil has already been thrice recognized in the first two chapters.

In the desolation described in the second verse of chapter one, we have a recognition of the presence of evil in the universe;—"the earth was waste and void." In the charge to Adam, to keep the garden, as well as to dress it, there was recognition of the presence of evil, not in the world, not on the planet, but in the universe. Finally, the sacramental symbol, the tree in the midst of the garden, was the indication of the possibility of disobedience, a recognition that the fact of human will admits the possibility of wrongdoing.

Thus we have seen the adumbration of evil resting on the first pages. The Bible does not begin with anything perfect, save that in the first verse it does indicate a perfect God, and a perfect primal creation.

Now we come to the chapter which deals with the beginning of sin in human history; and it is a microcosmic revelation in that it shows not merely the source of the poison, but also its method, its activity, and its issue.

We must remind ourselves again that we are looking at these things in the atmosphere of simplicity and not of complexity. I attempted to emphasize that by way of introduction last Sunday evening, when we considered the garden story, and saw man, perfect but not perfected, as to his being, his nature, his vocation, and his limitation. In all these stories we are away behind the complexities of life in the midst of which we live, dealing with the simplicity of elemental human character and nature.

We shall attempt to gather our thoughts around the three personalities revealed in this chapter; the personality of God, the personality of man, and the personality of Satan. These are taken for granted in the story that is told.

We are introduced in the beginning of the chapter to a clearly defined, yet mysterious personality, wholly evil, described here as the serpent. Then we are again face to face with man as we saw him in our previous study. And here also we are in the presence of God, described first by the name Elohim, and then by the title Jehovah Elohim.

Gathering our meditation around these three personalities, Satan, Man, and the Lord God, we shall attempt to examine the teaching of the story concerning the Satanic method; the Human experience; and the Divine attitude and activity.

Satan is here introduced to us as a personality doubly disguised. Neither the beast nor the Angel is clearly seen. "The serpent" appearing to Eve was not a snake in our sense of the word. "The serpent" means "the shining one," and the suggestion is that this temptation came through the medium of a person, new to the one being tempted; a person arresting, commanding attention, neither an angel of light in all the full glory of the revelation, nor wholly a beast of the field; but some strange personality in which there was the disguise of the beast and the disguise of the angel.

Those of you who care to follow the study, will take time to trace the word serpent, or shining one, through the Scriptures; noticing especially what light the New Testament flings upon it, and discovering the harmony of the teaching which the Bible gives concerning this person.

It is enough for our present purpose that we recognize that there came into that garden scene at which we looked last Sunday evening, one who was neither angel nor beast; a living one, for that is the real meaning of the word beast, not necessarily beast in our sense of the word, but a living one, somehow of the material, of that creation beneath man and under his government; and yet shining with a splendour that suggested other powers, subtle and supernatural.

Whatever the appearance may have been we are supremely interested in watching the method of the enemy. First, he questioned the goodness of God; secondly, he denied the severity of God; finally, he slandered the motive of God.

The enemy questioned the goodness of God, "Yea, hath God said, Ye shall not eat of any tree of the garden?" What I am about to say may appear a paradox, but hear me through. The question was not an inquiry; it was rather an attempt to convey a suggestion to the mind of the woman, by the method of interrogation. The thought suggested was that in that sacramental symbol of limitation, there was, on the part of God, an unkind withholding of something which might have been possessed by man. In the wilderness, long millenniums afterwards, I see another Man being tempted; and I hear this as the first temptation, "If Thou art the Son of God, command that these stones become bread." We seem here to be very far away from Eden. I am glad of this, because it reveals the fact that temptation comes in varied garbs to man, but that essentially it is ever the same. Coming to the wilderness to the Son of God, the second man, the last Adam, the tempter said, "If Thou art the Son of God, command that these stones become bread"; and the suggestion was that if He were the Son of God, God ought to feed Him, that God was withholding something that He ought to have; He was asked to use the power of His Sonship to change the condition in which God had placed Him for the moment.

Thus, the first suggestion of the Tempter is that God is unkind, that restriction is unkind. This was not declared, not announced, not affirmed, but it was suggested. That is always the beginning of temptation. For the purpose of immediate illustration, instead of thinking over the vast expanse of diversified human life as we know it today, let us think back within our own personal experience, and we shall find that whatever form the temptation of sin takes, at the heart of it there is suggested the idea that restriction which forbids the thing we desire is unkind on the part of God. That is the first suggestion of evil.

Evil is ever inconsistent. This is part of its method. A most contradictory word follows immediately. The woman said to the serpent "Of the fruit of the trees of the garden we may eat; but of the fruit of the tree which is in the midst of the garden, God hath said, Ye shall not eat of it, neither shall ye touch it, lest ye die." To that the Tempter emphatically replied, "Ye shall not surely die." If in the first movement, I have the questioning of the goodness of God, in the second I have the denial of the severity of God. The affirmation is a distinct negative of the emphatic declaration of God, made to this man when He put before him the sacramental symbol of the limitation of his liberty. This was a minimizing of sin, a declaration that disobedience will not have the effect which God has said it will have; and consequently, it was a minimizing of the value of holiness.

Thus while the first suggestion was that restriction is unkind; the second was that restriction is unreal. First, God is not good in that He deprives you of anything. Secondly, God is not severe, He will not punish you as He said He would if you take of the fruit of the tree.

Come to the wilderness again, and again the suggestion seems entirely different, while yet it is the same, "Cast Thyself down: for it is written, He shall give His angels charge concerning Thee." In one case; Take this fruit and eat it and you shall not die. In the other; Cast Thyself down, and Thou shalt not die. It is the very same temptation in its central meaning, though the method of declaration is different, that there can be no punishment as the result of trafficking with God and disobeying His clearly defined law.

Finally;—and here we reach the heart, the most awful revelation of evil—the motive of God is slandered; "God doth know that in the day ye eat thereof, then your eyes shall be opened, and ye shall be as God, knowing good and evil." One almost trembles even to interpret so evil and awful a suggestion, yet this is it. It was the suggestion of selfishness and jealousy on the part of God. It was the suggestion that God was keeping man outside his own kingdom.

The motive of God was thus slandered as the enemy declared in effect; He knows that you will be as gods knowing good and evil; He is jealous, He would keep you out of your kingdom.

I come again to the wilderness and hear the Tempter saying, "Here are the kingdoms of the world; You ought to have them all; You ought to be able to possess them; but You cannot possess them because of Your loyalty to the will of

God, because of Your poverty and Your lowliness, and Your refusal of the things that other men are seeking. Behold, I will give Thee the kingdoms of the world from which Thou art being kept by abiding within the law of Thy God." Again the principle is exactly the same.

The appalling thing is the element of truth in every lie that evil tells. In this third chapter of Genesis, I see the supreme illustration of that which Tennyson sang,

> A lie that is all a lie may be met with and fought outright;
> But a lie that is partly truth is a harder matter to fight.

Take each of these temptations, "Hath God said, Ye shall not eat of any tree of the garden?" That was the truth, but it was the truth so framed and presented, with veiled suggestion, that it was the most monstrous lie. "Ye shall not surely die"; that was true, but it was the interpretation of death on the level of the material; man sinning, did not immediately die after the fashion in which men use the word; that is physically only. "You shall be as gods, knowing;" you shall come into a kingdom from which God has excluded you. Directly as they sinned they came into the kingdom, and they knew.

Therein is revealed the subtlety of temptation. The Satanic method is that of uttering a partial truth, and suggesting a lie; of seducing men, by the uttering of a half truth, to yield themselves to that which is of the very nature of evil.

All this is testified to by common human experience. The first definite step of wrong to which we can look back, that act in which we overstepped the boundary within which we had walked in childhood, was taken after inward thought. That thought took the form which inspired to outward action of evil when we imagined that it was unkind of God to deny us something which we desired. Then followed the thought that violation of the law would not result in punishment. Finally, we persuaded ourselves that God was keeping us out of something which by right belonged to us, that He was unjust as well as unkind. In answer to such suggestions we acted in the hope of gaining our kingdom.

I hold in my hand a little book unveiling the soul of a man who gave himself to all the courses of evil. The tragedy of the book is that I am afraid it was not an honest book, as subsequent events proved. This man wrote:

> I became the spendthrift of my own genius, and to waste an eternal youth gave me a curious joy. Tired of being on the heights, I deliberately went to the depths in the search for new sensation. Desire at the end was malady, or madness, or both.

"I deliberately went to the depths in the search for new sensation." As though he had said, there were things from which God shut me out by His law. I felt I had a right to enter into those things, and I went to the depths! And what depths they were; depths not to be named in the company of clean men and women. That was an illustration of the outworking in the nineteenth century of this selfsame principle. Here is the method of Satan. It is unkind of God to keep you from those things that lure you. God is not severe after all; you will not die if you disobey. You have a right to know, even though you break His law to gain knowledge. These were the suggestions of evil.

Intimately related to these and immediately following upon them, we find the human experience. I shall waste no time in distinguishing between the sin of the woman and the sin of the man; they were one. There are three things at which we shall look. First of all the sense. What was felt by this human being? How did temptation appeal? We have, so far, been looking at the temptation as it came from the enemy. Now let us try to feel the sense, the experience of the woman under temptation.

The woman saw three things; that it was good for food, that it was pleasant to the eyes; and that it was desirable in order to make one wise. Let me interpret the story of Genesis by the language of the mystic Apostle John. The lust of the flesh; she saw that it was good for food. The lust of the eyes; she saw that it was pleasant to the eyes. The vain-glory of life; she saw that it was to be desired to make one wise. That was the threefold human emotion under the spell and power of which man capitulated in the presence of temptation.

The lust of the flesh; good for good. Get to the wilderness and watch the Man being tempted once again; "Man shall not live by bread alone."

Pleasant to the eyes; the lust of the eyes. "It is written Thou shalt not tempt the Lord thy God"; Thou shalt not live by sight, but by faith.

"To be desired to make one wise"; the vain-glory of life. "Thou shalt worship the Lord thy God, and Him only shalt thou serve," was the answer to the glamour of the kingdoms of the world, the vain-glory of life.

I have referred to the wilderness, for there we see temptation refused; but the human sense was the same; good for food, pleasant to the eyes, desirable to make one wise. There is no need for me to make application. Stand out in this great city and you have the whole picture; the lust of the flesh; the lust of the eyes; the vain-glory of life; that is how man is attracted. Let James put all the story in brief words. "Lust, when it hath conceived. . . ." That is the sense.

The second matter demanding attention is that of the act, the taking of the fruit. It was volition, acting in answer to the impulse of sight, wholly within the realm of the material. It was an act impelled by sight; by that which contradicts faith, or professes to be independent of it; it was an action of the will, inspired by wit, wisdom, cleverness, observation, sight.

It is wonderful how men can be deceived by their own cleverness. It is perfectly certain that two and two make four, but it may be unsafe to act upon that fact. If you are making your calculation, and say that two and two make four, your finding may be a blasphemy and a sin. Is it not true, then, you ask? Certainly; but supposing you ought to have said, two and two, and one; you have forgotten a quantity, failed to take account of another number; then your logical accuracy is your soul's damnation. You ought to have found five, and not four. "Soul, thou hast much goods laid up for many years; take thine ease, eat, drink, be merry; but God said unto him, Thou foolish one, this night is thy soul required of thee." "But God," that was the One he had forgotten. He said, two and two make four; and he tried to live upon the four, when it ought to have been five; the One was the forgotten principle. That demonstrated the madness of living by sight. That is the story of Eden. Volition by sight; action impulsed by the cleverness of human calculation; turning from faith in the forgetfulness of the supreme One, Who makes the quantity in your clever four, the eternal five.

That volition by sight on the basis of the material expresses itself in rebellion against God on the level of the spiritual; and finds as the result life passing under the bondage of Satan. That was the first act of sin. Let us again take James' word. In dealing with the sense we said "Lust, when it hath conceived." In dealing with the act we say "beareth sin."

Then we come to the issue of it all, the first issue was fear. That is where fear comes into the Bible. What was fear? In this case and always, it is lack of spirit-strength. They were afraid, afraid of God! Why? Had God changed? No, they had changed. In the mystery of that spiritual life which was the essential, they had lost their knowledge of God, and consequently, they had become afraid.

Then followed shame. To me this is a very remarkable word, "they knew that they were naked." Let us disabuse our minds of some very paltry and incidental interpretations of that statement. They became conscious of the material, conscious of the flesh, and were ashamed of it; because they knew that in that act they had violated the spiritual. "Who told thee that thou wast naked?" What made you conscious supremely of the material, and in your consciousness of it, what generated in your mind the sense of shame? That sense of shame is the one note of music here. It is the one gleam of light. If there had been no shame, how utterly hopeless it would have been ever to hope for their redemption. The shame is the evidence that there was still the opportunity for return. It was the sense of the material, and the fact that they had yielded to the temptation, surging through the soul. They were naked, and they tried to cover up the material because they had become ashamed of the sin.

The final fact was that of their utter and hopeless dejection. Not satisfied with the coverings they had woven for themselves of the leaves of the garden, they hid themselves amid the trees of the garden when they heard the sound of God going in the wind of the day.

For food the hand was stretched out, and in the grasping of that forbidden fruit there was loss of spiritual strength, which issued in fear. For that which was pleasant to the eyes the sin was committed, and immediately there surged upon the soul, not the pleasantness of life, but the shame of life. After wisdom the mind stretched out, and instead thereof there came the knowledge of good and evil experimentally, which was conviction of the most appalling madness and folly. Again we turn to James, and complete his declaration, "Sin bringeth forth death."

Briefly, let us notice the Divine action as answer to the Satanic method. The first suggestion was that God was not good, that He was unkind. God vindicated His goodness in His administration of justice. The very fact of His inquisition is a revelation of His goodness; He came to their level, and talked to them, asked them questions, allowed them to talk to Him, made opportunity for them to speak out the story of their wrong. The method of the inquisition traced the sin back to its source. I suppose we are always inclined to feel contempt for the man as he attempted to place the blame upon the woman, and even upon God, for the emphasis of his answer is this, "the woman whom Thou gavest me"; and we have the same feeling for the woman when she tried to plead her own weakness, "the serpent beguiled me." Ere you indulge in contempt for Adam or Eve, remember that God asked the questions and accepted the excuses. When in reply to God's question Adam named the woman, He turned to her and asked, "What is this thou hast done?" and when she replied, "The serpent beguiled me," He immediately turned to the serpent. In the form of whatever living creature he had disguised himself, that beast was then and there changed in its material fashion, and forevermore became a snake. You remember Ruskin's description of the snake, "that running brook of horror." Whenever men look upon a snake they feel the revulsion that sin ought to make in their minds. Sentence was pronounced at the center of the wrong. Yet there was a sentence upon the woman, full of grace; "in sorrow thou shalt bring forth children." The crowning glory of her being, motherhood, was to be sanctified through sorrow, travail, and pain. Do not let us be afraid of looking at that. What holy sanctification has come into the world, and been maintained therein by the awful and appalling mystery of motherhood through pain. There was a sentence on man, full of purpose; the highest dignity of thy being, toil, shall be gained through stress and strain and weariness. Side by side with that most sacred thing of all, the sanctity of the pains of motherhood, is the sanctity of the weariness of toil. If these things had been unnecessary to perfect men and women, they were necessary for the remaking of imperfect men and women. So that His severity was exercised in patience, and the direct lie of evil was answered.

Finally, His motive was unveiled in mercy. The devil had suggested selfishness as His motive, and that He answered in the word that prophesied the ultimate triumph through travail; the seed of the woman "shall bruise thy head, and thou shalt bruise His heel"; that was the prophecy of the ultimate good of the creature, and it revealed the love that motived the whole government of God. Such was the Divine activity in the presence of sin.

This is the Bible account of the origin of the sin and sorrow of humanity. If you reject it, then what? From the facts of sin and sorrow and suffering you cannot escape. How do you explain them? Do you tell me that all I see in the world of sorrow and suffering and sin are parts of an upward movement; that gradually humanity is rising superior to these things and will leave them behind? Then, my masters, what an appalling and unutterable beginning there must have been! I cannot write over the beginning, if the beginning was such as is necessary to that view, "In the beginning a good God." I must put away the idea of good altogether, and write God down a monster. But again; if you tell me that this is part of an upward movement, where are the evidences in individual or national life of a natural upward movement apart from external influence brought to bear? I affirm there are no evidences. Wherever you find an individual rising, a tribe rising, a nation rising, it is not the result of a natural movement from within; it is the result of some external touch of quickening and redeeming power.

If I accept this story, what then? I have found the theory corroborated in all human experience, absolutely corroborated in my own. I know temptation did not come to me by way of a tree, because I do not live in a garden. I saw no shining one taking the form of a beast, or beast transfigured into the form of a shining one. Yet the temptation came in the same way, by the suggestion that God was unkind, that He was not severe, that He was not fair. My heart was persuaded to imagine that because I could not do this and could not go there, I was being kept out of some kingdom that I ought to be able to enter.

So temptation came, and the sense which resulted in my capitulation to the temptation, was the same, good for food, pleasant to the eyes, to be desired to make one wise; the lust of the flesh, the lust of the eyes, the vain-glory of life.

It is the same story. You can change the garments and the environment, and the language, but the facts abide. The story is true to life in London today.

If this story be true, herein is the vindication of the Christian evangel. Herein is the inspiration of all Christian endeavor. Man as we meet him is not as God meant him to be. He is what he is as the result of temptation and sin. Yet thank God, over all the darkness and sorrow and sadness there is the word of God, the seed of the woman shall at last crush the head of the serpent and master evil, even though in the process His own heel be wounded.

THE BEGINNING OF SIN

Tonight we are not looking on in hope, we are looking back to accomplishment. We have seen the seed of the woman crushing the head of the serpent, to the bruising of His heel; we know the perfect Victor, Who is the perfect Saviour.

www.ingramcontent.com/pod-product-compliance
Lightning Source LLC
Chambersburg PA
CBHW052143300426
44115CB00011B/1493